Eat Your
Way
Across the
U.S.A.

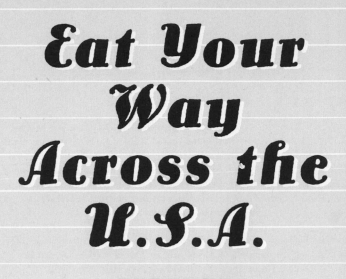

Eat Your Way Across the U.S.A.

---

500 Diners, Farmland Buffets,

Lobster Shacks,

Pie Palaces, and Other

All-American Eateries

Revised and Updated

Jane and Michael Stern

Broadway Books, New York

Broadway Books titles may be purchased for business or promotional use or for
special sales. For information, please write to: Special Markets Department,
Random House, Inc., 1540 Broadway, New York, NY 10036.

BROADWAY BOOKS and its logo, a letter B bisected on the diagonal, are
trademarks of Broadway Books, a division of Random House, Inc.
Visit our website at www.broadwaybooks.com.

Library of Congress Cataloging-in-Publication Data

Stern, Jane.
Eat your way across the U.S.A. : 500 diners, farmland buffets,
lobster shacks, pie palaces, and other all-American eateries / Jane
and Michael Stern. — Rev. and updated, 1st ed.
p.   cm.
ISBN 0-7679-0093-6 (pbk.)
1. Restaurants—United States—Directories.   I. Stern, Michael,
1946–   .   II. Title.
TX907.2.S837   1999
647.9573—dc21   98-33233
CIP

REVISED EDITION

Designed by Kathleen Herlihy-Paoli, Inkstone
Maps by Stanley S. Drate, Folio Graphics

01 02 03 10 9 8 7 6

CONTENTS

★ ★ ★

New England

★

Mid-Atlantic

★

Mid-South

★

Deep South

★

Midwest

Southwest

Great Plains

West Coast

Sidebars

★ ★ ★

Acknowledgments

★ ★ ★

One nice thing about our job is how many people want to help. The more we write about our favorite places to eat, the more enticing suggestions we get. Tipsters via U.S. mail, e-mail, and word of mouth have helped us build a database of good eats prospects that make every road trip an appetizing adventure.

It has been especially exciting to be associated from the start with Broadway Books, where we once again know the steady hand of old friend and publisher Bill Shinker. John Sterling's enthusiasm has inspired us all along the way, and editor Harriet Bell has made our lives as writers all too easy. And when something needs to get done, we know we can count on Alexis Levenson. As ever, Binky Urban, our four-star agent, manages to take the worry out of publishing.

Some of the choicest places in this book were discovered while researching "Two for the Road," our column that appears in *Gourmet* magazine. It is inspiring to be part of *Gourmet*, an oasis of civility and high spirits in the publishing world, where every month we have the pleasure of working with a team of brilliant editors. In particular, we thank Gail Zweigenthal for her unfailing support and Alice Gochman, the world's best dining companion.

Inspiration to keep eating has also been provided by our dear friends at Public Radio International's "The Splendid Table"—Lynne Rossetto Kasper, Sally Swift, and Tom Voegeli—to whom we deliver fresh sound bites for the Saturday show; and we are also indebted to the laissez-faire editors and staff of Epicurious.com, the website for which we write a "Wish You Were Here" postcard from wherever we happen to be each week.

Finally, heartfelt thanks to Bunny Kyle and Jean Wagner, who care for our beloved Lewis, Minerva, and Clementine when we are on the road, as well as to John Porto and Karen Rue, who mind our equine pals Piegan and K.T. every day.

Introduction

✫ ✫ ✫

Eat Your Way Across the U.S.A. is a guide to the best food in America. Whether your goal is to savor regional specialties all across the country in neighborhood cafés, seaside shanties, and backwoods supper clubs, or simply to find something decent to eat while on a road trip or in an unfamiliar city, this book is designed to be your appetite's favorite travel companion.

It will lead you to unforgettable (but often unsung) restaurants, delicious (but mostly inexpensive) meals, and the kinds of culinary roadside experiences that can transform breakfast, lunch, and dinner into the high points of any trip. We intend for this book to be a way to know the diversity of America through its food: Texas beef parlors, Yankee shore dinners, Creole gumbo lunchrooms, Great Lakes fish fries, High Plains farmers' cafés, the Basque dinner halls of the Rockies, Georgia soul food buffets, Border Town chile cheeseburgers, Milwaukee milk shakes, and Seattle seafood.

Although we hope that armchair gourmets will find pleasure merely browsing through the national bounty reflected herein, our primary goal in writing and designing the book has been to create a traveler's tool as useful as a road map or Swiss Army knife. We want *Eat Your Way Across the U.S.A.* to be easy to consult when you need a dining tip anywhere in the country—a valued resource to be packed in briefcase, knapsack, or automobile glove compartment, to be consulted in small towns and big cities, along interstates, back roads, and blue highways.

A vast majority of the 500+ places reviewed are very inexpensive, for the simple reason that in most parts of this country, the truly wonderful food is *not* the pricey fare sold in linen-tablecloth dining rooms. From the po'boys of Cajun country and the pig pickin's of the Carolinas to the pie palaces of the upper Midwest and the old-time pizza parlors of the Northeast, America's most distinguished food tends to be of-the-people fare, eaten without pomp-and-circumstance and fine wine, but with a large stack of paper napkins and a tumbler full of iced tea or a cold beer on the side.

We have indeed included a handful of expensive restaurants in this book—cattle country steak houses, lobster shore dinners, a few high-fashion dining rooms in big cities—because these special places do provide the kind of unforgettable deluxe dining experience that we travelers often crave. In every case, the top-dollar meals we have included are, in their own way, true reflections of local culinary character. Every restaurant in the book has been rated for price.

We should state a point that we hope is obvious to any reader: This is a very personal book. We really love the places we have included, and we hope you love them, too. This is not the kind of guidebook that is compiled by committee or survey. For us, eating is a passion, and reading about it—whether for vicarious pleasure or to get some practical advice—ought to be inspiring.

Although we depend on (and are profoundly grateful for) tips, suggestions, and advice we get from readers of our previous books and our "Two for the Road" column in *Gourmet*, as well as from net-surfers who log onto our Epicurious.com postcards, we have always done all the eating and traveling and writing ourselves. When considering restaurants for inclusion in this book, we used no stringers and no hired eaters. We personally ate everywhere. We dined anonymously and we paid for the meals out of our own pockets. And as it turned out, perhaps one out of ten restaurants we visited was good enough to include.

Since we started traveling around the country looking for good food in 1974, we have driven more than three million miles and we have eaten in tens of thousands of restaurants. *Eat Your Way Across the U.S.A.* is the culmination of that quest, reflecting what we have learned in a quarter century of American meals. A few of the restaurants listed here are old favorites that we have returned to dozens of times over the years; many are recent discoveries. Each and every one has won our heart, and never just because it serves delicious food. For us, the joy of eating our way across the U.S.A. has been something more than sustenance. It has shown us the soul of a nation. It is our hope this book will help readers find—and savor—that soul.

WHAT IS NEW AND DIFFERENT ABOUT THIS 1999 EDITION

✩ ✩ ✩

There are more than 100 restaurants included in this edition that were not in the last one. To make room for them while keeping *Eat Your Way Across the U.S.A.* glove-box size, we have eliminated some of the sidebars. Of course, we also cut any restaurants that went out of business or changed for the worse. And we have even removed some still-thriving eateries that we like very much—mostly deluxe ones—since it is our belief that serious eaters can find them listed in other, more traditional guide books.

HOW TO USE THIS BOOK

★ ★ ★

☛ If you are planning a special trip to any restaurant in this book, *please* call ahead to make certain it is open. Hours of operation change and proprietors sometimes go fishing. (Be aware that telephone area codes are being reassigned all the time, and although we have updated all the numbers herein, chances are good that some will have changed yet again—i.e., a "not in service" number does not necessarily signify an out-of-business restaurant.)

☛ Many heartland restaurants do serve dinner, but you should be aware that dinner hour can end as early as six or seven o'clock. Also, some of the best specialties are seasonal: Michigan cherries, Dungeness crab, caramel apples, etc.

☛ Most of the restaurants require no reservations and are come-as-you-are. Some pricier ones do have a dress code and a few require a reservation. We've tried to make note of which ones get insanely crowded, and what you can do about it. But again, if in doubt, please call ahead.

☛ Our approximate cost guide is as follows:
$ = one full meal is under $10
$$ = one full meal is between $10 and $25
$$$ = one full meal is over $25

☛ We use the abbreviations B (breakfast), L (lunch), D (dinner) and BYOB (bring your own alcoholic beverage) throughout.

☛ We welcome tips for inclusion in future editions, comments, and even complaints. Please address any such correspondence to us c/o Broadway Books, 1540 Broadway, New York, NY 10036. Or e-mail us: mstern01@snet.net

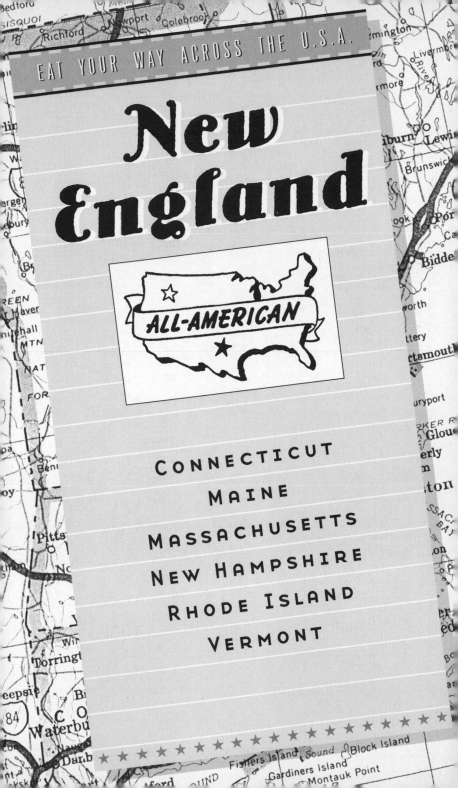

New England

ALL-AMERICAN

CONNECTICUT

MAINE

MASSACHUSETTS

NEW HAMPSHIRE

RHODE ISLAND

VERMONT

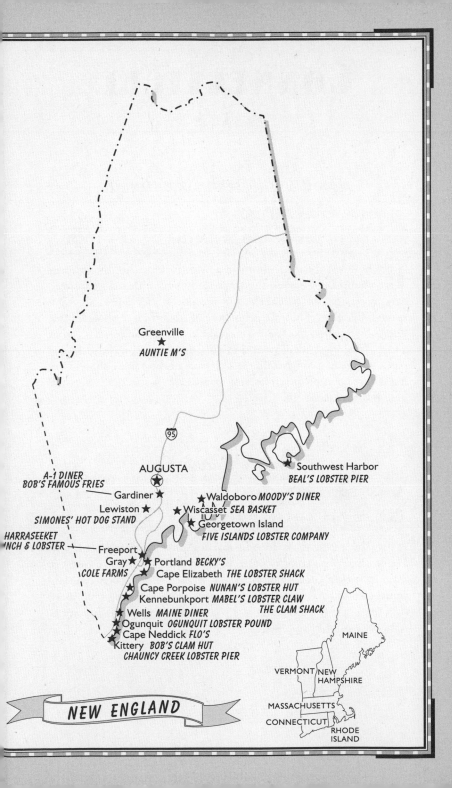

Greenville
★
AUNTIE M'S

95

AUGUSTA

A-1 DINER
BOB'S FAMOUS FRIES
Gardiner ★
Lewiston ★
SIMONES' HOT DOG STAND

★ Waldoboro *MOODY'S DINER*
★ Wiscasset *SEA BASKET*
★ Georgetown Island
FIVE ISLANDS LOBSTER COMPANY

Southwest Harbor
BEAL'S LOBSTER PIER

HARRASEEKET
NCH & LOBSTER → Freeport
Gray ★ ★ Portland *BECKY'S*
COLE FARMS Cape Elizabeth *THE LOBSTER SHACK*
Cape Porpoise *NUNAN'S LOBSTER HUT*
Kennebunkport *MABEL'S LOBSTER CLAW*
THE CLAM SHACK
★ Wells *MAINE DINER*
Ogunquit *OGUNQUIT LOBSTER POUND*
Cape Neddick *FLO'S*
Kittery *BOB'S CLAM HUT*
CHAUNCY CREEK LOBSTER PIER

NEW ENGLAND

MAINE

VERMONT NEW
HAMPSHIRE

MASSACHUSETTS

CONNECTICUT RHODE
ISLAND

CONNECTICUT

★ ★ ★

Abbott's Lobster in the Rough

117 Pearl St., Noank, CT (860) 536-7719	$$
(May to Labor Day, then weekends through Columbus Day)	LD

The chowder is bracing—briny and loaded with clams; the steamers are plump and luscious; there are pearly pink littlenecks and steel-gray oysters on the half shell; and the hot lobster roll sandwich is swoonfully buttery; but the prime lure of Abbott's is a whole lobster. Order any size you like (once you make it to the head of what can be a long, long line); then, twenty minutes later, crack, pick, suck, and pluck your way through a timeless pleasure of the Yankee shore. Dining is alfresco at picnic tables and utensils are plastic, but it is a million-dollar meal. BYOB.

Denmo's Snack Bar

Main St., Southbury, CT	$
(203) 264-4626	LD

This jolly, picnic-table drive-in makes clam platters and clam rolls piled high with crunchy heaps of nectarously sweet ocean nuggets, sided by wicked-good onion rings. To cleanse the palate between clam courses, consider a brace of Denmo's excellent foot-long chili dogs; then top it all off with a double-dip cone of rich chocolate ice cream. Ahh, the cuisine of summer!

Dr. Mike's

158 Greenwood Ave., Bethel, CT	$
(203) 792-4388	ℒ𝒟

Dr. Mike's ice cream parlor doesn't have a lot of flavors: eight are listed on the blackboard at any one time, and the roster may change if that day's cherry vanilla or mint chip gets eaten up. The essentials are almost always available: rich chocolate, chocolate lace and cream, and vanilla.

Getting some of this made-daily, small-batch ice cream can be dauntingly difficult—a fact that does not dissuade us Dr. Mike diehards, who are convinced that we have found the best on earth. The place is cramped, hidden away in a back alley with accommodations for dining that consist of exactly three rickety tables on a porch, forcing most customers to eat leaning against their cars in the parking area. On a weekend afternoon, you'll wait forever to place your order at the tiny counter where there is barely room for two employees.

Cones are the perfect ice cream delivery system, but if you really want to indulge, get a Dr. Mike's sundae. A full-size one totally fills a cardboard pint container once a shovelful of fresh whipped cream is gobbed across the top. Among the toppings, take special note of the tart-sweet dark cherries, especially if chocolate malt ice cream happens to be on the board that day.

The Goulash Place

42 Highland, Danbury, CT	$
(203) 744-1971 (closed Mon)	ℒ𝒟

Just minutes off the interstate in a residential neighborhood, the Goulash Place serves old-world home cooking. It is a paper-napkin lunchroom, run by the same couple since the 1970s (he cooks, she waits tables), during which time the prices have stayed firmly in the single-digit range. Loyalists come for satisfying plates of such Hungarian classics as chicken paprikash, pork-stuffed cabbage, goulash (three varieties), or roast duck (on weekend evenings) with all the

trimmings including either squiggly little nockerli dumplings or tasty
seasoned mashed potatoes. Soups are definitively comforting; the best
dessert is palacsinta—Magyar crepes folded around sweet apricot
filling.

Jerry's Pizza	
885 Washington St., Middletown, CT	$
(860) 346-5335	*LD*

This little storefront in a shopping center is an unlikely looking
source of grand food, but since 1968 Jerry Schiano has been our
main man for breathtaking pizza in central Connecticut. He makes all
kinds of fine thin-crust ones, as well as hot oven sandwiches and
spaghetti with red sauce; but his triumph is a specialty he calls the
white Sicilian. It is a medium-thick pie heaped with a mishmash of anchovies, garlic, parsley, oregano, and hot red pepper plus olive oil; and
it is strong. Its crust is elegant: crunchy at its edges, yet cream-soft
within, and with a yeasty dignity that offsets the giddy topping. Just as
it takes a full ninety minutes to make, you must allow a good long
while to savor this pizza, then more time to bask in its afterglow.

Kitchen Little	
Rte. 27, Mystic, CT (860) 536-2122	$
D Thur–Sat; (later hours on summer weekends)	*BL* daily

Tiny isn't a little enough word to describe this cute breakfast shop,
where the seats are so close together that private conversations are
virtually impossible. We once accidentally shared mugs (inscribed IS
THERE LIFE BEFORE COFFEE?) with our neighbor at the counter. Weekends year-round and every day in summer, throngs wait outside to be
called for a precious table or stool. Once inside, happy eaters plow
into pancakes, omelets, and such elaborate egg concoctions as a

"S'medly," which is two scrambled eggs atop home fries, sausage, mushrooms, and onions, all blanketed with melted cheese, or a "Portuguese fisherman," scrambled eggs with sausage, peppers, and jalapeño cheese.

Lunch is mostly sandwiches—there is a meaty lobster salad roll—and the wonderful clam chowder unique to southern New England, which is clams and bits of potato packed into a bracing clear broth.

Lenny & Joe's Fish Tale	
1301 Post Rd., Madison, CT (203) 245-7289;	$$
and at 86 Boston Post Rd., Westbrook (860) 669-0767	LD

Lenny & Joe's is famous for its whole-belly fried clams—hefty mouthfuls with brittle crusts—and its crunchy onion rings and just about any other summertime shoreline food that fits in a fry kettle: shrimp, scallops, oysters, scrod, and calamari. But there are many superlative nonfried things to eat in this pair of happy-go-lucky joints, foremost among them a lobster roll, which is nothing but chunks of lobster meat sopped with butter in a hot dog bun. Chowder is delicious—Yankee-style with plenty of clams—and there is a full repertoire of such virtuously cooked seafood as broiled swordfish steak and filet of sole, even Connecticut River shad in the spring, served with boiled redskin potatoes.

Louis Lunch	
261–263 Crown St., New Haven, CT	$
(203) 562-5507	BLD

Whether or not the hamburger was invented in this tiny cook shop in 1900 (as some historians contend) has no real bearing on the fact that the burgers served at Louis Lunch today are delicious. What fun it is to watch them be made, one by one, from balls of ground beef dusted with salt and flattened on the carving board, then broiled in an antique cast-iron implement that suspends patties sideways in a grate (so grease drips away). To sink your teeth into one of these lovely hunks of beef with dark crusts and juicy pink insides is a timeless joy. Ask for the "works" and onions are grilled right along with it; sliced tomatoes are available (but not ketchup), as is a schmear of Cheese Whiz. Instead of buns, Louis Lunch sandwiches its burgers in toast made in a vintage assembly-line toaster.

Orem's Diner	
209 Danbury Rd. (Rte. 7), Wilton, CT	$
(203) 762-7370	BLD

For us, Orem's is old reliable—the local diner where we go whenever we're home and too lazy to cook. It is a comfortable place with a counter and booths and a gigantic menu that has something for everyone. Our favorites are the crusty hash browns that come with morning eggs, hearty homemade soups, gravy-bathed hot turkey sandwiches with drifts of creamy mashed potatoes, and a chicken souvlaki plate served with killer-garlic cream on the side.

There is nothing fancy about the old wooden-sided hash house, which has been dishing out honest eats since 1921, when Route 7 meandered north through bucolic farmland. Now the road is crowded with businesses, and there is usually too much traffic, but Orem's remains the kind of quick-service, decent-food stop that takes you back to simpler times.

O'Rourke's	
728 Main St., Middletown, CT	$
(860) 346-6101	BLD

Tucked among the storefronts at the north end of Main Street, O'Rourke's 1946 diner is a silver jewel in the rough. Proprietor Brian O'Rourke started working here for his uncle as a potato peeler in 1958, when he was seven. He has kept the best diner traditions, and added many of his own, including a tremendous repertoire of home-made breads (Norwegian rye, Portuguese sweet bread, potato bread, pain noir, banana bread, and muffins) and spectacular Sunday break-fasts, including seasonal garden omelets and Irish soda bread pancakes topped with cream, sabayon, and fruit.

O'Rourke's menu ranges from sophisticated chili (Brian grinds the peppers himself) to Connecticut shad and shad roe in season, but there is one local specialty better here than anywhere else on earth: the steamed cheeseburger. The steamer, a central Connecticut passion, was invented in Middletown about a half century ago at Jack's Lunch (now defunct). It is a medium-thick burger cooked to ultimate juiciness in a small metal steam box. The meat is topped with an oozing blob of melted cheddar that has been prepared in its own separate steam box tray. The drippy duo are set forth upon a fluff-centered hard roll and garnished with a thick slice of crisp raw onion and yellow mustard. Not to be missed!

Pepe's Pizzeria Napoletana

157 Wooster St., New Haven, CT	$$
(203) 865-5762	D

Crust is what makes a Pepe's pizza our food-god. Cooked at high tem-perature on the brick floor of an ancient oven, it is brittle, especially around its edges, which are burnished gold and occasionally blistered black, and yet there is a profound resilience in every bite. The pizza men aren't persnickety about scraping the oven floor, so it is likely the pizza's underside will be speckled with burnt grains of semolina and maybe even blotched by an oil spill where another pizza leaked, all of which give the mottled oval a kind of reckless sex appeal that no tidy pie could ever match.

The best of the menu is white clam pizza, for which the crust is dotted with freshly opened littleneck clams, a scattering of grated sharp Romano, a salvo of coarsely minced garlic, and a drizzle of oil. Mozzarella with onion (but no tomatoes) is another long-time fa-vorite, as are the more traditional sloppy configurations with tomato sauce, cheese, pepperoni, and sausage. Broccoli and spinach recently have been added to the kitchen's repertoire; on a white pie with moz-zarella and garlic, they're delish.

Phillip's Diner

Rte. 6, Woodbury, CT	$
(203) 263-2516	**BLD**

Chicken pie is a nearly lost tradition in Connecticut. Time was, farmers' wives made them to sell out their back doors, and they were on the menu in neighborhood cafés throughout the state. Phillip's still makes and serves these time-honored beauties, with big chunks of tender chicken in well-seasoned gravy, accompanied by great flakes of crust.

The other overpowering allure to this humble town diner is donuts, which are eat-'em-by-the-dozen fine. They are pure, fresh, and sweet, eminently suitable for dunking. The ones that send us into ecstasy are the basic round brown ones, unfilled and unfrosted, with a faintly chewy crust gilded with a sandy coat of cinnamon-sugar.

Sally's Apizza

237 Wooster St., New Haven, CT	$$
(203) 624-5271 Tues–Sun	**D**

New Haven pizzaphiles debate whether Sally's or Pepe's is better, but we are not so fussy about these two Wooster Street culinary landmarks. Either place we can get a table is fine with us (seats at both are extremely scarce at mealtime). Cooked on the brick floor of an ancient oven, Sally's pie has soul. Sally's does have some things Pepe's does not, most notably a photograph on the wall of Sally's brother Tony standing with Frank Sinatra, as well as two outstanding specialty pizzas: fresh tomato pie (made only in the summer) with thick circles of tomato, creamy mozzarella, garlic, and chopped basil; and broccoli rabe pie, heaped with bitter greens when they are available at the Long Wharf produce market.

Sea Swirl

Rte. 1 at junction of 27, East of Mystic, CT (860) 536-3452	$
closed from late fall to late spring	£D

Sea Swirl's whole-bellied fried clams feel debonair, light, and lithe when you heft them from their cardboard container; and yet their taste belies their elegance. They are luscious and briny—assertive seafood, not for sissies or nutritional prigs, but pure delight for clam cognoscenti. Sea Swirl, which is a soft-serve ice cream stand, also offers impeccable clam shack atmosphere, with its picnic tables sandwiched between Route 1 and an auto supply store, and its best seats providing a view of giant drums of Eat-It-All Twinkle Cote topping that is used on sundaes.

Swanky Franks

182 Connecticut Ave., Norwalk, CT	$
(203) 838-8969	£D

This wooden diner at the end of the Exit 14 ramp off I-95 serves lusty hot dogs. They are *deep-fried*, meaning they emerge from the hot oil with crisp skin that makes their garlicky insides seem all the more plush. Nestled in a soft bun and slathered with a good dollop of Swanky's chili sauce, they are an odoriferous delight, especially satisfying when accompanied by a big basket of dark-cooked French fries as well as the constant roadside repartee that goes on among counter kibbitzers and waitresses.

The Sycamore

282 Greenwood Ave., Bethel, CT	$
(203) 748-2716	BLD

A Dagwood burger (two griddle-cooked, crisp-crusted patties with the works), French fries, homemade root beer: that's all you need to know about the Sycamore, a neon-ringed drive-in where service at counter and booths is speedy, and carhops are available for those of us who prefer to dine off window tray and dashboard.

Whistle Stop Muffins

20 Portland Ave. (Branchville Station), Georgetown, CT	$
(203) 544-8139; also in the Wilton train station,	BL
7 Station Rd., Wilton, CT (203) 762-9778	

In the charming little waiting room of the train station, commuters line up for coffee and big-topped muffins—about a dozen kinds made every day, plus scones and coffee cake of various configurations. It is all first-rate stuff; we like the caramel sticky buns, banana walnut muffins, and apricot scones best of all, especially very early in the day when they are almost too hot to hold. Most customers get breakfast to go; veterans know how to make their own change from piles of coins and dollar bills strewn across the counter during the busy rush hour; but there are also a few cozy seats where those in no hurry can sip, munch, and dunk while enjoying the morning papers at their leisure.

Windmill Restaurant

400 Hollister St., Stratford, CT	$
(203) 378-6886	LD

Plump hot dogs, slow cooked on a grill behind the bar, lure lunch-time customers to the Windmill from miles around. Smothered with onions and mustard, sauerkraut and a finely shredded chili sauce, the dogs are especially well complemented by a cold draft beer or two.

Middle European specialties are served on weekend evenings—wiener schnitzel, smoked pork chops, stuffed cabbage—but it's dogs at midday we like best. They are just the right thing to eat in a vintage neighborhood place (since 1934), where the decor is bowling trophies and mounted game animals, and where daylight streaming in through glass-brick walls suffuses booths with a nostalgic glow.

Yankee Doodle

260 Elm St., New Haven, CT	$
(203) 865-1074 (limited weekend hours in the summer)	BL

At the ancient stove and griddle in a short-order hash house, eggs are scrambled at lightning speed every morning and pigs in blankets (hot dogs wrapped in bacon, accompanied by hot relish) and Dandy Doodle Double burgers are sizzled in the blink of an eye at noon. Checks are issued with the food; and it feels quite normal to be in and out, with a satisfying meal under your belt, in under five minutes. Twelve stools at a counter are the only accommodations, so the place gets crowded at mealtime, when people-watching is superb. Clientele include a curious mixture of eccentric townies and culturally adventurous Yalies, for whom these good cheap eats are a great equalizer.

Chowder Variations

New England restaurants offer soup, stew, and chowder, all on the same menu. Soup needs no explanation, but stew and chowder have unique regional meanings. *Stew* (oyster, fish, clam, or lobster) is warm milk or cream seasoned with salt and pepper, pooled with melted butter, and containing nothing but large morsels of seafood: no potatoes, no vegetables of any kind. You'll get soda crackers on the side. *Chowder* always has potatoes in addition to its featured ingredient, which may or may not be seafood, and it can be milky, creamy, or clear.

NEW ENGLAND–STYLE CHOWDER

A milk or cream-based gallimaufry, rich with the flavor of salt pork and thick with chunks of potato. Clams are the usual main ingredient, but farmhouse chowders can be made with corn or even root vegetables. As a rule, this is a rib-sticking dish, traditionally served as a meal unto itself.

RHODE ISLAND–STYLE CHOWDER

A creamy bisque made with just enough tomatoes to turn it blushing pink, traditionally served with crusty clam cakes on the side. (This is not to be confused with "Manhattan-style" chowder that is basically a vegetable soup with clams in it and no cream or milk whatever.)

SOUTHERN NEW ENGLAND–STYLE CHOWDER

This very popular but seldom-documented variation on the theme is frequently served at clam shacks and lobster pounds in Connecticut and into Rhode Island. Made without any milk or cream but with a scattering of potatoes and onions and plenty of minced clams and their nectar, it is a bracing, steel-gray brew made to pique your appetite prior to a grand shore dinner.

MAINE

★ ★ ★

A-1 Diner	
3 Bridge St., Gardiner, ME	**$$**
(207) 582-4804 (closes Sun after brunch)	**BLD**

A 1946 Worcester dining car with a lovely interior of burnished wood, tile, and stainless steel, the A-1 has a multiple personality. It is, in part, old-fashioned diner, with fine, inexpensive breakfasts and lunchtime franks 'n' beans and meat loaf with mashed potatoes of the highest order; but it is also a sophisticated restaurant with such exotic specials as Senegalese shrimp stew, Gorgonzola risotto cakes, and cardamom chicken stew. We've had good experiences on both sides of the menu. The dessert list is both nostalgic and sophisticated, too, including such items as Maine Whoopie Pie (sort of like a gigantic Oreo), Indian pudding, and red devil's food cake, plus Bourbon Street fudge cake and swank gingerbread with silk-smooth lemon sauce.

Auntie M's	
Main St., Greenville, ME	**$**
(207) 695-2238	**BLD**

Auntie M's folksy dining room is where locals come for breakfast and to fiddle with the communal jigsaw puzzle when it's still dark outside in winter months. Donuts are freshly made, the egg platters are piled with crusty fried spuds, and the coffee keeps coming. At lunch, summertime treats include good fried clam platters; and year-round you can count on soups and chowders and such daily specials as meat loaf with (genuine) mashed potatoes, tuna casserole, lobster rolls, and chicken à la king, followed by handsome hunks of pie—chocolate cream, pecan, pumpkin, peanut butter, banana split, apple, or blueberry.

Beal's Lobster Pier

Clark Point Rd., Southwest Harbor, ME	$$
(207) 244-7178 or 244-3202 (summer only)	£D

Picnic tables overlook the harbor; from them, you can see the mountains of Acadia National Park in the distance and listen to the water rippling against the hulls of berthed fishing boats.

Inside, select a lobster from the tank; while waiting for it to boil, eat your way through a bucket of steamer clams or dip into a cup of chowder. If a handsome whole lobster is too challenging a proposition, you can also get a lobster roll—tightly packed, with plenty of fresh, sweet meat atop a cushion of shredded lettuce.

Becky's

390 Commercial Street, Portland, ME	$
(207) 773-7070	BLD

Becky's is a good old diner that opens at 4 AM every day of the year except Christmas and Thanksgiving (when it is closed); and its clientele in the predawn morning hours is a colorful conglomeration of men and women who work on or near the waterfront. The waitresses themselves are a lively bunch, always palavering with each other and the cooks behind the pass-through window (where orders are hung on a clothesline) and refilling your coffee cup until you are ready to float away.

Lunch is swell—the baked beans and franks are as classic a platter as you'll find anywhere in New England, and the Italian sausage sandwiches are true heroes. But breakfast is the great meal of the day. Fresh muffins can be had merely toasted or, for those of wanton taste, split and buttered and cooked on the same grill where millions of orders of bacon and eggs have grilled, thus absorbing the luscious flavors of breakfast past. Hash browns are soft and chunky; eggs are expertly cooked and arrive glistening with butter. On the side, Italian toast is the best available bread, served in hefty oval tiles that are buttered and crisp-cooked.

We cannot help but mention the newly posted smoking policy,

which is worthy of a Washington politician. It forbids cigars, clove cigarettes, and roll-your-owns; it limits each customer to two cigarettes per meal; and it requests that those in the smoking section extinguish their light before walking through the non-smoking section to pay their bill at the cash register.

Bob's Clam Hut	
Rte. 1, Kittery, ME	$
(207) 439-4233	LD

Bob's Clam Hut is an eat-in-the-rough stand by the side of the road that makes a specialty of seafood baskets: shrimp, haddock, oysters, and clams (whole bellies or strips). A basket includes French fries, which are fine pale twigs, but pay extra for a side of onion rings, which are huge and crunchy—a perfect complement for fried seafood. Bob's lobster roll is also top drawer, cool and expensive (about two dollars more than a fried clam roll), in a bun that is buttered and grilled until toasty golden brown on both sides.

Bob's Famous Fries	
Water Street near Bridge St., Gardiner, ME	$
Generally open from April through July	LD

Guess what's the house specialty at Bob's Famous Fries? Hamburgers and hot dogs are also on the menu, and they are quite all right. But it's French fries that make this old blue bus an eater's destination in inland Maine. Throughout the summer, starting before noon every day, Water Street is perfumed by the alluring smell of fries emerging from hot cooking oil. They are pale, thick twigs with a creamy interior, available by the bowl ($1.50) or large plate ($3.00). Bob cooks them to order and hands them out the bus window with a folded paper towel that serves as a napkin. Dip them in the cup of ketchup provided or, better yet, give them a spritz with one of the spray bottles of vinegar (white or apple) that Bob sets on the outside counter where summer spudhounds congregate.

Chauncey Creek Lobster Pier

16 Chauncey Creek Rd., Kittery, ME	$$
(207) 439-1030 (summer only)	£ D

The lobster is fresh and sweet, available in sizes well over three pounds; the pier setting is magnificent: here is a major Maine meal, with even a few frills in the form of mussels steamed in wine, clams on the half shell, and tasty lobster rolls. BYOB, and bring your own salad and bread, too, if you want that. On a cool summer evening, this is a picnic to remember.

The Clam Shack

Dock Sq., Kennebunkport, ME	$
(207) 967-2560 (summer only)	£ D

Here they are: the best fried clams in Maine and the best lobster roll on earth. An ebullient hut no bigger than a newsstand with nowhere to sit inside or out, the Clam Shack is perched at one end of the Kennebunkport Bridge and is crowded all summer long. Customers cluster in the sun devouring clam baskets, chowder, and lobster rolls off the hood of their car or leaning against the whitewashed bridge rail. Either way, you must contend with greedy birds eyeing unattended onion rings (crunchy hoops with luscious warm insides). A posted sign warns: BEWARE OF SEAGULLS. THEY LIKE OUR FOOD AS MUCH AS YOU DO.

When you sink your teeth into a Clam Shack lobster roll, you know instantly you are tasting greatness. Six to ten big pearlescent chunks of fresh-from-the-shell tail and claw are arranged in the bun; some are so succulent you can hear the juices ooze when you bite them. You have a choice of mayonnaise or butter; what that means is the meat is assembled on the bun and only then is the condiment spooned on. The result is an array of pure pink lobster merely frosted with a dollop of mayonnaise or veiled in a shimmering mantle of melted butter. One July afternoon as we ate from the hood of our car, a lawyer visiting from Idaho polished off a lobster roll and an order of onion rings and stood on the sidewalk announcing to travelers and Kennebunkporters who ambled past, "We've got nothing like this in Boise! Nothing at all!"

Cole Farms

Rte. 100, Gray, ME	$
(207) 657-4714	BLD

Off the coastal tourist trail, Cole Farms is a big, informal restaurant that locals have frequented for decades. They come for honest inland food: hot muffins in the morning, farmhouse corn chowder, good fish chowder with clam cakes on the side, hot dogs and baked beans, American chop suey, and old-fashioned puddings (Indian, Grape-Nuts, tapioca, etc.) for dessert. It is straightforward food, freshly made, satisfying, and cheap.

Five Islands Lobster Company

Rte. 127 (at the end), Georgetown Island, ME	$$
(207) 371-2990	LD

From a picnic table on the dock, the sweeping view encompasses five small pine-covered islands just off the rocky coast. Nearby trawlers rock gently at their mooring, gulls squawk overhead, and the briny ocean air is tinged by the sweet smell of fresh-cooked lobster meat.

"Come on back, let's pick one out," is the greeting at the counter in the red clapboard shed on the pier when you walk in and say you'd like a lobster. Find one the right size and it is boiled to order, along with corn on the cob or potatoes; and the only other thing to get right here is a square of "Patti-cake" (made by Patti) that is loaded with tiny Maine blueberries. Next door is a grill, where a broader menu offers crisp-fried crab cakes, onion rings, fish and chips, et al for lobster-frowners (or for those of us who need things to eat while we wait the twenty minutes for our lobster to cook).

The lobsters are beautiful and delicious, served on trays with drawn butter and accompanied by a large smooth stone for cracking shell.

The Maine coast lobster-eating experience gets no better than this.

Flo's

Rte. 1, Cape Neddick, ME	$
(daily except Wed)	£

On a scale of one to ten, how hungry are you? Walk into Flo's. Shout your number out. In five minutes, you will get that many hot dogs presented to you at the narrow pass-through window between the counter and the kitchen in this tiny roadside diner. You'll also have to tell Gail Stacy—Flo's daughter-in-law and now the proprietor—what condiments you want, and about this there can be no choice. YOU WANT HOT SAUCE. Not too hot, it's more a sweet and sour onion relish. Ladled on snapping-plump steamed wieners in their soft white buns and sprinkled with a dash of celery salt (Gail does that for you, adding just the right zest), it is one part of a transcendent combo—the finest little hot dog on the East Coast.

For those with any kind of appetite at all, a half a dozen go down easy. But no matter how many you eat, as you drive away from Flo's, you'll wish you had gotten more. And when you are far from this roadside gem, you will dream of Flo's hot dogs, longingly. There is nothing like them anywhere else.

Harraseeket Lunch & Lobster

Town Landing, Freeport, ME	$
(207) 865-3535	£D

One summer afternoon at a picnic table under the striped blue tent outside Harraseeket Lunch & Lobster, we looked down at our trays of food and sighed with the sheer joy of the moment. Here before us were a couple of irresistible shoreline meals: a mountain of crisp fried clams, a lobster roll overstuffed with great chunks of pink meat, crusty clam cakes, and a curious fry-basket delicacy called onion middles (little sweet nuggets that are deep-fried along with the more traditional rings). Plus, homemade whoopie pies for dessert—big, gooey devil's food discs sandwiching marshmallow creme. We ate slowly, listening to gentle waves lap against the wharf and to an American flag flapping crisply overhead in the July breeze. All the money in the world could not buy a culinary experience more purely pleasurable than this cheap-eats boon.

The Lobster Shack	
246 Two Lights Rd., Cape Elizabeth, ME (207) 799-1677	$
mid-April to mid-October	£Ð

A gorgeous setting for summer seafood, the Lobster Shack has a picturesque indoor dining room as well as picnic tables that overlook a rockbound coast, perfumed by ocean breezes. Pick your own whole lobster from the tank, or if you are too impatient to wait twenty minutes for it to boil, have a bowl of the Shack's delicious lobster stew, a milky-orange brew loaded with big hunks of meat. There is a full eat-in-the-rough menu: chowder and lobster stew, boats and plates and sandwiches of fried clams, plus puddings for dessert and strawberry shortcake during strawberry season in July. It is an unassuming place to eat but it has found a spot in our thoughts as a perfect taste of Maine.

Mabel's Lobster Claw	
124 Ocean Ave., Kennebunkport, ME	$$
(207) 967-2562	£Ð

Mabel Hanson's wood-paneled walls are decorated with autographed pictures of the many celebrities who favor her restaurant, including local householders George and Barbara Bush (he likes baked stuffed lobster; she goes for eggplant Parmesan). You don't have to be famous to feel at home in this comfy dining room, which has an old-fashioned, summer-resort ambiance and a staff of swift waitresses in rubber-soled nurse shoes who just naturally suggest that any piece of pie you order ought to be had à la mode.

The bread, cakes, and pies are made by Mrs. Hanson every morning; her peanut butter ice cream pie with hot fudge topping is rapturous; and however you like your lobster, Mabel does it right. Her lobster stew is legendary; if you want a really large whole lobster for dinner, she will go next door to the Port Lobster Company and fetch you a five-pounder. The lobster roll is as deluxe as they come, served with fries and slaw on an actual china plate (although the roll itself is sheathed in a cardboard case). The meat in the roll is juicy, fresh, and copious, some chunks so large that you feel a little embarrassed picking it up and eating it out of hand; a knife and fork seem more suited to the task.

Maine Diner	
Rte. 1 N, Wells, ME	$
(207) 646-4441	*BLD*

This ship-shape blue-and-white eatery is a landmark on the lobster trail. It is best known for lobster pie, an ambrosial family recipe in which big chunks of lobster meat are mixed with the lobster's own tomalley and some buttery stuffing, then baked in a casserole. The Henry Brothers, who run the place, have won awards for their seafood chowder, but it is that luxurious pie and the lobster rolls that keep us coming back.

Two kinds of lobster rolls are listed on the menu: the traditional one made with big chunks of knuckle, claw, and plenty of succulent tail meat with mayo in a toasted, grilled bun, and the "hot lobster roll," which is nothing but unadorned warm lobster meat piled into the toasted bun, accompanied by a cup of drawn butter. "Somebody from Rhode Island suggested the buttered roll many years ago," proprietor Dick Henry said. "But we found that if we served the meat already buttered, the bun fell apart." So you can either pour the butter on the sandwich, risking bun disintegration, or you can simply pick chunks of meat and shreds of toasted bread from the plate and dip them in the cup of butter as you wish.

Moody's Diner

Rte. 1, Waldoboro, ME	$
(207) 832-7468	BLD

The Formica counter is the same, as is the old wooden phone booth, but Moody's counter stools have been reupholstered, and the expanded diner, which first opened as a roadside stand in 1935, now seats a hundred people—a welcome change for those of us who have spent time waiting to get inside for breakfast. Corned beef hash, home-fried potatoes, and blueberry muffins are the choice morning foodstuffs in this roadside landmark, which exudes plenty of quirky downeast character despite its sprucing up. At lunch, count on such staples as meat loaf, franks 'n' beans, American chop suey, and stew. The many regional specialties include what connoisseurs consider the finest fish chowder in the state. Whatever you eat, top it off with pie—mincemeat, custard, or irresistible walnut cream.

Nunan's Lobster Hut

Rte. 9, Cape Porpoise, ME	$$
(207) 967-4362 (summer only)	D

A practical restaurant made for lobster eating: tables with ribs around the edge so debris doesn't fall off, big wash-up sinks and paper towels in the dining room, and marine paint on the floor for easy swabbing. It isn't in any way pretty, but there is a certain utilitarian charm about it, like an old army Jeep or vintage coffee grinder. Lobster dinners—the only thing to eat—are presented on large metal pans. The perfectly boiled crustacean is accompanied by uninteresting rolls and a bag of potato chips. For dessert: brownies or blueberry pie.

That's all you need to know, except the fact that Nunan's is extremely popular and can be maddeningly hard to get in. We recommend going at 5 PM when they open, or very late, preferably on a weekday.

Ogunquit Lobster Pound

Rte. 1, Ogunquit, ME (207) 646-2516	$$
(summer only)	LD

Pick your lobster from the pool, sit at a green-painted picnic table under a gazebo in a shady tall-pine grove, and savor a summertime pleasure unchanged by the commercial growth that has transformed so much of Rte. 1 into a bargain-hunters' strip mall. Set far back from the road, the Ogunquit Lobster Pound has been a good place for civilized shoreline dining since 1944. You'll pay a few dollars more here than at most wharfside lobster pounds; but there are more choices—steamers, lobster stew, fried clams, and broiled fish in addition to steamed-to-order lobsters (and don't forget deep dish pie for dessert)—and there is an irresistible charm to the setting, particularly at the outdoor tables. It's like an old-time picnic, or summer camp for the whole family.

Sea Basket

Rte. 1, Wiscasset, ME (207) 882-6581	$$
Wed—Mon (closed Tues and all of January and February)	LD

Sea Basket lobster stew is exquisite. Milk-rich but not thickened or heavy, it is loaded with hunks of knuckle and claw meat and has a glistening butter slick on top. Fish and clam chowder are similarly excellent; and the baskets of fried shrimp, clams, and haddock are all fresh and crisp. To our taste, Sea Basket scallops are especially delicious—sweet, tender, and veiled in a crust that virtually melts when bitten.

Sea Basket is a functional roadside café, outfitted with laminate booths and tile walls. Service is "eat in the rough" style: place an order and wait for your number to be called. Nutritional worrywarts will be happy to know that the menu includes a light lobster roll (made with lo-cal mayonnaise) and baked potatoes with fat-free sour cream.

Simones' Hot Dog Stand

99 Chestnut St., Lewiston, ME (207) 782-8431	$
Mon–Sat	BL

Simones' serves the reddest little wienies we have ever seen, about the color of a maraschino cherry. Each is nestled in a steamed-soft split bun, and "the usual" configuration is relish, chopped raw onion, and ketchup. Sauerkraut, cheese, and chili are also available and salt and pepper shakers are accompanied by a shaker of celery salt—a favored hot dog seasoning throughout Maine.

At less than a dollar apiece, these little steamers are fun dogs, not epicurean ones, and Simones' is a merry little café with a chatty counter. Wednesday is bargain day, when the price drops to seventy-five cents per dog. The one-sitting eating record of thirty-six has stood for decades. (Simones' itself dates back to 1908.) The waitresses informed us that those who try to break it inevitably make the mistake of drinking soda pop at some point in their marathon. The carbonation fills them up and they always lose their appetite somewhere near the two dozen mark.

MASSACHUSETTS

★ ★ ★

Baxter's Fish N Chips

177 Pleasant St., Hyannis, MA (508) 775-4490	$
closed from Columbus Day until early spring	£D

Overlooking the Hyannis harbor, Baxter's is an ultracasual fish-fry where customers call out their order and tote their food to picnic tables indoors and out. Clams are grainy-textured, luscious, and oily with a nice ocean savor; fish is tender; scallops are sweet; and the clam fritters, served with syrup for dunking, are superb. To drink, get your own tonic (Massachusettsese for soda pop) at the bar, where a sign warns: NO CHECKS, CHARGES, CUFFING.

Yankee Drink Lingo

North of New York City (in which a "coffee, regular" means coffee *with* cream), soda fountains have strange terms for familiar drinks, especially confusing because the slang varies from place to place.

What the rest of America knows as a *milk shake* (ice cream, milk, and syrup blended smooth) is known throughout Rhode Island as a *cabinet*, and farther east along the coast as a *frappé* or *velvet.*

A *milk shake,* in most downeast sweet shops, means milk and flavored syrup, but no ice cream.

A *soda* is a soft drink (what the Midwest knows as *pop),* except in eastern Massachusetts, where soft drinks are known as *tonics.*

Butler's Colonial Donut House

461 Sanford Rd., Westport, MA (508) 672-4600	$
only on Fri, Sat, Sun	BL

Weekends only, starting at seven in the morning and until the day's supply is gone, here's a little place on the road to Rhode Island Sound that is a donut-eater's delight. Glazed or raised, circular with holes or long and filled with jam and whipped cream, they're probably not what you need to eat before going swimming; but after too much time doing healthy things in sun and surf, nothing quite fills the bill as nicely as a half dozen of these handsome sinkers.

The Clam Box

206 High St., Ipswich, MA	$
(978) 356-9707	LD

A roadside marvel in business since 1935, the Clam Box is shaped exactly like a trapezoidal cardboard clam box, but thirty feet high. Its clams are some of the North Shore's finest, their sea-salt smack sheathed in a frail crust that blends perfectly with the plump clam inside. A Clam Box platter features shatteringly crisp onion rings and fried potatoes as well as coleslaw so finely chopped you want to eat it with a spoon.

Durgin-Park

Faneuil Hall Marketplace, Boston, MA	$$
(617) 227-2038	LD

Durgin-Park is an antique mess hall mobbed by tourists and locals who come for unaffected Yankee fare dished out by brusque Yankee waitresses. It is a raucous place where food gets slapped onto plates without concern for how it looks, then slammed down on long communal tables with no regard for etiquette; but the disdain for dining nicety only adds to the sense of authenticity. Beantown standbys, all served in abundance, include blocks of downeast corn bread, oyster stew made with milk and cream, stone-crock baked beans, wondrously dark Indian pudding, and strawberry shortcake made with fresh berries on an old-time biscuit. For many regular customers, the only thing to eat is prime rib—thick as the Boston Yellow Pages and oozing juice—and we wouldn't think of ending a meal without hot apple pandowdy with ice cream on top, along with a dish of Durgin-Park's own weird, wonderful coffee Jell-O.

J. T. Farnham's

88 Eastern Ave., Essex, MA	$
(978) 768-6643	£D

A cute little roadside diner, Farnham's has always been the kind of place favored by locals more than tourists; now under new management, service is a bit more formal (regulars no longer bus their own tables after breakfast), but the fried clams remain grand. They are tender, light-crusted, easy to eat, and with a faint nut-rich flavor; and the snapping-firm, sweet-fleshed fried shrimp are equally inspired. A plate of either is a mountain, and the onion rings are big and meaty with ragged crunchy crusts. To accompany such feasts, Farnham's offers all the usual brands of tonic (local lingo for soda pop), plus sarsaparilla and Moxie.

Four Seas

360 S. Main, Centerville, MA	$
(508) 775-1394 (summer only)	£D

Four Seas is beloved by generations of Cape Cod residents and vacationers for its delicious ice cream, served in cones, cups, and sundaes. Posted on the wall each day are the available flavors: vanilla, chocolate, strawberry, of course; maple walnut, black raspberry, and other fairly familiar names; plus such curious house specialties as penuche pecan and frozen pudding; and, on occasion, fresh cantaloupe. Likewise, the list of sundae sauces ranges from the familiar—hot milk chocolate (aka hot fudge) and hot butterscotch—to such soda-fountain Victoriana as claret, wild cherry, and soft walnuts in maple syrup. Frappés and milk shake flavors are also itemized—all are available plain, minted, or malted—and if you're not from around here, you need to know that a milk shake means nothing but a flavored syrup and milk; a frappé is what most of the rest of us know as a milk shake: flavoring, milk, and ice cream blended together.

Lindsey's Seafood Restaurant

3138 Cranberry Hwy., Buzzards Bay, MA	$$
(508) 759-5544	LD

Years ago, Lindsey's sold clam baskets to beach-goers, and although it has grown from a roadside shack into a large, modern clamatorium, it still serves lovely platters of fried seafood, with crunchy clams a specialty. Start your meal with milky-sweet New England chowder and end with warm Indian pudding. For fish frowners (who have no business on Cape Cod to begin with), there are actually some fine farmhouse suppers on the menu, including turkey pot pie and roast beef, with tasty mashed potatoes on the side.

Ma Glockner's

151 Maple St., Bellingham, MA (508) 966-1085	$$
closed Mon (closed several weeks in winter)	LD

Berch-fried chicken," Ma Glockner's claim to glory, involves a mysterious cooking process (not frying!) the details of which are known only to the kitchen staff, but we can tell you that the result is a crisp-skinned half-bird that fairly drips buttery flavor. It is served with French fries, cranberry sauce, and delectable hot rolls swirled with cinnamon-sugar, followed by coconut cream pie. This well-nigh perfect meal has drawn crowds to the old-fashioned family restaurant with the neon hen roosting on top since the 1930s.

Mike's Donut Shop

115 Broadway, Everett, MA (617) 389-9415	$
closed only midnight to 6 AM, Fri and Sat	B

Here is Beantown in the raw, round the clock. Frequented by truckers, cabbies, insomniacs, and fried-dough addicts, Mike's is a pleasure of the soul that only culinary outlaws really understand. The donuts are hand-cut and freshly cooked, but they aren't elegant. The plain ones have a dense, cakey texture just right for dunking; and the French crullers are airy enough to eat a half dozen at a shot, easy. Boston creams, loaded with cool whippo and blanketed with chocolate, are just the kind of sweet treat the nutrition police are always warning us about, so it is only natural to break out into a mischievous smile as one scarfs down a bunch of them in this rogues' gallery of a donut shop.

We recently received an e-mail from Matthew L. Bashore, who has the fortune (good or bad?) to live near enough Mike's to eat there whenever the craving strikes. "For future editions of your book, I suggest a warning to the uninitiated," Matthew wrote. "My wife has become addicted to Mike's pink coconut donuts. Her three AM fixes are becoming more frequent, and she lives her life in a weary blur, anticipating the next taste of that rosy ring of delight."

Mildred's Chowder House

290 Iyanough Rd., Hyannis, MA	$$
(508) 775-1045	LD

Once a roadside clam shanty, now an immense eating hall, Mildred's continues to serve the simple Cape Cod cooking that made it famous. Chowder, of course, is the house specialty, and it is a classic: creamy, vaguely porcine, generously dotted with clams and little tender chunks of potato. Mildred's seafood stew is well worth spooning into, simplicity itself. Lobster stew, for example, is nothing but a broad bowl of warm cream and melted butter in which float large, tender pieces of lobster meat. What could be more comfortable than that? There is plenty of good local fish on the menu, and there are some fancy-pants casseroles, but we suggest travelers in search of Yankee flavors stick to basics. For dessert, of course, that means pudding. There is good, old-fashioned Indian pudding, made of long-cooked cornmeal and molasses, as well as a fine Grape-Nuts custard, gentle as baby food.

No Name

15¹/₂ Fish Pier, Boston, MA	$$
(617) 338-7539	£D

No Name isn't an undiscovered haunt of fishmongers and mariners anymore. In fact, it's quite a tourist attraction. The old lunch room on the pier among the fish warehouses and lobster companies has become a large institutional restaurant. But the transformation has not changed the fact that this is still a fine place to eat fresh Boston seafood at reasonable prices.

The chowder is superb, thick with fish but not overly rich. Scrod is served simply broiled in a pool of butter on a silver plate, its surface faintly crusty from the broiler. Poke it with a fork and it falls into big, sweet hunks, pure as fish can be. Fried clams, scallops, shrimp, or fish are all exemplary, served with milky coleslaw and an especially tasty tartar sauce. Our exuberant waiter, who barked out orders amidst the clatter of this overgrown luncheonette, gleefully explained why the tartar sauce is so good, holding his fingers to his lips and puckering up with an air kiss aimed at the chef back in the kitchen: "The Greek touch!"

White Cap

141 High St., Ipswich, MA	$
(978) 356-5276	£D

White Cap has gone upscale and introduced table service since it was an eat-in-the-rough clam joint, but its simple shoreline fare is still first-class. Its clams are golden blistered squiggles, rich and satisfying, meltaway light. There are various sizes on the plate, and they are impossible to stop eating until they are gone. The fried onions are lovely, too, and the clam chowder is superb: milky-smooth more than creamy-thick, it is sweet as a sea breeze and deeply satisfying. There are some pieces of potato in it, but what is amazing is how many chunks of diced clam each spoonful yields.

Woodman's of Essex	
121 Main St., Essex, MA	$
(978) 768-6451	£D

Woodman's is a raucous enterprise, a helter-skelter complex of eating areas including a tent for clambakes, a raw bar, and a sprawling enclosed dining room where wooden booths and tables are almost always packed with carefree eaters. There are signs taped and tacked everywhere. Some announce menu items: LOBSTER ROLL SPECIAL, CLAM STRIPS. One near the take-out window says, ATTENTION: ALL COLESLAW, TARTAR SAUCE, AND BUTTER MONEY GOES TO THE L. DEXTER WOODMAN SCHOLARSHIP FUND, THANK YOU. Another near the order window alerts customers: OUR FRIED CLAMS ARE RUNNING BIG TODAY.

The fried clams, which were invented here in 1916 by Lawrence Woodman, are beauties: light gold with a suave crunch to their surface and a velvety interior that is pure pleasure on the tongue. You can buy them by the pint or, an even better choice, as a clam plate, piled so ridiculously high that it would seem impossible for it to hold one more clam, onion ring, or French fry. Besides impeccable fried seafood, Woodman's sells beauteous whole lobsters. It is also well worth sampling Woodman's clam cakes and chowder . . . although not at the same time you are eating a clam platter. Either choice is a full meal, and then some.

NEW HAMPSHIRE

Bishop's Ice Cream	
183 Cottage St., Littleton, NH	*$*
(603) 444-6039 (April to Columbus Day)	*LD*

A Victorian house across from a three-horse cemetery, Bishop's makes ice cream every morning and dishes it out to hordes of happy hungries all day long. There are good baroque concoctions available, Bishop's Bash in particular (chocolate chips, nuts, and brownie chunks in dark chocolate), but the best flavors have the carefree quality that ice cream used to have before the era of superpremium amalgams loaded with cookies and candy. Vanilla is pure and white; chocolate is only gently chocolatey and not too serious; coffee is creamy more than caffeinated. Here, too, is the old Yankee favorite, Grape-Nuts ice cream, with little nubs of cereal softened to grainy bits of salubrious texture in the smooth ivory custard.

There is something unusually civilized about coming to Bishop's for ice cream. You'd think that such a happy-time product would stimulate yelps of exuberance and that the interior of the shop would ring with rapture. On the contrary, there is a reverential hush about it, even when Bishop's is jammed and every little table is occupied with ice cream eaters and a hundred are waiting to get inside. Our favorite place to lick cones is just out front, where a bench affords a pleasant view of the street and an American flag flaps on a pole high above.

The Brick Store

Rte. 302, Bath, NH	$
(603) 747-2074	BLD

Not a restaurant, but a valuable source of many good things to eat in the car or at a picnic, The Brick Store is the oldest general store in America, dating back to the eighteenth century. It is appetizing just to walk in and smell two hundred years of food and soaps and sundries, as well as smokehouse bacon and sausage, muffins and donuts, and maple candy. Among the emporium's attractions are slant-front counters (so ladies with hoop skirts can step close and inspect the merchandise) as well as benches on the front porch where passers-by are invited to sit a spell and watch the world go by. We walked out with bags of old-fashioned store crackers, soldier beans for slow-cooking, and a jar of maple cream (for slathering on waffles) made by local householder and chanteuse Patti Page.

George's Diner

10 Plymouth St., Meredith, NH	$
(603) 279-8723	BLD

We like the motto of George's Diner—"Just Good Food"—but there are daily specials that are more than ordinary meat and potatoes. For example, you can eat a classic, although now hard-to-find, New England boiled dinner every Friday night (that's corned beef with all the fixin's), as well as mighty tasty corn chowder every Monday at lunch. Breakfast, served until two in the afternoon, is notable, including homemade muffins, excellent home fries to accompany eggs, and (on frequent occasions) red-flannel hash, which is traditionally made from leftover boiled dinner. Any day, the franks and beans are dandy (those beans don't come from a can!); and the pie selection resembles a good church bake sale.

Lindy's Diner

19 Gilbo Ave., Keene, NH	$
(603) 352-4273	BLD

You have probably seen Lindy's many times, but always in the background. It's the all-American Main Street diner across from the bus station where candidates for president of the United States come to be seen hobnobbing with ordinary citizens and enjoying such of-the-people meals as bacon and eggs for breakfast, and franks and chili, creamed chipped beef, or pot roast for lunch. During primary season, the place is frequented by an inordinate number of out-of-town journalists, politicos, and campaign camp followers, but once the citizens of New Hampshire have cast their ballots, Lindy's reverts to being an honest, blue-plate diner that deserves your vote.

Miss Wakefield Diner

Rte. 16, Sanbornville, NH	$
(603) 522-6800	BL

We are NOT a fast-food operation," warns the menu in this lovely 1949 diner resuscitated by the Benner family a few years ago. That's a fact: no fast-food outlet serves mashed potatoes like this, piled into a mountain with gravy cascading down the side, to accompany excellent meat loaf; and the warm bread pudding is diner fare *par excellence.* Indeed, you will wait a bit if you order your corned beef hash extra well done; and a burger with bacon, mushrooms, and blue cheese takes a while to assemble. But service is brisk enough; and the taste and quality of Miss Wakefield's homey food is a quantum leap beyond anything mass produced.

Breakfast is especially right—handsome blueberry or cranberry pancakes with real maple syrup, Texas French toast, giant muffins, tawny home fries with eggs—but we must also thank traveling epicure Dorothy S. O'Connor for alerting us to the fine grilled cheese sandwich at lunch, served with homemade soup. Such comfort food cannot be franchised.

Polly's Pancake Parlor

Rte. 117, Sugar Hill, NH (603) 823-5575	$
(seasonal) April through October; weekends only in November	B L

Ever since "Sugar Bill" Dexter and his wife, Polly, converted the carriage shed of their farm into a tea room in 1938, this rustic White Mountain eatery has been a showcase for maple products at their finest. Pancakes are the specialty of the house; they are made from stone-ground flours or cornmeal, accompanied by crystalline maple syrup and maple butter spread. You can also get maple muffins, maple Bavarian cream, and a wondrous slivered apple and maple syrup ice cream topping known as Hurricane Sauce (named after the hurricane of '38, which blew so many apples off the trees that they had to figure out a way to use them up fast). Polly's opens after mud season in the spring, when many of the surrounding maple trees are hung with taps and buckets; the spectacular time to visit is autumn, during the sugarbush's chromatic climax. (Warning: during tourist season, you will wait for a table.)

RHODE ISLAND

4th Street Diner

184 Admiral Kalbfus Rd., Newport, RI	$
(401) 847-2069	B L D

The jonnycakes Trish Warner makes at the 4th Street Diner are nearly see-through thin, just the way people in this part of Rhode Island like them (and spell them—without the *h*). Served alongside just about any meal, but especially at breakfast, the elegant corn cakes are reason enough to find a seat in this mid-century diner that provides a reality check for anyone overwhelmed by the rich people's "cottages" that attract tourists to Newport. In this joint, you rub elbows with locals and eat such of-the-people fare as biscuits with sausage gravy, Portuguese soup made with kale and beans, chorizo sausage–stuffed quahog clams, and freshly roasted turkey made into hot sandwiches and Thanksgiving-style suppers every day.

Allie's Donuts

3661 Quaker Lane (Rt. 2), North Kingstown, RI	$
(401) 295-8036 5AM–5PM Mon–Fri; 6AM–1PM Sat	BL

Allie's is a big building out in the country where hundreds of dozens of donuts are made every morning. There are two entrances and two adjoining order counters, and the excitement and activity behind the counter as well as in the lines of waiting customers is a thrilling appetizer. The variety of available donuts is more impressive than any chain, but the big difference is that these donuts are delicious. Plain, raised, and filled, small donut holes and hefty sugar sticks are all beautifully hand-made, modest-sized, with faintly crunchy exteriors and cakey insides that are sweet but not cloying. Beyond exemplary donuts is a whole repertoire of ancillary delicacies including turnovers, French apple squares, chocolate-pecan brownies, coffee cakes, cupcakes, cookies, and twists.

Angelo's Civita Farnese

141 Atwells Ave., Providence, RI	$
(401) 621-8171	LD

Atwells Avenue is the main artery of Federal Hill, one of America's most delicious Little Italys, a brick-street neighborhood of aromatic bakeries, pizzerias, cheese shops, and sidewalk cafés. Among the many good restaurants, Angelo's stands out for its southern Italian home cooking: honest pastas, braciola (Tuesdays and Wednesdays only), veal or eggplant parmigiana, and utterly comforting pasta e fagiole soup. It is an unassuming place with large tables shared by strangers, friendly service by waiters in well-worn aprons, and good cheap wine by the jugful.

Aunt Carrie's

Point Judith, Narragansett, RI (401) 783-7930	$
June through early September	LD

This breezy beachside dinner hall and clam shack takes you back a half century to carefree days along the ocean shore. Salt breezes blow in across the parking lot, where barefoot sun worshipers eat crunchy fried clams, shrimp, and scallops by the plate or pint, then head down toward the sand and surf. There is also a lovely wood-paneled dining room where contemplative customers enjoy bounteous soup-to-nuts shore dinners that include clam cakes, chowder, steamer clams, brown bread, filet of sole, corn on the cob, lobster, and Indian pudding. In early summer, look for rhubarb pie, an Aunt Carrie's specialty for decades.

Bocce Club

226 St. Louis Ave., Woonsocket, RI (401) 762-0155	$$
Wed–Sun (Sun from noon)	D

Gigantic dinners of roast chicken and pasta, served family-style, are a Rhode Island custom and the specialty of at least a half-dozen institution-sized eating halls around the state. The Bocce Club, a modest restaurant in a homey Woonsocket neighborhood, is where the tradition began in the 1920s when a group of Italian-Americans gathered for supper after their afternoon bocce game. The chicken, seasoned with rosemary and bathed in butter and olive oil, is succulence incarnate. It is preceded by antipasto, accompanied by crusty bread, pasta in a meaty red sauce, and a motley heap of French fried *and* oven-roasted potatoes. Pass the platters, and eat until you cannot move: that is the Bocce Club way.

Caserta's Pizzeria

121 Spruce St., Providence, RI	$
(401) 272-3618	LD

If you have any doubt that New England is Pizza Central, come to Caserta's in Providence, Rhode Island, and you will achieve blissful certainty. On a side street just off Atwells Avenue in Federal Hill, Caserta's is an old-world godsend. Here the pies are built upon thick, yeasty crusts, spread with fragrant tomato sauce and luxuriously creamy cheese or topped with whatever round-the-world hodgepodge you favor. One locally liked interpretation of the flat pizza pie is known hereabouts as a popeye (elsewhere, a calzone), in which the dough is folded over to make an immense sandwich. Caserta's own variation on this theme is called the Wimpy: spinach, mozzarella, and disks of pepperoni, all folded inside a big pocket of the flavorful crust. It's pizza paradise.

Common's Lunch

The Commons, Little Compton, RI	$
(401) 635-4388	BLD

There are many good things to eat in this comfy town lunchroom, which is the kind of place where the day's newspapers are passed along from one bunch of morning coffee hounds to the next. Stuffies—quahog clams with oceanic cracker-crumb stuffing—are moist and satisfying. Buttery clam chowder is accompanied by crusty clam cakes. We once had a prune apple pie here that was grandmotherly good. But the main culinary lure is jonnycakes, corn griddle cakes made the way cooks in the eastern part of the state prefer them: light and lacy, and so thin you can practically see through them. They are served for breakfast, just like ordinary pancakes with bacon or sausage and syrup on the side, but their slightly gritty texture and steamy corn flavor is a unique Yankee taste experience to remember.

Haven Brothers

Fulton and Dorrance Sts., at Kennedy Plaza,	$
Providence, RI	D
5 PM–3 AM Mon–Thur; until 4 AM Fri and Sat; closed Sun	

Love it or leave it, Haven Brothers is not for the culinarily squeamish. It is a movable lunch truck that comes to this spot and parks every night, six nights a week, just as it has done for more than a century. An old-time dog wagon *par excellence*, Haven Brothers sparkles with sass and attitude as hash slingers dish out hot dogs and baked beans, cheap sandwiches with "coffee milk" on the side, and beef patties that loyal customers know, with affection, as murder burgers. Seating is limited—there are three stools—but that doesn't stop crowds from gathering around in the middle of the night to consume their meals on foot and partake of New England's most colorful late-night junk-food binge.

Jigger's Diner

145 Main St., East Greenwich, RI (401) 884-5388	$
(D Fri only)	BL

Jigger's had been neglected for ten years when chef Carol Shriner restored the vintage 1950 dining car in 1992. She varnished wood booths until they gleamed, she polished stainless steel in the open kitchen, she buffed the green-and-white tile on the walls and found matching pale valances for the windows, and she crafted a menu of blue-plate specials and regional delights way above ordinary diner standards.

Fine-textured meat loaf is accompanied by genuine mashed potatoes or hefty steak fries and (for a dollar extra) tart homemade applesauce. There are gravy-topped turkey croquettes, cheese steaks on good torpedo rolls, even trendy specialty sandwiches such as pesto chicken and deluxe turkey (with roasted red pepper). Start with a cup of comforting soup, conclude with baked-here pie, cake, or a stellar bread pudding with rum sauce; you can even accompany the meal with a tall milk shake (known in these parts as a cabinet) served in a silver beaker.

Breakfast is grand, too (especially so on weekends): hot muffins, chunky home fries, hand-crafted sausage patties, and jonnycakes, which are Rhode Island's unique style of cornmeal griddle cakes, made here the South County way—plump and moist inside with a fine sandy crust.

On Fridays only, this convivial place stays open for dinner, serving fish and chips, clam cakes, and chowder.

Prairie Diner	
416 Public St., Providence, RI (401) 785-1658	*$*
Mon–Sat	*BL*

There is one good reason to come to the Prairie Diner, a weathered eatery in a less-than-lovely part of Providence, and that reason is snail salad. Since mid-century, chef Albert Iannone's zesty mélange of thin-sliced snails in a marinade with onions, chopped celery, and olives has built a loyal clientele of diners and take-out customers who savor this only-in-the-Ocean-State salad as an antipasto before hot Italian platters, alongside cornucopic sandwiches or stuffed clams or chowder, and as a cool meal unto itself.

Silver Top Diner	
13 Harris Ave., Providence, RI (401) 272-2890	*$*
11 PM to 6:30 AM daily	*DB*

For night owls only, Silver Top is a genuinely old wooden dining car in the working part of town. Recently refurbished, it specializes in big, simple meals that appeal to peripatetic appetites with middle-of-the-night munchies. The omelets are massive, the char-cooked steak sandwiches are served on good buns, and the "Caveman" burgers are a guaranteed half pound of beef, served with good garlicky home-fried potatoes. Of course, the true appeal of this intensely lively place is people-watching. The clientele is a fascinating mix of club-hoppers, tattoo collectors, cops on and off the beat, and insomniacs on the prowl, all doing their own thing along the counter as the jukebox throbs and the grill sizzles until dawn.

VERMONT

★ ★ ★

Blanche and Bill's Pancake House

Rte. 4, Bridgewater Corners, VT	$
(802) 422-3816 Wed–Sun	BL

Blanche Toth makes pancakes from a recipe created by her late husband Bill. The batter's ingredients are secret, but Blanche told us that she ages it three days (five days for waffles). The result are lacy cakes with a faint bite reminiscent of sourdough but not nearly as

Yankee Arcana

Most of America's regional cuisines have enjoyed a certain vogue in recent years—California, Cajun, Tex-Mex, Gulf Coast, etc. One that never was chic, and likely won't be, is New England. In this part of the world, the fuddy-duddy ways of the kitchen don't lend themselves to high-fashion interpretation by trendy chefs. But they sure make for interesting eating along the road. These are some of the tasty regional oddities still fairly common at ordinary cafés, diners, and roadside stands:

<u>American chop suey</u> A parsimonious school-lunch-type meal of elbow macaroni mixed with ground beef and tomatoes.

<u>Boiled dinner</u> Corned beef boiled with cabbage, beets, carrots, and new potatoes. Look for this at the table of an old inn.

<u>Brown Betty</u> Cracker-crumb pudding sweetened with molasses or maple syrup.

<u>Fried dough</u> Disks of quick-fried dough topped with cinnamon-sugar or tomato sauce and eaten on the stroll at Grange fairs and draft horse competitions. Similar items, but not so flat, are often served with seafood along the southern shore in Massachusetts, where they are known as doughboys.

tangy: elegant flapjacks! The round, small-hole waffles are fragile, crisp, and toasty, served with a liberal dusting of powdered sugar. Sweet Vermont maple syrup is provided, or you can order any breakfast accompanied by Blanche's own wild blueberry sauce, which is warm and tart.

This estimable little pancake house is a jolly rectangular place, its walls festooned with Red Sox encomia as well as dozens of felt-penned signs, some announcing specials of two, four, or six 'cakes with various pig meats, others posted just for humor's sake: FREE DIRECTIONS ANY TIME. ACCURATE DIRECTIONS, 77 CENTS. One sign says, IGNORE ALL SIGNS! And out in the parking lot, the car of Tina the cook boasts three nearly matching bumper stickers: I ♥ VERMONT, I ♥ JESUS, and I ♥ ELVIS

Grape-Nuts pudding A sweet custard in which the cereal softens to create streaks of grain.

Indian pudding Cornmeal and molasses, cooked forever, to become a dark, spicy samp-like breakfast cereal, but eaten for dessert. Served hot with ice cream on top.

Jonnycakes Little corn cakes made from hard flint corn. On the eastern side of Narragansett Bay, they tend to be broad and thin. To the west, they are silver-dollar size, moist, and plump. Eaten for breakfast, but also as a side dish with supper.

Red flannel hash Made from leftover boiled dinner, named because the beets make it blush.

Sugar on snow During maple sugaring season, warm syrup is poured on fresh-fallen snow, forming chewy maple candy. Sugar on snow (also known as frogs or leather aprons) is so intensely mapley that it is customarily eaten with dill pickles, which help revive an exhausted sweet tooth. Not served in restaurants, but sometimes available at sugar houses in the spring.

Whoopie pie Snack cakes made of two disks of chocolate cake with sugary white goo between them.

Brooksie's	
Rte. 132, Sharon, VT	$
(802) 763-8407	𝓑𝓛𝓓

Billed as "The Cadillac of Diners," and located yards from Exit 2 off I-89, Brooksie's is a low-slung town café where Vermonters come to chat 'n' chew at the counter and at aluminum-ribbed dinette tables spread across the tile floor. Decor includes pictures of local scenery and a vintage "Shake With Uncle Sam" test-of-strength arcade game that long predates Brooksie's genesis in 1948.

Home cooking rules inside the friendly dining room, where one winter day's specials included kielbasa and buttery escalloped potatoes, shepherd's pie, and spicy cabbage soup loaded with broccoli, carrots, celery, and barley. You can come any time for a fine roast turkey dinner with lumpy mashed potatoes and stuffing; and the pie repertoire includes apricot, peach, raspberry, and cherry double-crusters.

In warm weather, Brooksie's is also a drive-in featuring burgers and fried clams and much car-to-car shenanigans among the locals. We prefer visiting off season, though, when the action is all indoors and the clientele has a calmer mien. "I saw Mabel drive by just a while ago," says a waitress to a regular as she pours a sixth cup of coffee one morning after breakfast. "So she must be OK. Haven't seen her in here all week."

The Bryant House	
Rte. 100, Weston, VT	$
(802) 824-6287	𝓛𝓓

At a wooden table in the Bryant House, you can order a bowl of crackers and milk: good old cracker-barrel crackers, a bowl of milk to crumble them in, and a hunk of local cheddar on the side. There's a forthright meal for you! Other Yankee treasures on the menu include chicken pie topped with a broad, flaky biscuit, apple crisp redolent of maple syrup, and Indian pudding as respectable as adult breakfast cereal, not too sweet, served warm with vanilla ice cream melting fast on top.

This tidy little café is affiliated with the adjacent Vermont Country Store (of mail-order fame), which is itself a bonanza of such local culinary peculiarities as five-pound bags of mush cereal, cans of fiddlehead greens, and penny candy by the piece.

Curtis' Barbeque	
Rte. 5 (exit 4 off I-91), Putney, VT (802) 387-5474	$
Wed–Sun, April through November	£𝕯

There are picnic tables but no dining room at Curtis Tuff's unusual roadside attraction, which he bills as the "Ninth Wonder of the World." Mr. Tuff has transformed a couple of immobilized school buses into a kitchen and built a smoke pit to the side. Here he sells delicious barbecued pork ribs and chicken, accompanied by zesty baked beans or baked potatoes. The air smells of burning wood and sizzling pork, and if you are lucky, you will meet Mr. Tuff's pet pig, who roots around the woodpile or the tables looking for a snack.

Gilman's Fairlee Diner	
Rte. 5, Fairlee, VT	$
(802) 333-3569 𝕭£ Daily; 𝕯 Thur and Fri	𝕭£𝕯

Twenty years ago The Fairlee was a beacon of good eats for motorists on their way to or from the Northeast Kingdom. It fell on hard times and finally closed; but now the Gilman Family has revived it. Once again this pretty little diner is a travelers' delight and a locals' fave.

It's a cozy place with just six varnished wooden booths (coat hooks on posts between them) and a dozen stools at the counter. In the morning, regulars eat small piles of homely little donuts—great for dunking—and help themselves to coffee refills from the urns. The lunch menu ranges from burgers and a modern chicken-topped Caesar salad to the locally favored specialty, fried tripe. Lunchcounter buffs will love the hot turkey sandwich, made of delicious white and dark meat and accompanied by a stout swirl of mashed potatoes; also note the spicy meat loaf with golden-dark French fries and lots of gravy. Among the several locally made pies available, we favor apple raspberry crumb.

P & H Truck Stop	
Exit 17 off I-91, Wells River, VT	$
(802) 429-2141	BLD

The aroma in the P & H is not of axle grease and diesel fuel, it is of fresh-baked bread and pot roast blanketed with gravy. The moment you walk in, past shelves of white and cinnamon-raisin bread for sale, you know you have found a kitchen that means business.

Soups and chowders are especially inviting: tomato-macaroni soup is thick with vegetables, ground beef, and soft noodles; corn chowder is loaded with potatoes and corn kernels and flavored with bacon. We love the falling-apart pot roast and any kind of sandwich made using thick-sliced P & H bread, but the mashed potatoes (*purée de pommes de terre* on the bilingual menu, written for French-Canadian truckers) taste like they were made from powder, and the meat loaf is strictly for diehard diner fans. The homemade dessert selection is huge, including fruit pies, berry pies, custard pies, meringue pies, Reese's pie (a peanut-cream), a few types of pudding, and maple-cream pie thick as toffee and topped with nuts.

Putney Diner	
Main St., Putney, VT	$
(802) 387-5433	BLD

Beautiful breakfast and fine pie are the main lures to this pleasant little town café only a few minutes away from I-91. In the morning, big plates of sausage and eggs or three-egg omelets are accompanied by broad-topped muffins that are split and toasted on the grill. At lunch, after hearty meals of meat loaf or roast turkey and stuffing, nearly everyone tops things off with a "baked by Karen" pie, the varieties of which include apple, candy-sweet maple walnut, chocolate

Great American Breakfasts

For us, breakfast is the best meal on the road. It is an opportunity to eat good things not available back home, such as red-eye gravy in a Shenandoah Valley ham house, beignets in New Orleans's French Quarter, huevos rancheros in a bordertown café, or fancy grade maple syrup in a White Mountains sugar shack. Plus, it is the best time of day to soak up local color. In small town cafés and urban diners, regular customers come to trade news and gossip at the counter; cops stock up on donuts; truckers fill thermoses with forty-weight java to get them through the day.

These are some of the country's most colorful breakfast spots:

- Al's Breakfast, Minneapolis, MN (p. 210)
- Becky's, Portland, ME (p. 16)
- Blanche and Bill's Pancake House, Bridgewater Corners, VT (p. 42)
- Blue Heaven, Key West, FL (p. 135)
- Café du Monde, New Orleans, LA (p. 155)
- Chatter Box Café, Sutter Creek, CA (p. 335)
- Classen Grill, Oklahoma City, OK (p. 299)
- The Cottage, LaJolla, CA (p. 336)
- The Diner, Yountville, CA (p. 337)
- Doidge's, San Francisco, CA (p. 337)
- Dot's Diner, Bisbee, AZ (p. 277)
- Durango Diner, Durango, CO (p. 282)
- Goody Goody Diner, St. Louis, MO (p. 219)
- Hob Nob Hill, San Diego, CA (p. 341)
- Jigger's Diner, East Greenwich, RI (p. 40)
- Kitchen Little, Mystic, CT (p. 6)
- Loveless Café, Nashville, TN (p. 98)
- Mrs. Rowe's Restaurant, Staunton, VA (p. 103)
- Old Smoky's Pancake House, Williams, AZ (p. 280)
- The Original Pancake House, Portland, OR (p. 354)
- Otis Café, Otis, OR (p. 354)
- Paris Coffee Shop, Fort Worth, TX (p. 316)
- Polly's Pancake Parlor, Sugar Hill, NH (p. 36)
- Romney Coffee Shop, Lafayette, IN (p. 195)
- Sears Fine Foods, San Francisco, CA (p. 348)
- Silver Spur Café, Sheridan, WY (p. 269)
- Up For Breakfast, Manchester, VT (p. 48)
- Waldorf A'Story, Story, WY (p. 270)
- Whistle Stop Muffins, Georgetown, CT (p. 12)
- Wolfie Cohen's Rascal House, Miami Beach, FL (p. 145)
- Yankee Doodle, New Haven, CT (p. 13)

cream, banana cream, and crumb-top four berry. In the summer, look for superb strawberry rhubarb. The Diner's pie is not big and flashy; it is served in farm-simple little slices—plain-looking, but delicious tasting: pie made by a pro. One day after breakfast, we ordered four pieces between the two of us and our waitress arched her eyebrows but managed to contain her incredulity. "And four glasses of water, too," we asked.

"Don't push it!" she said with the grin of a seasoned accomplice.

Up For Breakfast

4235 Main St., Manchester, VT	$
(802) 362-4204	B L

Green Mountain pancake paradise! Three kinds are available, with or without blueberries in the batter: buttermilk, buckwheat, and sourdough. Good muffins, too: tender-textured quick breads with broad-risen tops and cream-colored insides, the best of them chock-a-block with blueberries and nuts. More elaborate breakfasts include multi-ingredient fritattas, omelets filled with goat cheese and avocado, French toast made using big slabs of marvelous applesauce pecan spice bread, and chicken-duck-cilantro sausage. Wild turkey hash—wildly assembled, not made from wild turkeys—is a cook's tour de force that combines big shreds of roasted turkey with peppers, onions, potatoes, and pine nuts, all griddle-cooked until crusty brown on the outside and topped with poached eggs and a film of fine hollandaise.

Beware: seats in this café can be mighty scarce, especially on weekends or during leaf-peeping season, when an hour's wait is not uncommon.

Wasp's Snack Bar

67 Pleasant St., Woodstock, VT	$
(802) 457-9805 Mon–Sat	BL

Many sightseers visit Woodstock for its Green Mountain charm, quaint shops, and rarefied gourmet meals (at the Woodstock Inn and the Kedron Valley Inn). But few of them find their way to the ten-stool counter in this shoebox-shaped, wood-shingled diner. "The Wasp" is a hangout for townsfolk—workers, housewives, dowagers, artists, and eccentrics—who come for eggs, hash browns, and coffee at 6 AM, for hot dogs and hamburgers at lunch, and for bull sessions and to catch up on local gossip any time. Although it took down its sign several years ago so as not to encourage accidental tourists, the Wasp has always seemed a friendly place to us, and we love the grilled cheese sandwiches and chicken soup at lunchtime, with chocolate cake for dessert. It's an honest meal for a couple of dollars, with a taste of old Vermont thrown in for free.

The Wayside Restaurant

Barre-Montpelier Rd., Berlin, VT	$
(802) 223-6611	BLD

An oasis of genuine regional cooking in a state with too many mediocre "gourmet" inns, the Wayside is a place to sample salt pork and milk gravy (Thursday), fresh native perch (during ice-fishing season), old-fashioned boiled dinner (when it's cold out), and several kinds of hash, including red flannel hash, made with beets. We especially like the Wayside on Wednesday, which is chicken pie and meat loaf day. What a feast the chicken pie is, piled into a big crockery boat with dressing and a crusty biscuit, with a great heap of gravy-dripping mashed potatoes on the side. Wayside meat loaf is outstanding, too: a two-inch-thick slab with a sticky red glaze along the rim and rivulets of stout brown gravy dripping down its sides.

Homespun desserts include Grape-Nuts custard, mince pie, apple pie in a fork-crimped crust, and a radiant maple cream pie that comes dolloped with whipped cream.

Mid-Atlantic

ALL-AMERICAN

DELAWARE

DISTRICT OF COLUMBIA

MARYLAND

NEW JERSEY

NEW YORK

PENNSYLVANIA

White Haven
FAMILY DINER ★

★
Conyngham
TOM'S KITCHEN

HARRISBURG ★

MAMA'S
★ Bala-Cynwyd

Philadelphia
(see below)

Pittsburgh ★
PRIMANTI BROTHERS

Gettysburg ★
FARNSWORTH HOUSE

Leipsic *SAMBO"S*
★ *TAVERN*

Baltimore
(see below)

DOVER ★

Grasonville *HARRIS CRAB*
★ *HOUSE*

Silver Spring
CRISFIELD ★
★ ANNAPOLIS

Washington D.C.
FLORIDA AVENUE GRILL
SHOLL'S COLONIAL CAFETERIA

St. Michaels *CRAB CLAW*

Crisfield ★
CAPTAIN'S GALLEY

Philadelphia

JIM'S STEAKS
OLIVIERI'S PRINCE OF STEAKS
PAT'S KING OF STEAKS
SHANK & EVELYN'S

Baltimore

ATTMAN'S DELICATESSEN
GUNNING'S CRAB HOUSE
OBRYCKI'S
WOMAN'S INDUSTRIAL EXCHANGE

NEW YORK

PENNSYLVANIA

NEW JERSEY

MARYLAND DELAWARE

WASHINGTON D.C.

Rochester *NICK TAHOU*

Tonawanda *TED'S JUMBO RED HOTS*
Buffalo *ANCHOR BAR*
West Seneca *SCHWABL'S*

ALBANY

*RED ROOSTER
DRIVE-IN*
Brewster

DURYEA'S
Montauk

Beacon
QUINN'S LUNCHEONETTE

Amagansett
THE LOBSTER ROLL

New York
(see below)

Brooklyn (see below)

BAHR'S LANDING Highlands
RAY'S SEAFOOD RESTAURANT Colt's Neck

Sea Bright

Long
Branch

*HARRY'S
LOBSTER
HOUSE*

TRENTON

*THE
LIGHTHOUSE*

Atlantic City
*DOCK'S OYSTER HOUSE
WHITE HOUSE SUB SHOP*

Brooklyn

*LUNDY'S
PETER LUGER
TOM'S LUNCHEONETTE
TOTONNO'S PIZZERIA*

New York

*BARNEY GREENGRASS
BENNY'S BURRITOS
CAFÉ EDISON
CARNEGIE DELI
EISENBERG'S SANDWICH
FINE & SCHAPIRO
KATZ'S DELI*

MID-ATLANTIC

DELAWARE

★ ★ ★

Sambo's Tavern

Front St., Leipsic, DE	$$
(302) 674-9724 (customers must be over 21)	LD

Crab feast! Newspaper tablecloths, paper-towel napkins, piles of hard-shelled crabs, radiating peppery spice: all the elements of the Delaware Bay delectation are at the ready in this friendly crab house with a view of the slow-moving Leipsic River. If pick and hammer and bib are not your favored tools for dining, Sambo's Tavern also makes fork-and-knife fine crab cakes and platters of tasty fried fish.

DISTRICT OF COLUMBIA

★ ★ ★

Florida Avenue Grill

1100 Florida Ave. NW, Washington, D.C.	$
(202) 265-1586 Tues–Sat	BLD

Taxi drivers originally staked out this modest corner café near Howard University back when it opened in the mid-1940s. It has since been discovered by *everybody,* high and low, black and white, famous and unknown. The midday menu is a roster of soul food classics including stuffed pork chops, fried fish, and chitterlings, but the great meal to eat in a ramshackle Grill booth or at the scenic counter (where staff and customers trade hash house repartee) is breakfast. Country ham is sizzled to perfection and served with eggs, grits, and gravy, and heaps of sinfully sweet fried apples with hot biscuits on the side.

Sholl's Colonial Cafeteria

1990 K St. NW, Washington, D.C.	$
(202) 296-3065	BLD

No power tables here, no lobbyists or politicians or trendy foodies, either. Sholl's is a rare enclave of culinary democracy in the heart of Washington, D.C. An old-fashioned cafeteria serving three square meals a day, it is plain, simple, and cheap. And the food is good, extraordinarily so when it reflects the southern-rural kitchen traditions that surround the capital, such as crisp fried chicken, savory greens, and a repertoire of creamy-sweet pies. Our favorite meals are the squarest ones: meat loaf with real mashed potatoes, beef stew with corn bread on the side, chicken and biscuits. And for dessert, when we can pass up the rainbow selection of Jell-Os, the rice pudding is superb.

MARYLAND

Attman's Delicatessen

1019 E. Lombard St., Baltimore, MD	$
(410) 563-2666	LD

When the craving for good corned beef (or brisket or pastrami) on rye strikes you in the Baltimore area, go to Attman's in the part of town once known as Corned Beef Row for all its delis. The neighbor-

Diner Slang 101

"Adam and Eve on a Raft" . . . . Poached eggs on toast
"Barn paint" . . . . Ketchup
"Bird seed" . . . . A bowl of cereal
"Cat's eyes" . . . . Tapioca pudding
"Crow slab" . . . . Chocolate pie
"Dog soup" . . . . A glass of water
"Gob stick" . . . . Spoon
"Hounds in hay" . . . . Hot dogs with sauerkraut
"Slippery Joe" . . . . Coffee with cream
"Whiskey toast" . . . . Rye toast

hood is a bit run-down (although Attman's has been remodeled), and the culinary experience is axiomatic. Work your way along a line of fragrant Jewish fare, which is placed onto a tray by the staff, after which you carry your meal into the "Kibbitz Room" to enjoy. In addition to piled-high hot sandwiches, knishes, pickled herring, and matzoh ball soup, Attman's serves wonderful oversized all-beef kosher hot dogs.

Captain's Galley

1021 W. Main St., Crisfield, MD (410) 968-1636	$$
in summer; shorter hours off-season	BLD

The Captain's Galley is a pleasant, polite restaurant that serves much delicious seafood native to the mid-Atlantic region, including sautéed soft-shelled crabs and luxurious oyster fritters. But the one thing you need to eat in Crisfield is crab cakes, and there are none better than the Captain's. Served two-by-two, creamy-sweet and fresh as ocean spray, tender but with a nice little snap to their golden crust, they are the best along the Chesapeake Bay, ergo, the best on earth. The house crab seasoning is sold to take home, but the real secret, of course, is the utter freshness of the local backfin crabmeat.

Crab Claw

Navy Point, St. Michaels, MD	$$
(410) 745-2900	£Ð

Overlooking the harbor and outfitted with open-air tables for sunny-day dining, the Crab Claw has been a favorite fixture of the Eastern Shore for decades. Locals and vacationers alike crowd into the nautically themed dining room to eat piles of hot-spiced Maryland blue crabs, crab cakes, and soft-shells accompanied by pitchers of beer and stacks of paper napkins. It is an informal place, boisterous and fun. If you arrive by boat, there is a house dinghy to help you get ashore.

Crisfield

8606 Colesville Rd., Silver Spring, MD	$$
(301) 588-1572 Ð only Sat and Sun	£Ð

In this new location, the legendary name "Crisfield" applies to a polite fish house that serves consummate mid-Atlantic seafood, including Chesapeake Bay striped bass, luscious stuffed shrimp, and wantonly creamy crab imperial in the shell, as well as Norfolk-style sautéed-in-butter crabmeat. Don't come here to eat the kind of lean, meager seafood the nutrition police are always telling us we ought to eat. Even the broiled fish seems impossibly rich: huge fillets of flounder, moister and sweeter than anywhere on earth. Nor is this the restaurant for gracious amenities—don't expect fawning service—but for a good ol' fish feast, Crisfield cannot be beat.

Gunning's Crab House

3901 S. Hanover St., Baltimore, MD (410) 354-0085;	$$
also at 7304 Parkway Dr., Hanover (410) 712-9404	£D

Steamed crabs, highly spiced and served by the dozen with plenty of beer on the side, are the essential Maryland meal; and no one presents it with more panache than the impertinent staff of Gunning's. With deep-fried pepper rings, faintly sugar-sweetened, to put a twist on the luscious marine feast, it is a culinary adventure not quite like any other, and one all adventurous eaters need to know about. Dine near the bar or in the open-air crab garden when weather permits, and be sure to wear clothes you can wipe your hands on. No amount of napkins is ever sufficient.

There is a newer Gunning's in Hanover, operated by the family that opened the original one but sold it. The crabs and fried green pepper rings are every bit as good, and the staff is every bit as sassy.

Harris Crab House

433 N. Kent Narrows Way, Grasonville, MD	$$
(410) 827-9500	£D

The long tables are covered with brown wrapping paper. The sound in the big, airy dining room and on the outdoor deck is of crab shells cracking and people slurping up the sweet pink meat. There are ribs and chicken on the menu for crab-frowners, as well as a good array of fresh, local seafood, but steamed crabs are the primary lure to this family-oriented crab house on the waterfront. During the week, Harris offers an all-you-can-eat feast; on weekends, buy 'em by the dozen.

Obrycki's

1727 E. Pratt St., Baltimore, MD (410) 732-6399	$$
(closed November through April)	£D

You'll pay handsomely to eat in an old row house now spruced with colonial trim (brass chandeliers, wall sconces), but no matter how much the management turns on the fine-dining charm, the great Obrycki's meal is a sloppy one. Hard-shell crabs, steamed and brilliantly spiced, can only be eaten with sturdy hammers and picks like the tools of a combat engineer. So wear a bib . . . and prepare to feast. On days when Obrycki's can get no good Chesapeake Bay crabs (call ahead if that's what you have your heart set on), they serve a mighty fine pan-fried soft-shell crab sandwich. And we even like the crab imperial—a creamy, goopy comfort-food concoction utterly at odds with today's cruel lite-is-good nutritional dogma.

Woman's Industrial Exchange

333 N. Charles St., Baltimore, MD	$
(410) 685-4388	BL

There isn't a nicer restaurant anywhere for an old-fashioned ladies' lunch: chicken aspic, deviled eggs, and biscuits, for example, served by a staff of uniformed, kindly waitresses in a dining room unchanged for decades. Or you can choose a mild chicken salad sandwich on white bread, meaty croquettes with gravy, or fine-spiced crab cakes. Accompany the dainty fare with a glass of lemonade, top them off with layer cake or meringue pie. Then, when you're done, you can buy jams, jellies, and handwork made by deserving local women, who have been beneficiaries of this stalwart institution since it started serving meals in 1882.

NEW JERSEY

☆ ☆ ☆

Bahr's Landing	
2 Bay Ave., Highlands, NJ	$$
(732) 872-1245	£D

When the Bahr family started serving soup to fishermen from their Highlands houseboat in 1917, the New Jersey shore was a string of little villages and long, sandy beaches. The villages have sprawled but the beaches are still beautiful, and Bahr's has become a big barn of a place catering to hungry families. With a picture window overlooking the Shrewsbury River, a museum's worth of nautical decor, and a long menu of shore dinners, it is the quintessential vacation-time seafood restaurant. Start with "famous chowder" made with tomatoes and vegetables and mountains of chopped clams, or a big bowl of steamers served with broth and butter. Then move on to lobster, flounder, or maybe fried clams. Keep it simple—the stuffed, sauced preparations are best ignored—and you can have a fine, familiar, and satisfying tourist meal.

Dock's Oyster House	
2405 Atlantic Ave., Atlantic City, NJ (609) 345-0092	$$
Tues–Sun, late March to mid-November (reservations advised)	D

For impeccable seafood in civilized surroundings at reasonable prices, Dock's is Atlantic City's best bet. You can have freshly opened clams and oysters or a good-sized boiled lobster, but don't ignore preparations that require more formidable kitchen skills. Fried seafood is gorgeous, sheathed in a frail, savory crust; oyster stew is lush and comforting; and there isn't a finer linguine with garlicky clam sauce this side of Hoboken.

Jewish Deli Lexicon

Waiters in the urban delis of the Northeast are crabby all the time, but they treat you even worse if you act like a greenhorn. So here are ten basic terms you should know before ordering:

Blintzes: sweet pot cheese rolled in crepes and fried in butter

Chicken-in-a-pot: a stew/soup in golden broth with tender vegetables

Kasha varnishkes: bow-tie noodles with buckwheat groats

Knish: a potato dumpling with the atomic weight of lead

Knoblewurst: garlicky salami

Kugel: noodle pudding that can be either sweet or savory

Latkes: potato pancakes, served on the side of sandwiches or as a meal

Novie: Nova Scotia lox—sliced smoked salmon that isn't too salty

"Oy vay": an expression of exasperation; the waiter's mantra

Schmaltz: rendered chicken fat, often spread on dark bread like butter

Harry's Lobster House

1124 Ocean Ave., Sea Bright, NJ (732) 842-0205	$$$
(reservations advised)	D

The Jersey shore has many, many places to eat steamers, lobsters, clams, and crab. Most are breezy and casual and serve decent-enough food. Harry's Lobster House is deluxe (no beachwear allowed!) and serves excellent food. There isn't a better stuffed lobster anywhere, loaded with pearly hunks of sweet crabmeat, and the flounder, either simply broiled or crab-stuffed, is a delight. Start with a dozen raw oysters and/or clams and you have an unimprovable mid-Atlantic feast. The pleasure of a Harry's meal is due in great part to the charm of the place itself, open since 1933 and located in a plain wood-sided building on the main drag of an old vacation town. In its simple, white-walled dining room (without the usual nautical jim-crack decor), loyal customers enjoy a kind of resort-town luxury that has faded away nearly everywhere else.

The Lighthouse	
65 New Ocean Ave., Long Branch, NJ	$
(732) 229-1222 (summer only)	£ D

For quick refreshment along the shore, the Lighthouse is a dandy place to know about. It is a small stand with no seating other than three picnic tables in the parking lot and a menu of hot food limited to hot dogs and meatball sandwiches. But the reason everybody stops here is Italian ice: cool, not too sweet, the perfect summer pick-me-up during a hot day at the shore. Flavors include chocolate, vanilla, cherry, orange, and lemon.

Ray's Seafood Restaurant	
29 Rte. 34 S., Colt's Neck, NJ	$$
(732) 303-1396 £ Tues–Fri; D daily	£ D

Located in the lovely green New Jersey that interstate travelers do not see, Ray's is a civilized country restaurant surrounded by horse farms and orchards. And yet it is just miles from the shore, and its forte is seafood. Plain (baked flounder in lemon butter) or fancy (salmon in puff pastry with crabmeat and brie), the fish on Ray's menu is always fresh and delicious. We particularly like the mussels—marinara or bathed in garlic and wine—and anything with crabmeat. Crab cakes with sweet mustard sauce, flounder stuffed with crab, or crab imperial are all four-star meals . . . not cheap, but worth every penny.

After a meal at Ray's, go across the road to Delicious Orchards, a u-pick-'em apple stand and stupendous country market that is proof positive New Jersey deserves its sobriquet, the Garden State.

White House Sub Shop

2301 Arctic Ave., Atlantic City, NJ	$
(609) 345-1564	£Ɗ

The White House invented the submarine sandwich. Apparently, the great moment occurred during World War II when the sandwich hereabouts known as a hoagie was rechristened as an ode to the men in the Navy who served in loaf-shaped underwater boats. Today's edible White House subs set the gold standard for gigantic sandwiches. They are piled into bakery-fresh lengths of crusty bread, and their configurations range from the White House Special (a sheaf of Italian cold cuts well-oiled and decorated with lettuce and sweet pepper) to messy hot boats loaded with meatballs. Ambiance is Americana in the raw: the walls are plastered with pictures of celebrities who have come to gobble down the gorgeous sandwiches, and the counter help is full of Jersey sass.

NEW YORK

Anchor Bar

1047 Main St., Buffalo, NY	$$
(716) 886-8920	£Ɗ

In the kitchen of the Anchor Bar in 1964, Teressa Bellisimo invented the Buffalo chicken wing. For years, the fried-crisp, hot-sauced little munchies remained a local obsession, but in the early 1980s, they went national in a big way. Anchor Bar wings, which are part of an otherwise unexceptional menu in this corner tavern, are served just the way they were in 1964, in the now-classic configuration with celery stalks (to relieve the palate from their heat) and a bowl of creamy blue cheese dressing to dip them in. They are available hot or mild; the former really is hot, and will set your lips tingling and reaching for a beer. That, of course, is the idea of bar food, of which these zesty wings are a definitive mouthful.

Barney Greengrass	
541 Amsterdam Ave., New York, NY (212) 724-4707	**$$**
until 6 PM	**BLD**

Smoked sturgeon is a staple at good delicatessens everywhere; nowhere is it better than at Barney Greengrass, a family business since 1908. Each cool slice of sturgeon is firm and white, lean and luscious, the sweet flesh insinuated with a whisper of smoke. Have it on a sandwich between slices of rye bread, or on a smoked fish platter with silky pink salmon, pickled herring, and sable. Other good things to eat include whitefish salad, flamingo-pink borscht served in a glass, excellent chopped liver, and triple-decker masterpieces of tongue, pastrami, brisket, and/or corned beef. Perhaps the greatest single dish at this old Formica-table West Side luncheonette is scrambled eggs laced with nuggets of Nova Scotia salmon and oily onions.

Beware of long lines to get in, especially on weekends.

Benny's Burritos	
113 Greenwich Ave., New York, NY (212) 727-0584;	**$**
also at 93 Ave. A (212) 254-2054	**LD**

You might not think of burritos as a real New York food, but they are, thanks to Benny's. When this boisterous joint opened about a decade ago, it started a major eating trend, and now burritos are as much a part of the city's culinary scene as pizza by the slice and hot dogs from a cart. The two Benny's and their uptown sibling, Bertha's (at Broadway and 76 St.), are rightly famous for delicious behemoth burritos loaded with high-quality ingredients ranging from classic meat and cheese to spinach and even tofu. The margaritas are immense, the setting is hip, the people-watching is a gas. It all adds up to a dining experience that is downtown New York at its most beguiling.

Café Edison

228 W. 47th St., New York, NY	$
(212) 840-5000	B L D

At the table up front in the area roped off for celebrities, we swear we saw Neil Simon having matzoh ball soup with William Burroughs (in the summer of '97). And was that magician David Copperfield in the back, making his cheese blintzes disappear off the plate in record time? Everybody who eats at the Café Edison in the Edison Hotel just off Broadway looks like somebody famous, even if they're not.

Please, don't get the impression that this is a ritzy spot. It used to be, in the 1920s, when it was the hotel's grand ballroom. Now the glamour has faded, the bas-relief salmon-colored walls are taped with signs advertising daily specials (TRY OUR BAGELS!), and the waitresses give everyone an equal-opportunity hard time. Still, celebrities flock to this unlikely neighborhood haunt for its genuine Jewish food served without pomp or pretense. So if you are in midtown Manhattan and crave a plate of braised brisket or a bowl of beet borscht, pickled herring, or homemade gefilte fish—at low-low prices, and in the company of celebrities in search of a culinary reality check—find a booth or a counter seat at Café Edison (but do not occupy the front table: that's reserved for playwright August Wilson, who says the coffee-shop clatter inspires some of his finest work).

Carnegie Deli

854 Seventh Ave., New York, NY	$$
(212) 757-2245	B L D

The Carnegie Deli is not for everyone. It can be raucous and rude in a way that some visitors find unbearable. On the other hand, if you are looking for the biggest (and most expensive) pastrami sandwich in town, and a true New York experience—for better and for worse—a seat at one of these overcrowded communal tables has no equal.

Apparently, hand-sliced pastrami is a thing of the past. At least our waitress would not allow us to order our sandwich that way. But even the Carnegie's machine-sliced sandwiches are pretty astounding—so tall that the top piece of rye bread appears to be merely an afterthought applied to the tower of meat. It is virtually impossible to eat the ordinary way, by picking it up in your hands and taking a bite; instead, most customers go at it piece-by-shred, directly from the plate. To accompany this heap of meat and bread, the Carnegie supplies perfect puckery accoutrements—half-sour and sour dills and pickled green tomatoes.

The pickles are arrayed in silver bowls on long tables where strangers are crowded elbow-to-elbow as in a school cafeteria. Forget privacy, peace, and quiet when you sit down here; a Carnegie meal is a down-to-earth communal experience shared by blasé regulars, wide-eyed tourists, and genuine show-biz celebrities (whose pictures line the walls).

Duryea's

65 Tuthill Rd., Montauk, NY	$$
(516) 668-2410	£D

Eat in the rough: choose what you want from a photocopied menu, place your order by the cash register, then wait until your name is called. Tote your own plastic tray full of food (on paper plates) to a table on the lobster deck with a lovely view of Montauk Bay. Then, feast on an absolutely simple but expertly prepared shore dinner: whole lobsters, fresh and sweet, are served with good baked potatoes and rugged coleslaw; big lobster rolls come on toasty buttered buns. Bring your own beer or wine, and it will be a summertime meal to remember.

Eisenberg's Sandwich

174 Fifth Ave., New York, NY	$
(212) 675-5096 Mon–Sat	BL

What's not to like at this neighborhood luncheonette, famous for its tuna sandwich on rye toast? There are other good things to eat—chicken salad, egg salad, corned beef, and pastrami, as well as a hot entree each day—but it's the tuna that has attracted repeat customers since the 1930s. A few years ago, *New York Eats* author Ed Levine secured the sacred recipe: one can of Bumble Bee solid white tuna and Hellmann's mayonnaise (plenty of it), mixed with a big spoon, not a fork.

Like its impeccable tuna, Eisenberg's charm is all about simplicity. One narrow room with a long counter on one side and minuscule tables-for-two along the other, it is a guileless taste of old New York, with a big bowl of pickles on every table.

Fine & Schapiro	
138 W. 72nd St., New York, NY	$
(212) 877-2874	*LD*

We fell in love with Fine & Schapiro for its chicken in a pot, a meat and vegetable soup/stew of grandmotherly succor. Matzoh ball soup is fine, too. And the pastrami sandwiches, while not the mile-high behemoths of the more famous Jewish delis of New York, are exemplary.

Fine & Schapiro is truly kosher, not just kosher style. Its ambience is geared to contemplation. A radio tuned to a soporific lounge-singer station provides mood music to aid digestion. Service is provided to booths by a team of unflappable waitresses who, although never aggressively smiley, worry out loud if you don't finish all your sandwich and fuss over regulars like their own children. At lunchtime, several booths are occupied by old people in the company of nurses and caretakers.

Katz's Deli	
205 E. Houston St., New York, NY	$
(212) 254-2246	*BLD*

A vintage lower East Side dining experience, Katz's (since 1888) is a line-up-and-order delicatessen where the size of your sandwich and even the quality of meat in it is determined by your rapport with the counterman. Tipping is supposedly not allowed, but if you manage to slip your man a little something as he forks the corned beef onto the cutting board, he'll give you fat or lean, whichever you prefer; he may even offer a few forkfuls to nosh while he slices. Pastrami, corned beef, and brisket on fine, fresh rye bread are all deli paradigms, as is the garlicky salami known as knoblewurst, and the all-beef hot dogs are New York's best.

A sign above the cash register on the way out advises SEND A SALAMI TO YOUR BOY IN THE ARMY.

The Lobster Roll	
Rte. 27, Amagansett, NY	**$$**
(516) 267-3740 April-October	**LD**

On any sunny day, you will wait too long in line, and the wood-benched tables scarcely provide a view of the highway let alone the ocean. But despite these hardships, the Lobster Roll is one of the essential seafood shacks in the Hamptons. It has been here forever, operated by a family that settled on Long Island in the seventeenth century, and the menu is traditional family-fun vacation food. Chowder, steamers, plump lobster rolls, and fried puffers are the staples; but it is dessert that is great, pie in particular. It is glorious pie, pie that reminds you of Long Island's farmland heritage, with a fine flaky crust and bounteous filling. Midsummer, when the sky is blue and the waves lap against nearby sands, what could be better than a lunch of chowder and lobster followed by a slab of fresh strawberry-rhubarb or raspberry pie?

Lundy's	
1901 Emmons Ave., Brooklyn, NY	**$$$**
(718) 743-0022	**LD**

For seafood feasting the old-fashioned way, Lundy's is tops. Opened in 1918, known as the largest restaurant in America into the postwar years, it closed in 1979 and reopened in 1995, one-quarter of its former size, now seating a mere 800 customers at one time. It remains a boisterous Brooklyn dining hall, staffed by hordes of white-jacketed waiters toting warm baking powder biscuits, bowls of chowder, and giant tureens full of steamer clams to start a meal, then the great, juicy lobsters that star in the house's famous shore dinners, followed by enormous wedges of pie and cake for dessert. Portions are big, service is brash, customers are loud, and the good times roll just as they did fifty years ago. It is possible to have a downscaled, less-expensive meal in Lundy's clam bar or in an adjoining sidewalk café.

Nick Tahou

2260 Lyell, Rochester, NY (716) 429-6388	$
always open	BLD

Western New York is America's wiener world, and Nick Tahou of Rochester dishes out some of the wickedest. Upstate franks are not slim aristocrats like you might get from a cart in New York City, nor are they crowned with baroque bouquets of condiments like the all-beef red hots of Chicago. Tube steaks in this part of the world tend to be raunchy but irresistibly seductive. Nick Tahou, a round-the-clock eat place where the air is redolent of spice and oil, dishes out several good varieties: red hots, Texas hots, pork hots radiating pepper, and regular pink weenies that are split and grilled to attain maximum lewd character before they are loaded into buns and heaped with a fine-grained chili. *Specialité de la maison* is the garbage plate: baked beans, home-fried potatoes, macaroni salad, a pair of grilled dogs, raw onions, and chili sauce all heaped upon a thick cardboard plate. At sunrise, after a long, hard night, a garbage plate at Nick's just might be what you need.

Peter Luger

178 Broadway, Brooklyn, NY (718) 387-7400	$$$
(reservations required)	£D
(Peter Luger credit cards are the only ones accepted)	

Peter Luger is the archetypal neighborhood restaurant of a bygone New York. Although the neighborhood is now moribund, the heavy oak tables of this robust tavern are packed every night with happy carnivores quaffing dry martinis and gliding knives into butter-tender slices of prime beefsteak. White-aproned waiters, most of them seasoned veterans, seldom bother to let customers know that lamb chops and prime rib are also available (a written menu is given only if you ask for it) because nearly everyone comes for porterhouse, which arrives sliced on a platter to which all at the table help themselves. The meal starts with freshly baked onion rolls and tomato and onion salad (tasty in tomato season). On the side, you want crusty hash browns and creamed spinach; then cheesecake or apple strudel for dessert. It is a classic meal, well-nigh perfect.

Quinn's Luncheonette

330 Main St., Beacon, NY	$
(914) 831-8065	BL

People sometimes forget that there is more to New York than New York City. There are plenty of small and medium-size towns upstate, where the livin' is easy and the restaurants are homey and affordable. Such a place is Quinn's of Beacon, where for many years now, locals have congregated at lunch for bowls of soup (turkey noodle is especially excellent), oven-fresh bread, and made-from-scratch macaroni and cheese. At Quinn's, the waitresses call you "Hon" and give you their honest assessment of the day's repertoire of pies. The hustle of the Big Apple seems light-years away.

Red Rooster Drive-In

Rte. 22, Brewster, NY	$
(914) 279-8046	£𝒟

Hamburgers sizzled on a smoky charcoal grill and served on a tender bun—deluxe, please, with lettuce and tomato!—are accompanied by French fries and milk shakes (or floats or egg creams). Cheeseburgers are especially satisfying, and if you like grilled onions, thirty cents gets you a great extra heap of them atop the chunky beef patty. Also on the menu are hot dogs, cheese dogs, and chili cheese dogs. Eat in your car, at one of three tiny booths inside, or outdoors at a slew of picnic tables spread across the lawn in back. Adjacent to the open-air dining room is a modest miniature golf course where kids and carefree adults while away pleasant evenings in the Red Rooster's afterglow.

Schwabl's

789 Center Rd., West Seneca, NY	$
(716) 674-9821	£𝒟

One of the essential things to eat in the Buffalo area, other than fried chicken wings and charcoal-cooked hot dogs, is the sandwich called beef on weck. Several places make a specialty of it. Schwabl's, an old leather-table beef house, is the one we like best. The beef is roasted to pink, sliced thin, and piled high inside a salty-topped roll that is spangled with caraway seeds (known as kummelweck). Unless you want it dry, the man who carves the beef and assembles the sandwich behind the bar dips the top of the roll in natural gravy—not so deeply that the sturdy bread falls apart, but long enough for juice to ooze when you heft the sandwich from the plate. Horseradish, the preferred condiment for beef on weck, is provided at each table and at the bar.

Ted's Jumbo Red Hots

2312 Sheridan Dr., Tonawanda, NY	$
(716) 836-8986	£D

Western New York is probably more fanatical about frankfurters than any other place in the country. From the pale "white hots" of Rochester to the charcoal-grilled red hots of Buffalo, tube steaks are an upstate passion. We think some of the best are dealt by Ted's of Tonawanda (and about a half dozen other locations in the Buffalo area). Ted's dogs come smothered in powerful, peppery relish and sided by hard-crusted onion rings, but what makes them great is the way they are cooked: over coals that infuse each link with pungent smoke flavor and burnish its taut skin with a seared crust. The locally favored drink to accompany a grilled red hot is a loganberry-flavored beverage that tastes like bug juice at sleep-away camp.

Tom's Luncheonette

782 Washington Ave., Brooklyn, NY	$
(718) 636-9738 Mon–Sat	BL

A few years ago, Tom's was declared New York's best breakfast restaurant by *New York* magazine, which praised its "festive atmosphere" as the basis of good karma that make bacon and eggs transcendent. A 1930s-vintage, Formica-clad diner, Tom's attracts Prospect Heights residents early in the morning for banana walnut pancakes, egg sandwiches, grits 'n' eggs, and hot oatmeal. Customers rub elbows and nurse cups of coffee while exchanging pleasantries with the kindly staff. At noon, the place smells of good hot lunch: burgers frying, cheese sandwiches grilling, slabs of meat loaf and slices of beef brisket on plates with swirls of mashed potatoes. Wash down these satisfying meals with fresh lemonade, a cherry-lime rickey, or the classic New York egg cream, made by swirling together just the right amounts of milk, chocolate syrup, and seltzer water.

Totonno's Pizzeria

1524 Neptune Ave., Brooklyn, NY (718) 372-8606	$
Wed–Sun	LD

In a neighborhood that has disintegrated all around it, Totonno's (pronounced "T-t-own's") remains a true and good neighborhood pizzeria. Dough made fresh each morning is pounded out and topped with slices of creamy mozzarella and fresh tomato sauce. It emerges from the coal-fired brick oven crisp and chewy, with a savor no franchise can touch.

It used to be that Totonno's sometimes closed by 5 or 6 PM when it ran out of dough; it is now a certainty that pizza will be available through dinner hour.

PENNSYLVANIA

Family Diner

302 Main St., White Haven, PA	$
(717) 443-8797	BLD

A gem just minutes off I-80. There is something for everyone at the Family Diner, from liver and onions or ham steak with a pineapple ring to short-order sandwiches and a giant-size, dolled-up "diner hamburger with a college degree."

The great meal is breakfast, served until 2 PM. Inelegant, ribsticking pancakes are as big as the plate, heaped with hot blueberry or apple topping. Creamed chipped beef is sided by home fries or bitesize potato cakes. Eggs are available any way (including soft-boiled and poached) with a choice of five different kinds of pig meat. In addition to the usual bacon, ham, and sausage, there is luscious pork roll and the even more luscious Pennsylvania treat—scrapple, sizzled to a crisp.

Farnsworth House

401 Baltimore St., Gettysburg, PA	$$
(717) 334-8838	£D

Game pie, country ham, peanut soup, and crocked spoon bread are some of the vintage savories on the evening menu in this old brick home at the most famous battlefield in America. Farnsworth House was in the thick of the fight; more than 100 bullet holes in its south wall bear testimony to the hostilities of the three days in July 1863 during which Confederate snipers occupied what was then the Sweeney family home.

As Civil War–era tunes play (quietly), you dine by candlelight at walnut tables set with heavy pewter service plates and glasses, surrounded by paintings and Matthew Brady photographs of the battle's heros and framed letters written by Generals Lee and Pickett. The game pie is not actually gamy, but a robust melange of shredded pheasant, duck, and turkey mixed into a casserole with mushrooms, bacon, and wild rice and topped with a disk of pastry crust. Pumpkin fritters are an ideal side dish: plump, crunchy fried orbs with melting sweet insides.

Jim's Steaks

400 South St., Philadelphia, PA	$
(215) 928-1911	£D

Jim's, since 1939, is a deco-tiled cheese steakery that actually offers a choice of cheeses on your sandwich. Cheese Whiz is standard; if you don't tell the counter people otherwise, your tender beef is globbed with it (which some aficionados contend is the only proper topping), but more refined palates can request provolone or American, laid on in precut slices that turn soft from the warmth of the beef and give the sandwich a relatively epicurean twist. The bread is excellent, the fried onions are appropriately slippery, and the optional hot peppers are breathtaking. Have a Dr. Brown's soda on the side, and you've got a cheap-eats meal to remember.

Mama's

426 Belmont Ave., Bala-Cynwyd, PA	$
(610) 664-4757	LD

In an unlikely suburban pizzeria with help that actually verges on being polite (heresy!), you find superb cheese steak sandwiches. Lengths of delicious fresh Italian bread are piled with shaved beef that is well spiced and luxuriously juicy and laced with plump ribbons of sweet sautéed onions, then draped with a layer of provolone cheese. For forty years now, Mama's has been making this Philly classic, not to be missed by anyone in search of cheap-eats greatness.

Submarine-Spotter's Guide

The "hero" sandwich, piled high on a crusty loaf, has variants coast to coast, from the oyster po' boy of New Orleans to the lamb-stuffed Fresno sandwich of the San Joaquin Valley. You can eat a "Cuban" in Miami or a "Garibaldi" in Wisconsin, Italian beef in Chicago or French dip in Los Angeles.

Such sandwiches have the most aliases between the Delaware Valley and New London, Connecticut. These are a few names for the jaw-stretching pleasures you'll find along the roads of the Northeast:

LOCAL NAME	WHAT IT IS, WHERE IT'S FOUND
Hoagie (or Hoagy)	Usually signifies cold cuts, lettuce, and tomato, in Pennsylvania
Submarine	Served hot—meatballs or veal Parmesan—with tomato sauce
Wedge	A sub in Westchester County, New York; usually hot
Torpedo	A sub in the Bronx; hot or cold
Zep or Zeppelin	A sub in western Pennsylvania; hot
Grinder	A sub in New England
Bomber	A sub in western New York; hot or cold

Olivieri's Prince of Steaks

Reading Terminal Market, 12th and Arch Sts.,	$
Philadelphia, PA (215) 925-4320; Reading Market	£
general information number (215) 922-2317 Mon–Sat	

Cheese steak connoisseurship is a complex passion. Is the beef tender? You don't want it gristly, but beef that is *too* fine or fancy works against the outlaw savor of this most impudent of street sandwiches. Is the bread fresh? (It must be.) Is the cheese plebeian? (Deluxe cheese would be ridiculous.) Most important, is the service brash? One place you can answer an unqualified yes to all these vital questions is Olivieri's, where the bustle and commotion of the Reading Terminal Market provide just the right background for ingesting the regal sandwich that is Philadelphia's greatest contribution to American gastronomy.

Pat's King of Steaks

1237 E. Passyunk Ave., Philadelphia, PA (215) 468-1546	$
always open	ℬℒ𝒟

A mountain of shaved beef sopped with gravy and laced with slippery onions, piled into a good Italian loaf and gobbed with molten Cheese Whiz: the Philly cheese steak, it is said, was invented at this ultraurban food stand in 1930. No dining environment could be better for enjoying it, especially at 3 AM under harsh fluorescent lights, standing on a sidewalk (no tables here) where, according to a brass plaque strewn with dropped French fries and beef juice, Sylvester Stallone once stood and ate.

Primanti Brothers

46 W. 18th St., Pittsburgh, PA (412) 263-2142	$
always open	BLD

Pittsburghers like mixed-up food. Steak salad is a favorite local meal: chopped beef nestled in lettuce and garnished with French fries; ham is deliriously "chipped-chopped" for sandwiches; and sometimes French fries, coleslaw, and tomatoes are heaped inside the bread right with the meat. The place that invented the latter configuration is Primanti's, an open-all-night joint in the produce district. A gigantic fry and slaw stuffed ham sandwich at about 2 AM in the company of fruit haulers, swing-shift factory personnel, and glazed-eyed night owls is a dining experience no other city on earth can match.

Shank & Evelyn's

932 South 10th St., Philadelphia, PA (215) 629-1093	$
Tues–Sat; D upstairs	BLD

Great only-in-Philly neighborhood Italian food, with plenty of attitude, is what you'll get at the counter and tables of this family-run luncheonette. Homemade? Don't ask! Of course it's all homemade, and lovingly so: the meatballs, the veal scallopini, the eggplant parmigiana, the juicy chicken cutlet sandwiches on good bread topped with broccoli rabe, the pasta e fagioli soup. Breakfast is more ordinary bacon-and-egg fare, but the ebb and flow of characters at the counter and behind it is even more fun when the day is new and the coffee is strong. In the evening, more elegant meals are served upstairs.

Tom's Kitchen

Rte. 93, Conyngham, PA	$
(717) 788-3808	*BLD*

Here's an honest three-meal-restaurant not far off Interstate 80 through Pennsylvania. We've staked it out for trucker-size breakfasts starting at dawn as well as such meganutritious dinners as pork with sauerkraut, stuffed peppers, and meat loaf by the slab. Desserts are large, sweet, and satisfying: cream and fruit pies and an apple-season-only dumpling that is crusty and warm. Tom's also boasts fountain service, so you can accompany these mighty meals with shakes, floats, and ice cream sundaes.

Mid-South

ALL-AMERICAN

KENTUCKY

NORTH CAROLINA

TENNESSEE

VIRGINIA

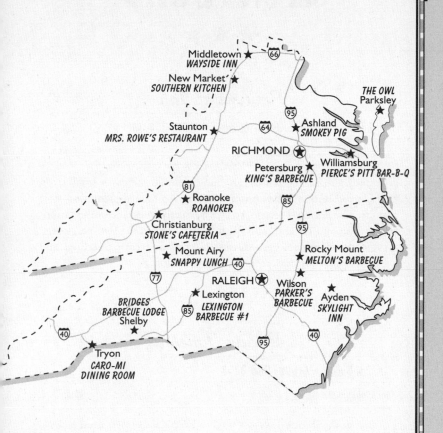

Middletown
WAYSIDE INN

New Market
SOUTHERN KITCHEN

THE OWL
Parksley

Staunton
MRS. ROWE'S RESTAURANT

Ashland
SMOKEY PIG

RICHMOND

Petersburg
KING'S BARBECUE

Williamsburg
PIERCE'S PITT BAR-B-Q

Roanoke
ROANOKER

Christianburg
STONE'S CAFETERIA

Mount Airy
SNAPPY LUNCH

Rocky Mount
MELTON'S BARBECUE

RALEIGH

Wilson
PARKER'S BARBECUE

Lexington
LEXINGTON BARBECUE #1

Ayden
SKYLIGHT INN

BRIDGES BARBECUE LODGE
Shelby

Tryon
CARO-MI DINING ROOM

MID-SOUTH

KENTUCKY

Beaumont Inn

638 Beaumont Inn Dr., Harrodsburg, KY (606) 734-3381	$$
no lunch Mon (reservations suggested)	£D

Formerly a finishing school for young ladies in the sweet small town of Harrodsburg, the Beaumont Inn is now a refined plantation-style hostelry. The setting is serene, service is courtly, guest accommodations are spacious and tasteful, and in the dining room, the two-year-cured smoked country ham, served with biscuits and corn pudding, and sweet layer cake for dessert, is a Dixie paradigm.

Boone Tavern

Rte. 25, Berea, KY (606) 986-9358	$$
(dress code in the evening)	BLD

Dinner at the Boone Tavern wants to be gracious (men need jackets, which the house will supply if you come without one), but the enthusiasm and occasional uncertainty of the staff, who are mostly students from Appalachia working their way through Berea College, make the occasion a beguiling mixture of formality and fun. The evening meal begins with warm spoon bread, fluffy as a soufflé, then moves into an eclectic repertoire that features upscale mountain-home cooking: cured ham with sweet lemon sauce, chicken flakes Elsinore in a crisp potato nest, Kentucky turkey with fresh cranberry relish, and fried chicken so neatly cooked you actually want to eat it with a fork and knife.

Bourbon Bowl

Hwy. 68, south of Paris, KY	$
(606) 987-3161	D

Friday night is the one amazing time to dine at the Bourbon Bowl: that's "Cosmic Bowling" night, featuring glow-in-the-dark bowling. The cuisine is pretty much the same every night, a traditional snack bar menu virtually unchanged in the forty-plus years Bourbon Bowl has been in business. For a hot cheeseburger and a cold beer to the sound of crashing tenpins, there's not a nicer place on earth.

George's Bar-B-Q

1346 East Fourth St., Owensboro, KY	$
(502) 926-9276	BLD

George's pit-cooked mutton is one reason Owensboro can make a legitimate claim to its title as the "Bar-B-Q Capital of the World." In this humble place, where a country and western jukebox provides suitable background music, the long-smoked lamb, cut into shreds, is juicy and high-flavored, imbued with powerhouse sauce. The Q menu also includes pork shoulder or ribs, beef, ham, and chicken; but the one other dish you need to know about is burgoo. A western Kentucky specialty originally brought from Wales (via Virginia, where its modern progeny is now known as Brunswick stew), burgoo began as hunter's potluck containing the varmint du jour. George's burgoo is thick with shreds of smoky mutton, vegetables, and an explosive dose of spice. No varmints that we could see.

Inn at Pleasant Hill

3500 Lexington Rd., Harrodsburg, KY	$$
(606) 734-5411	BLD

The last of the Shakers died in 1923 (they were celibate), and their Kentucky paradise lay idle until it was restored as a hotel and historical landmark in the 1960s. Guest rooms are furnished with reproduction furniture (plus phones, showers, and TVs), and they smell of the hewn wood of which they're made. It is impossible to describe the tranquillity that settles in the evening when you stroll the pathways among the solid brick buildings. Cattle low in nearby fields, an owl hoots overhead, a faint clatter is heard from the kitchen in the Trustees' House dining room, where cherrywood tables are set with candles in hurricane lamps.

Shakers ate well because they needed fuel for all the hard work they did (and also, one supposes, as a substitute pleasure for the sex they weren't allowed to have). Choose from such entrees as crisp fried chicken, aged country ham, and turkey with dressing made from Shaker sage. Relishes, hot corn sticks, and vegetables, including a luscious salsify casserole, are served in bowls that get passed around the table family-style. To end this meal, there is a fine chess pie or the classic Shaker specialty, lemon pie, which is an eye-opening little wedge of supreme sweetness and sour citrus tang. There is no liquor or wine served; the Shakers weren't tipplers, and anyway, Shakertown's county is dry.

Lynn's Paradise Café

984 Barret Ave., Louisville, KY (502) 583-3447	$
BL Tues–Sun; D Thur–Sat	BLD

Once a grocery store, Lynn's is a wacky wonderland of concrete animals, thrift-shop lamps, and a corncob mural on the outside wall. But there is nothing silly about the satisfying plates of meat loaf and mashed potatoes, fried chicken, and black bean chili over rice, or Lynn's repertoire of first-class hamburgers.

Breakfast is served until early afternoon. You can eat impeccable eggs, grits, and biscuits or opt for more exotic fare, which usually includes such taste wonders as fruit-sauced tropical French toast, bourbon-ball French toast, or banana split pancakes. Our best memory is of a sausage-pepper-egg scramble loaded with kielbasa, sided by delightful buttermilk biscuits and baked apple slices.

Moonlight Bar - b - q Inn

2840 W. Parrish, Owensboro, KY	$
(502) 684-8143	£Ð

The Moonlight is the best place to eat barbecued mutton, which is western Kentucky's favorite smokehouse meat. It is strong-flavored stuff with more oomph than beef, certainly more than pork, but the long cooking process insinuates enough smoke to turn it wonderfully tender.

Mutton at the Moonlight is served at a vast buffet that also includes barbecued pork and beef, lots of southern-style vegetables, and the local melting-pot stew known as burgoo. Once your plate is piled high, you can choose among several degrees of hot sauce to further adorn the meat; but good as the sauces are, we like the basic stuff that the mutton comes with . . . all the better to savor its unique tang.

Old Stone Inn

6905 Shelbyville Rd., Simpsonville, KY (502) 722-8882	$$
£Ð Tues–Sat; Ð only Sun	£Ð

Decades ago, the Old Stone Inn earned a reputation as a House of Square Meals, Kentucky-style. It was the place to go for fried chicken or country ham accompanied by corn bread and luxurious vegetables. When it closed a while back, traveling chowhounds pined for its scalloped eggplant, corn pudding, and broccoli-cheese casserole; but now it is back in business, and once again the kitchen is cooking all the good ol' Dixie classics. Beyond ham and chicken, we have very much enjoyed crisp-cooked catfish and pork chops with fried apples on the side; and the supersweet desserts are a fit finale: buttermilk chess pie, pecan pie, and coconut cake.

The Inn dates far back into the last century; its dining room, while easy-going, has an antique patina that colors dinner with the romance of history.

Schneider's Homemade Candies	
420 Fairfield Ave., Bellevue, KY	$
(606) 431-3545	£𝔇

I f, like us, you consider it your duty to find (and eat) all of America's greatest caramel apples, you need to know about Schneider's. Crisp and fresh, gooey but edible without utensils, these mighty orbs-on-a-stick are apple epiphanies. Since 1939, the old-fashioned sweet shop on Route 8 has also been known for dainty cream-centered chocolates called opera creams (made only around Christmas) as well as ice ball ice cream, which is a scoop of homemade vanilla packed in ice, enveloped in syrup—a summertime favorite.

Skin Head's	
1021 S. Twenty-First St., Paducah, KY (502) 442-6471	$
Mon–Sat	𝔅£

D on't be alarmed by the name of this fine restaurant. It predates the era of talk-show neo-Nazis and refers to the bald noggin of the founder. "Remember now," the menu says, "short, fat, thin, or tall, 'Ole Skin Head' will try to feed y'all." We have been fans of Skin Head's hot grits and country ham with red-eye gravy since we first hit the road more than two decades ago. We love the big, puffy biscuits for breakfast and the skillet-fried catfish or brittle-crisp pork tenderloin sandwich at lunch. There isn't a more satisfying place to eat for miles around than at a rickety booth in this friendly "breakfast house of the South."

Vince Staten's Old Time Barbecue

9219 U.S. 42, Prospect, KY	$
(502) 228-7427	*LD*

Vince Staten wrote the book on barbecue. Literally. *Real Barbecue,* which he co-authored with Greg Johnson several years ago, is a fine guide to smokehouse meals from coast to coast. His expertise is reflected in his restaurant's menu, which includes seven different sauces inspired by American regional barbecue from "Texas Sweet" and "Tennessee Jack [Daniel's]" to "Legal Limit Hot Sauce" and one ultrahot one called "Death to Amateurs." The meat is far-ranging too: pulled pork, chicken, or beef, plus baby back ribs cooked Memphis-dry style (rubbed with spice). On the side there are saucy barbecue beans, corn on the cob, baked potato, or a dish called "I fought the slaw and the slaw won."

It isn't exactly an unspoiled, in-the-rough barbecue eating experience, but the sense of play and the extra amenities are welcome. We especially like the fact that Vince has a dessert menu (a rarity in most monomaniacal barbecue joints). The banana pudding is a Mid-South classic, and there is a similar one made with Oreo cookies. And, because this truly is a southern eat shack, there is moon pie.

NORTH CAROLINA

Bridges Barbecue Lodge

Hwy. 74 Bypass, Shelby, NC (704) 482-8567	$
Wed–Sun	*LD*

Bridges has the meditative atmosphere of the South's finest pork parlors. When we entered, we saw a sure sign of smokehouse excellence: five police officers at a table toward the back. Cops are an infallible guide to roadside food in all parts of the country; plates piled high with pork, these lawmen conversed in hushed tones, as if it would be sacrilegious to be raucous in so decent an eat-place.

There is no formal menu, just the slip of paper used by the waitress to take orders. You can get a sandwich, a tray, or a plate. A tray is barbecue and barbecue slaw; a plate also holds French fries, lettuce, tomato, and pickle. Both are accompanied by a basket of hush puppies, and whether you select sandwich, tray, or plate, you will have to decide if you want your meat chopped or sliced. It is a big decision: chopped meat is hacked into moist hash with some shreds of chewy crust, held together by a smidgen of tomato-based sauce with a strong vinegar tang. Sliced barbecue comes as big, soft flaps, mostly white, as tender as pork can be, just barely laced with the fragrance of the smoke pit.

Caro-Mi Dining Room	
1433 Hwy. 176 N., Tryon, NC (704) 859-5200	**$$**
Wed—Sun	**D**

As you wet your whistle from the relish tray, proprietor Charles Stafford explains the menu. He almost sings when he talks about his steaks, boasting that they are aged four weeks. The shrimps are big ones, he gloats, boiled and peeled with loving care. Rainbow trout is another house specialty, pan sautéed in butter to a parchment crisp. "Ours is real country ham," Stafford beams. "It is cured with salt—just enough—and brown sugar." If more than one person at the table orders ham, it is served family-style, stacked on a platter. It comes with grits and red-eye gravy, pork-speckled green beans, and sweet, slow-cooked apples.

The best part of a meal at Caro-Mi just may be the afterglow. When you are done with dessert (congenial things such as butterscotch or chocolate sundae or strawberry shortcake made atop a biscuit), step outside to the wide front porch where a dozen rocking chairs are marshaled in a row. Have a seat. Rock a spell. Listen to the river flow and the twilight crickets chirp. Maybe it isn't heaven, but this little spot in the western hills of North Carolina will do just fine until it is time to try the macaroni salad at the Pearly Gates buffet up yonder.

Lexington Barbecue #1

10 Hwy. 29–70 S, Lexington, NC (336) 249-9814	$
Mon–Sat	£𝕯

Lexington is a major barbecue town, with well over a dozen places serving hickory-smoked pork bathed in a vinegar-tomato sauce that teeters delectably between sweet and hot. Lexington #1, formerly known as Honey Monk's, is the daddy of 'em all. Its barbecue is hacked into a fine, tender hash peppered with crisp pieces from the outside of the roast, served in buns with fine coleslaw or as half of a platter along with crunchy hush puppies. The platters are easy to eat in your car: the sauced pig meat and hush pups are packed into a small cardboard boat, sort of like a trough.

Melton's Barbecue

631 Ridge St., Rocky Mount, NC (919) 446-8513	$
Closes at 3 PM Sun	£𝕯

Melton's is a lazy-looking place on a shady street overlooking a muddy river. Its specialty is North Carolina–style barbecue, which means elegant, ambrosial pork. A Melton's "pig pickin'" begins with a palate-teaser of tart mustard slaw, then moves directly to heaps of meat that are amazing in textural variety: moist, motley shreds, velvet-soft chunks, and succulent "outside" nuggets crusted with basting juice. The pork arrives with hush puppies, Brunswick stew, and potatoes, but it is unsauced—all the better to savor its porcine subtleties. Those who want to gild it concoct their own sauce from an assortment of Tabasco, pickled peppers, vinegar, and hot condiments set at every place. Eating at an unclothed table in this wood-paneled dining room helps you understand why native North Carolinians get overwhelmed with emotion on the subject of barbecue, and why Melton's, now seventy-five years old, is a culinary legend.

Parker's Barbecue

U.S. 301, Wilson, NC	$
(919) 237-0972	ℒ𝒟

A barbecue barn, an eating institution, a tarheel pork parlor to be reckoned with, Parker's is one grand roadside attraction. It is loud, noisy, and crowded, and the meals it serves are huge and porky. Barbecue feasts are its claim to fame: chopped meat piled high, boiled potatoes, corn dodgers, and coleslaw, all served individually or in family-style bowls, accompanied by iced tea. The pork is pale and exquisite, with a thin vinegar sauce nothing like the opaque ketchupy emulsions used on pig meat west of Lexington. It is said that this style sauce goes back to a time when cooks shunned tomatoes as poisonous. Whether or not that's true, Parker's barbecue is just the way people in this part of North Carolina have liked it for centuries.

Skylight Inn

South Lee St., Ayden, NC (919) 746-4113	$
Mon—Sat	ℒ𝒟

Coarse-shredded pork that has been tenderized and perfumed by wood smoke is served with just a soupçon of hot sauce, on a bun or on a cardboard tray with coleslaw and corn bread. Pete Jones's renowned barbecue is a simple meal about as close to perfection as pork gets, an archetypal taste of the downhome style of pig-pickin' unique to coastal North Carolina.

Snappy Lunch

125 N. Main St., Mount Airy, NC	$
(336) 786-4931	£D

Perhaps there are other restaurants that serve a pork chop sandwich, but none could be as delicious as the one you will eat at Snappy Lunch. A breaded, boneless slab of tenderized tenderloin enveloped in creamy batter is fried until crisp, some parts profoundly porky and other parts nearly all crust. This behemoth is sandwiched in a bun with ordinary tomato, onion, and mustard, plus extraordinary chile and slaw. The chile, which has the consistency of paste and a sweet zest that serves as a foil for the gentle-flavored chop, is layered in the sandwich with fine-cut cabbage slaw speckled with green peppers and onions. The total package is unwieldy in the extreme. Served in booths or at the counter with no plate but with a wax paper wrapper that serves as a holding place for fallen condiments, this sandwich requires two hands to hoist and eat. Dainty eaters use the plastic knife and fork provided to cut it in half; but even half is inevitably messy. There are no side dishes other than a bag of potato chips; and the beverage of choice is tea—iced and presweetened, of course.

A town gathering place since the 1920s, and operated by pork-chop master Charles Dowell since the 1950s, Snappy is a rare taste of small-town southern life (gents can get a good haircut in the barber shop next door). Mount Airy was the boyhood home of Andy Griffith, inspiration for his fictional TV hometown, Mayberry.

TENNESSEE

★ ★ ★

540 South Main, Memphis, TN (901) 526-5757	$
Tues–Sat; ℬℒ only Sun	ℬℒ𝒟

Take the trolley to the end of the line and travel to Memphis fifty years ago. Actually, this big old town lunchroom goes back further, to 1919, but its interior decor and its menu suggest mid-century America. Well-worn boomerang-pattern Formica adorns the long counter. In the second dining room, panoramic black-and-white pictures show a long-ago bustling downtown Memphis, and a vintage sign advertises a "STEAK PLATE DINNER," with drink, for forty cents.

The kitchen is a cache of southern probity, offering a rotating array of such plate lunch stalwarts as meat loaf and gravy, baked chicken with wild rice, pork chops, and (always) roast beef au jus. With each entree, you choose two vegetables from a daily array of a dozen; or you can do as we often do, which is make a lunch of three or four vegetables without meat. It's not that the meat is bad—we love the fried chicken every Thursday and Monday's meat loaf—but the vegetables and side dishes are sensational. Yams are deep, dark orange, bathed in syrup; mashed potatoes are stout, smooth, and laced with butter; macaroni and cheese is served with plenty of patches of chewy cheese among the softer stuff; and turnip greens are limp, leafy, and pungent. And there are sticks of corn bread with a delectable golden crunch of a crust and a faintly sour milk tang inside.

A humble restaurant, an everyday kind of place, but such unaffected food is a national treasure.

Barksdale Restaurant

237 S. Cooper, Memphis, TN (901) 722-2193	$
open until 6 PM	BLD

Most Memphians think of this wood-paneled corner café for lunch—pork chops (every Monday), country-fried steak (every day), and catfish (Friday) accompanied by a trio of well-cooked vegetables and followed by lemon icebox pie, banana pudding, or peach cobbler. You can't go wrong.

Barksdale breakfast is a treasure, too: aromatic country ham that is resilient but easy to slice, served with red-eye gravy to spoon on grits or dunk your biscuit in. Peppery milk gravy is also available, and it is superb.

The wall is lined with signed pictures of Barksdale fans who have 8 × 10 glossies to send, including musicians, local celebrities, and a few Elvis impersonators. Each inscribed the photo with a sentiment. One handsome face we didn't recognize wrote, *Thanks for the gravy fix!*

Buntyn

4972 Park, Memphis, TN (901) 458-8776	$
Mon—Fri only	LD

When we walked in Buntyn's door at 11 AM, the staff stood circled around a table in the front room, their heads lowered and hands joined as young Bill Wiggins led them in a prayer, asking God to help them bring joy into customers' lives. These people *believe* in what they do; and we guarantee that if you like good southern food, they will make a believer out of you.

Who couldn't love a waitress who begins a meal by telling her table what's available in words that sound to us like plate-lunch haiku:

> We've got corned beef and cabbage
> Gizzards and rice.
> The okra's boiled
> And corn's on the cob.

Home cooking better than Mom's is served on unbreakable partitioned plates. Shattering crisp fried chicken, crusty fried steak, soulful meat loaf in tomato sauce—such entrees are blue-plate paradigms. We would kill for that fried chicken, but it is their vegetables and side dishes that win our eternal loyalty. There is a list of well over a dozen to choose from every day, from pungent turnip greens and purple hull peas to macaroni and cheese, buttered squash, and dripping-sweet candied yams. Lime cream salad is a baroque jaw-dropper: sweet, creamy, pistachio-colored Jell-O packed with nuts and chunks of pineapple. Every meal comes with triangles of moist corn bread and/or the world's best hot-from-the-oven dinner rolls.

P.S. Buntyn desserts are exquisite. Coconut meringue pie, rising a jiggly six inches above the plate, and lemon icebox pie on a bed of crumbs are always on the menu. There is a different fruit cobbler every day, and Wednesday is banana pudding day.

Charlie Vergos Rendezvous	
52 S. Second St., Memphis, TN	$$
(enter through General Washburn Alley) (901) 523-2746	D
Tues–Sat	

This vast underground cavern of a beer hall with red-checked tablecloths and walls loaded with vintage Memphiana is a legend of American porklore. It is a good-times place ruled over by a staff of charmingly brusque waiters, mobbed with barbecue pilgrims and tourists. Midafternoon, when the kitchen gets in gear, the Rendezvous broadcasts the scent of sizzling, smoky meat throughout a significant part of downtown, even into the lobby of the Peabody Hotel across the street. The kitchen's main attraction is ribs, which are prepared with a "dry rub" rather than a wet sauce; thus their succulence is sealed inside a dizzyingly spiced coat. Pork shoulder and pork loin are less aggressively seasoned than the ribs, which will leave you parched till morning, and the pork shoulder sandwich is a classic.

Meat-and-Three: Plate Lunch Rules

Cafés throughout mid-Tennessee serve a midday meal known as meat-and-three. Customers choose one meat and three vegetables from the day's list, and the meal is generally served on a heavy unbreakable plate with raised partitions to keep the collard green juices from running into the yam casserole. Meat-and-three is always accompanied by biscuits or corn bread and a tall glass of tea, and generally followed by pie, pudding, or cobbler.

In our experience, the quality of the meat may vary, but the vegetables are almost always spectacularly southern, which means well-cooked, hog-jowl flavored, vigorously seasoned, cheese-enriched, bread crumb-gilded, and margarine-sopped. That is why many customers opt for meat-and-three without the meat, meaning an all-vegetable plate of three or four selections.

Cozy Corner Restaurant

745 N. Parkway, Memphis, TN (901) 527-9158	$
Tues—Sat	L D

Fluorescent lights, wood paneling, a large order area, and a few tables in a small dining room: all are signs of barbecue excellence, further suggested by the aroma of hickory burning in the pit oven, and utterly confirmed when you ease your teeth into a chunk of pitmaster Raymond Robinson's sublime pork shoulder. Sprinkled with plenty of pepper as it cooks, the meat develops a wicked blackened crust, which is not only savory itself but also performs the function of sealing in juices. Piled into a sandwich with a bit of coleslaw (that is the Memphis way), it is one of the most delicious things a person can eat—sloppy, drippy, lip-tingling hot, and downright sexy. Such supreme succulence is what makes Memphis the pork capital of America, and there is no better place to wallow in that fact than the Cozy Corner.

Ribs are sensational, too—big and meaty—and Mr. Robinson makes a specialty of barbecued Cornish hens and turkeys. The former are elegant little fowls with crisp mahogany skin and meat that pulls off the bone in soft, savory shreds. On the side comes good barbecued beans or profoundly soulful barbecued spaghetti—slim, droopy noodles bathed in smoky sauce.

Gridley's	
4774 Summer Ave., Memphis, TN	**$$**
(901) 761-0111 or 794-5997 for mail order	**£ⅅ**

Gridley's ritual barbecue meal always begins with bread—buttery little loaves that resemble the prefab ones served by some slothful restaurants but are in fact freshly baked and hot from the oven, and barbecue's ideal companion. Use them to mop a plate, cushion shreds of pork, and salve a tongue on fire from too much hot sauce.

You probably want to save all your appetite for pork, which is what Gridley's does best, but we must tell you that the seafood gumbo is a sensation—loaded with crabmeat, chunks of shrimp, and vegetables, served over rice, and deliriously spiced.

Slow-cooked over coals, the pork is moist and savory, available as shoulder meat that is chopped (nearly pulverized) or pulled (variegated shreds and hunks), or on the rib. It is mild, delicate-flavored meat . . . until you pour on some of Gridley's roaring-hot barbecue sauce, which will make your lips and tongue glow.

Barbecue salad is a regional oddity and yet another way to honor pork. A bed of cool lettuce is covered with large and small chunks of pulled pork shoulder that is lukewarm. On the side you get a cup of thick blue cheese dressing. And you can get barbecue pizza, too, topped with tomato sauce and shreds of pulled pork: what's not to like about that?

Also recommended: bar-b-q shrimp, which are served peel 'em and eat 'em–style with a buttery dipping sauce. And most wonderful of all, Mrs. Gridley's lemon icebox pie. Made with fresh lemons, it is extremely tart but also extremely sweet. Precisely what a tongue craves after a bout with barbecue of such grand character.

Interstate Bar-B-Que

2265 S. Third St., Memphis, TN	$
(901) 775-2304	LD

Inside and out, Interstate is perfumed by smoke from slow-sizzling barbecue. A modest-looking pork house serving ribs, shoulder meat, sausages, and bologna with all the proper fixin's, including addictive bar-b-q spaghetti (soft noodles in breathtaking sauce), it is a jewel in the crown of Memphis pits. Eat at a table in the simple dining room where a "Wall of Fame" boasts critics' accolades and 8 × 10s from celebrity fans; or enter next door and get it to go, by the sandwich, plate, or whole slab of ribs.

When you lift a rib, meat slides off the bone. It is chewy with a deep savor haloed by the perfume of wood smoke. Chopped pork shoulder has a few crusty outside shreds and tatters among the pillowy pile of interior meat; slices are less gooped with sauce, and not as messy, but not as succulent, either. A large chopped pork sandwich is the most Memphian dish on the menu, made as per local custom with a layer of cool coleslaw atop the well-sauced meat—a total mess that disintegrates as you eat it.

Leonard's

5465 Fox Plaza Dr., Memphis, TN	$
(901) 360-1963	LD

In 1922, pitmaster Leonard Heuberger invented the pig sandwich, which has since become a standard configuration in Memphis and beyond—pulled pork on a bun, drenched with tangy sauce and embellished with coleslaw. It was advertised with a wonderful sign that showed a pig in top hat and tails, captioned MR. BROWN GOES TO TOWN. "Mr. Brown" was the connoisseur's code for the dark, chewy, succulent meat from the outside of the pork roast, of which the sandwich had plenty. Mr. Heuberger and his smoke shack are gone, but the modern Leonard's still serves a superb pig sandwich and also sports the dapper neon pig.

Loveless Café

Hwy. 100, Nashville, TN	$
(615) 646-9700	BLD

On the highway heading west out of Nashville, the Loveless Café is a country-western diamond in the rough. For years it has been a favorite haunt among Grand Ol' Opry performers (it's not unusual to see a celebrity's tour bus at the back of the lot), but fame hasn't spoiled the Loveless one bit. It still serves its brittle-crusted fried chicken on red-checked tablecloths, and hot buttermilk biscuits are served with homemade blackberry and peach preserves. Even more than fried chicken and biscuits, ham is the pride of the Loveless kitchen. It is slow-cured country ham, fried on a griddle until its rim of fat turns translucent amber and the coral pink meat gets speckled sandy brown. It comes with a bowl of red-eye gravy for dipping, cream gravy, sorghum molasses, honey, and bowls of preserves. It all adds up to one of America's great breakfasts, any time of day.

Pope's Café

on the Square, Shelbyville, TN	$
(931) 684-7933	BLD

Pope's Cafe is a plate lunch parlor with a vegetable roster that customarily includes macaroni with stewed tomatoes, pinto beans, crowder peas, crisp disks of deep-fried squash, turnip greens soaking in their pot likker, mashed or steamed potatoes, and sliced fresh tomatoes. Desserts are delectably southern, too, including chocolate, coconut, and lemon meringue pie; Charlie Pride pie (named after a famous local horse who was named after the country singer); and a simple but irresistible chess pie. The most compelling reason to eat at Pope's is country ham—rank, complex, and very literally mouthwatering.

R & J Restaurant

Hwy. 45, Rutherford, TN (901) 665-6999	$
Mon–Sat	£Ɖ

Pork ribs, cooked over smoldering charcoal and hickory chips and bathed with secret recipe sauce, are R & J's main claim to fame, although we would never kick the tender chopped pork shoulder off our plate. In fact, anything smokemaster John Wayne James cooks in his open pit—including a strange, luscious prime rib—is a sure winner of a meal, complemented by superior coleslaw and crisp hush puppies.

The Ridgewood

900 Elizabethton Hwy., Bluff City, TN (423) 538-7543	$
Tues–Sat	£Ɖ

At the insistence of a reporter who needed a headline, we once declared the Ridgewood to be the best barbecue in America. We weren't lying, but it did seem a little crazy to choose just one restaurant out of the several dozen supreme BBQs from Chicago's South Side to the Texas Hill Country and from Kentucky's mutton parlors to the Basque smoke wagons of the Rockies' western slopes.

Still, we do adore dining at the Ridgewood; if it isn't the single best barbecue, it surely is in the uppermost echelon of America's pork palaces. The meat itself is sensationally tasty—tender, sweet pork sliced thick and piled high, then doused with a suave red sauce that is tangy but not painfully hot. It is heaped into a bun or on a plate with superb, meaty barbecue beans and fine French fries on the side. Adding to the pleasure of the food is the well-worn ambiance of this fifty-year-old country restaurant with its double-wide aisles to accommodate a staff of double-wide waitresses who can be perfectly polite, but who have been known to cut off the heads of any customer who dares question the time-honored Ridgewood codes of service (you'll likely wait in line; no extra sauce is provided with meals).

If you are a pilgrim in search of smokehouse greatness, the Ridgewood is a religious experience.

Things That Are Barbecued in Memphis

Memphis, Tennessee, is America's pork capital, with boundless variations on the duo of smoky pig meat and sweet sauce.

<u>Wet ribs:</u> glazed with enough spicy red sauce to require many napkins and moist towelettes

<u>Dry ribs:</u> rubbed with seasoning that forms a dry crust enveloping succulent meat

<u>Pig sandwich:</u> pork pulled off the smoked shoulder, drenched with tangy sauce and embellished with coleslaw in a broad bun

<u>Barbecue pizza:</u> hacked, shredded, sauced pork atop cheese and crust

<u>Barbecue spaghetti:</u> limp noodles in zesty sauce (meatless), served as a side dish like barbecued beans, often with barbecue coleslaw (cabbage salad with sauce)

<u>Barbecue salad:</u> similar to a chef's salad, but with chunks of pork instead of ham and turkey on the lettuce, topped with cool barbecue sauce or salad dressing or both

<u>Barbecue shrimp:</u> usually served "u-peel-'em" style, sopped with a buttery version of the house barbecue sauce—an unholy, irresistible mess to eat

<u>Hot links:</u> thick, porcine sausages glazed with sauce

<u>Turkeys and Cornish hens:</u> fabulous specialties of the Cozy Corner (p. 95)

Riverside Catfish House

10839 Hwy. 41, Chattanooga, TN	$
(423) 821-9214	D

For more than thirty years, Hattie Massengale's catfish parlor overlooking the Tennessee River has drawn customers from Chattanooga every night and from miles away for Sunday supper. While the menu lists chicken and shrimp, the only thing to have is catfish, preferably as part of the all-you-can-eat special with baskets full of hush puppies. Top it off with sweet buttermilk pie, and you will have enjoyed a timeless Tennessee feast.

Satsuma

417 Union St., Nashville, TN (615) 256-0760	$
Mon–Fri	£

Long ago, when we wrote a retro cookbook called *Square Meals,* the Satsuma was an inspiration. Serving ladies lunch since 1918, this gentle dining room knows all there is to know about such honest food as turkey à la king, freshly made chicken salad, and healthful turnip greens with hog jowl and corn sticks to mop up the gravy. Write your own order on the little pad provided every table, and don't forget a few servings of dessert, in which Satsuma is especially proficient. Lemon cake and chocolate meringue pie are our personal favorites, accompanied by a serving of the kitchen's immemorial sherry ice cream.

At the front of the main floor dining room one can buy baked goods and several cookbooks of Satsuma's recipes. We've had a great time making good things from them, but there is no way to take home the time-honored traditions of efficiency, courtesy, and southern charm that make this restaurant such a special place to eat.

Sylvan Park

2201 Bandywood Dr., Green Hills (Nashville), TN	$
(615) 292-6449 Mon–Sat	£D

Sylvan Park serves honest southern lunch at low prices in civilized surroundings. One day's menu offers sixteen different vegetables and side dishes including a great drift of flavorful turnip greens, luscious mashed turnips, luxurious macaroni and cheese, dainty niblets of corn in cream sauce, syrupy candied yams, pork-infused baby lima beans, and congealed (gelatinized) fruit salad. The meats include roast turkey and dressing, sugar-cured baked ham, and breaded pork cutlets. Every meat-and-three platter is served with a choice of hot, pale biscuits with creamy insides or weighty chunks of sour milk corn bread so buttery rich that it will make your fingers glisten when you pick one up. "Aren't they good?" asks our waitress when we request a second basket of these superb breadstuffs to mop the gravy off our plates. For dessert, there is hot cobbler or your choice of chocolate, pecan, or lemon icebox pie.

VIRGINIA

King's Barbeque

3221 W. Washington Rd., Petersburg, VA	$
(804) 732-5861 Tues–Sun	BLD

King's is a king-size restaurant that has been in the barbecue business for half a century. It serves both beef and pork, and the carvers at the end of the long counter will either slice or chop your choice for

platters or sandwiches. This barbecue spot has actual tables and silverware and even some food items not cooked over hickory wood, such
as fried chicken, ham steak, wonderful biscuits that go with everything, and even dessert in the form of hot apple pie. There are banquet
rooms for big parties and comfortable tables and chairs. Such amenities make King's a place unsuited to the barbecue purist who wants
nothing but smoky meat in a bare-bones setting; but if you're in the
area and you have a hankering for good slow-cooked pork with all the
trimmings, we highly recommend it.

Mrs. Rowe's Restaurant	
Rte. 250, Staunton, VA	$
(540) 886-1833	*BLD*

An essential fried-chicken-'n'-fixin's stop off Interstate 81 (at exit
57). The much-abused term "home-cooking" means something in
this big but friendly roadside restaurant, where the pan-fried chicken
is crisp (and takes an honest forty-five minutes to prepare) and the banana pudding is as gentle as baby food. All the pies are extraordinarily
good, especially apple and mince in the autumn, the latter topped with
rum sauce.

Breakfast is particularly nice. The sight of big, fresh sticky buns
and sweet rolls on the front-room counters and the aroma of country
ham sizzled on a grill and dripping red-eye gravy are like a farm
kitchen. The locally-favored morning meal is a brace of oven-hot biscuits topped with gravy, of which Rowe's offers three different kinds:
sausage gravy, tenderloin gravy made with big shreds of pork, and
creamy chipped beef. We recently fell in love with a new item on the
menu: pumpkin pancakes, which are earthy-orange and fetchingly
sweet—marvelous partners for a serving of Virginia ham.

The Owl

Rte. 13, N. of Accomac in Parksley, VA	$
(757) 665-5191	BLD

This modest roadside dining room, adjacent to a small motel, has been in business since the mid-1930s, and the homespun decor seems to have changed little over the decades. Roadside food connoisseurs have marked The Owl in their book of wonders for its crusty pan-fried chicken, Chincoteague oysters sheathed in brittle breading, crab au gratin, and cold-weather oyster stew. On the side of these tidewater comfort-food classics come such superb dishes as fried sweet potatoes (an autumn specialty), spoon bread cut into little quivery squares, and crisp squash fritters. Naturally, good biscuits are also served. The desserts are memorable: chocolate rum pie on a melting-light pale white meringue crust, and moist orange sweet potato pie, which is the tongue-soothing way to top off a meal of The Owl's vigorous country ham and gravy.

Pierce's Pitt Bar-B-Q

447 Rochambeau Dr., Williamsburg, VA	$
(757) 565-2955	BLD

Pierce's is one of the great pits of the East, and the last place you'll find good barbecue heading north out of pork country. It isn't much to look at—a cinderblock fast-food outlet in bright orange and yellow with a smokehouse out back—but the sandwiches are ravishing, available in jumbo or regular sizes with French fries, hush puppies, and slaw on the side. The meat, hacked into irregularly sized chunks and shreds, comes bathed in Pierce's sensational sauce, which is tomato based with a vinegar tang that will tease your tongue all the way up past the Mason-Dixon line.

Roanoker	
2522 Colonial Ave., Roanoke, VA	$
(540) 344-7746	*BLD*

The Roanoker lost its *intime* café charms when it moved and spruced up several years ago, transforming itself into a sanitary middle-class lunchroom, but breakfast of country ham with red-eye gravy and biscuits is still terrific, as are most of the large repertoire of southern-style side dishes that accompany lunch and dinner: crunchy corn sticks, candied yams, peppery boiled cabbage, congealed salads (aka Jell-O), and always a selection of high-seasoned greens and beans. One fine lunch we enjoyed not too long ago featured a heap of crisp-cooked chicken livers sided by "Swiss mix" (broccoli and cauliflower), dressing and gravy, and hot apple pie for dessert.

Smokey Pig	
212 S. Washington Hwy., Ashland, VA (804) 798-4590	$
Tues–Sun	*LD*

A strange barbecue parlor, located in a building that was once a general store, the Smokey Pig bills itself as "elegantly informal." We assume the elegant part of the equation refers to the fact that the kitchen goes beyond barbecue and offers crab cakes (mighty tasty), quiche, chicken salad sandwiches, and, on one occasion, a cup of gazpacho soup that was quite good. Daily specials include such other non-smoked meals as meat loaf (Tuesday) and pot roast (Wednesday), accompanied by choices from a broad vegetable repertoire and cocktails or wine from a list of four items: chablis, rose, burgundy, and blush. Despite such elegance, the great thing to eat at the Smokey Pig is, simply, smokey pig: delicious slow-cooked pork, chopped or sliced, served in a sandwich or as a dinner with slaw, potatoes, and hush puppies.

Southern Kitchen

U.S. 11, New Market, VA	$
(540) 740-3514	BLD

The Southern Kitchen is a fine town café where the clientele is a mix of locals and Shenandoah Valley tourists. The counter or pale green booths are good places to eat a quick country-ham breakfast; in the more demure adjacent dining room, families come for crisp fried chicken, local trout, and all-American hamburgers. The most distinctive menu item, and a true Virginia treat, is peanut soup, a smooth bisque with a faint onion zest that perfectly balances the opulence of the goober base.

Stone's Cafeteria

Roanoke Rd., Christiansburg, VA	$
(540) 382-8970	BLD

Since 1956, Stone's has been the upright restaurant east of town, its orange Naugahyde booths occupied by families who come for classic southern-style suppers such as baked chicken casserole and tender-crusted fried chicken. The ladies who dish out the food in the cafeteria line know the likes and dislikes of their regulars and keep up a steady patter with customers pushing their trays along. If you are a stranger, they are most solicitous about your preferences: "Extra gravy for those tenderloin tips? . . . yams on the side of that pork chop? . . . or would you prefer mashed potatoes? . . . or squash with bacon?" Such queries send us into cafeteria ecstasy, for all the food is fresh and homey. Topped off with a Stone's dessert such as coconut cream pie or layered strawberry pie, these are honest meals to remember.

Wayside Inn

7783 Main St., Middletown, VA	$$$
(540) 869-1797	D

Although the Wayside Inn declares itself "America's First Motor Inn," it opened long before the automobile. Located in the Shenandoah Valley on Route 11, which was known as The Valley Pike in the late eighteenth century, it is a history-rich, creaky-floored hostelry with a 1720-vintage tavern and a gracious dining room where Old Dominion food is star.

Start with peanut soup, a creamy delectation with an appealing tan hue and earthy taste, dotted with specks of nut. A Virginia ham plate is crowded with thin sheets of brick-red country ham—but not the super-salty kind—served in a puddle of translucent red-eye gravy. Normally, red-eye gravy is made by mixing ham drippings and coffee. The Wayside's chef adds a touch of brown sugar that nicely complements the ham's assertive savor. On the side come chunky mashed potatoes, but we recommend also ordering spoon bread. It is a dish of cornmeal pudding with a faintly grainy texture, crusty on the outside, smooth down below and just dry enough that it yearns to soak up the ham's sweet gravy.

For dessert: hot apple dumplings or apple-peach cobbler.

Barbecue Nation: What's Smoked Where?

There is no way to chart every different style of American barbecue (although such a quest would be a nice life's project), but it is important to have a general idea of what gets barbecued where so you don't commit the embarrassing *faux pas* of eating beef barbecue in Chattanooga or asking for a pig sandwich in El Paso.

That's the fundamental disparity: pork versus beef. Pork is king throughout the Mid-South and Deep South. Even if beef happens to be on the menu there, it should be ignored. Look for signs that show happy dancing pigs or "bink" spelled out in neon in the window. Bubba's of Eureka Springs, Arkansas, announced by a lovely sign in the shape of a pig, is a good example (p. 126).

Basic southern variations on the theme are found in

- North Carolina, where smoked pork is mixed with a spicy vinegar sauce (no tomato in it at all), as at Melton's Barbecue (p. 89)
- South Carolina, where many of the best sauces are mustard-based, as at Maurice's Piggy Park (p. 174)
- Memphis, where pork is hacked into "pig sandwiches" with coleslaw and where ribs are cooked either wet or dry. (Charlie Vergos Rendezvous, p. 94, and the Cozy Corner, p. 95, are two exemplary Memphis restaurants.)
- Georgia, where barbecue is frequently accompanied by Brunswick stew, a hearty gallimaufry of vegetables and pork shreds in gravy. Melear's (p. 150) is a classic.

In Texas and most of the West, beef is what's best—brisket, usually, but also succulent sausage links. There might be mounted cows' heads on walls,

John Wayne portraits, and cowboy-theme decor, but the greatest Southwestern barbecues are austere and without any frills to distract you from the meat. Louie Muller's of Tyler, Texas (p. 313) is the purest such place.

Oklahoma is a great beef state, but local smokehounds also favor barbecued bologna: thick slabs much spicier than the presliced supermarket variety. See Leo's Barbecue (p. 302).

Santa Maria–style barbecue in California is cooked directly over flames (of live oak wood), not indirectly over smoke. Although you'll find chicken, sausages, even filets mignon cooked this way, the traditional cut of choice is a beef tri-tip. (Good Santa Maria barbecue is available from street-corner vendors on weekends in many small towns in California cattle country. The Far Western Tavern in Guadalupe and the Hitching Post in Casmalia are two of the best restaurants that serve it, pp. 339 and 340.)

Western Kentucky is strange. It is mutton country, where mature lamb is slow-cooked over hickory wood and served as part of a ritual meal that includes barbecue-flavored beans, potato salad, onion slices, and white or tan bread suitable for mopping. Barbecued mutton also often finds its way into the Kentucky stew known as burgoo. The Moonlight Bar-b-q Inn has been a premier mutton house for decades (p. 85).

Many midwestern cities have great barbecue cooked by men and women who learned their trade in the South and serve superb pork (ribs in particular) with a sweet glaze. St. Louis has the added attraction of being the home of snoots—crisp-fried pig snouts bathed in sauce, as served at C&K (p. 216). Being more western, Kansas City smokehouses offer good beef brisket *as well as* good pork, and even mutton. Arthur Bryant Barbeque is the essential K.C. smokehouse (p. 215).

Deep South

ALABAMA

ARKANSAS

FLORIDA

GEORGIA

LOUISIANA

MISSISSIPPI

SOUTH CAROLINA

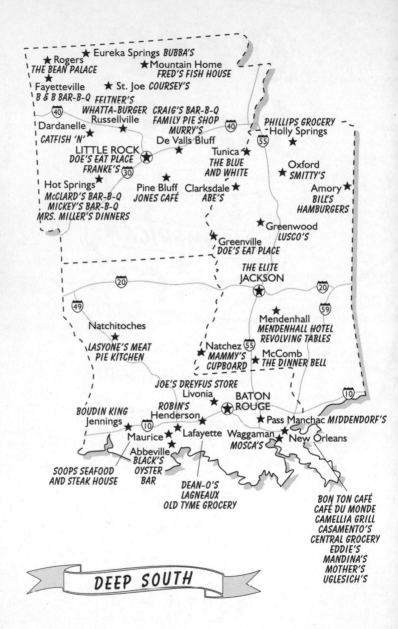

Rogers ★ Eureka Springs *BUBBA'S*
THE BEAN PALACE
★ ★Mountain Home
FRED'S FISH HOUSE
Fayetteville ★ St. Joe *COURSEY'S*
B & B BAR-B-Q *FEITNER'S*
WHATTA-BURGER CRAIG'S BAR-B-Q
Russellville *FAMILY PIE SHOP*
Dardanelle ★ *MURRY'S* *PHILLIPS GROCERY*
CATFISH 'N' De Valls Bluff Holly Springs
★
LITTLE ROCK Tunica
DOE'S EAT PLACE *THE BLUE* Oxford
FRANKE'S *AND WHITE* ★ *SMITTY'S*
Amory ★
Hot Springs Pine Bluff Clarksdale ★ *BILL'S*
McCLARD'S BAR-B-Q *JONES CAFÉ* *ABE'S* *HAMBURGERS*
MICKEY'S BAR-B-Q
MRS. MILLER'S DINNERS ★Greenwood
LUSCO'S
★ Greenville
DOE'S EAT PLACE

THE ELITE
JACKSON

Mendenhall
MENDENHALL HOTEL
Natchitoches *REVOLVING TABLES*

LASYONE'S MEAT Natchez McComb
PIE KITCHEN *MAMMY'S* *THE DINNER BELL*
CUPBOARD

JOE'S DREYFUS STORE
Livonia
BOUDIN KING *ROBIN'S* BATON
Jennings Henderson ROUGE
★ Pass Manchac *MIDDENDORF'S*
Maurice ★ Lafayette Waggaman ★ New Orleans
Abbeville *BLACK'S* *MOSCA'S*
OYSTER
SOOPS SEAFOOD *BAR* *BON TON CAFÉ*
AND STEAK HOUSE *DEAN-O'S* *CAFÉ DU MONDE*
LAGNEAUX *CAMELLIA GRILL*
OLD TYME GROCERY *CASAMENTO'S*
CENTRAL GROCERY
EDDIE'S
MANDINA'S
MOTHER'S
UGLESICH'S

DEEP SOUTH

ALABAMA

Bob Sykes Bar-B-Que	
1724 9th Ave., Bessemer, AL (205) 426-1400	$
Mon–Sat	£Ð

Three of the biggest rocking chairs ever made are positioned opposite the order counter at Bob Sykes, making it easy for even the widest customers to wait in comfort while the order they've given is assembled. Tote your own food to the table (veterans ask for a pitcher of extra sauce for dipping bread and sopping meat), then prepare to smack your lips over one of the choicest Alabama smokehouse meals. Finely chopped pork and especially succulent shredded beef are our favorite things to eat, although Sykes's ribs are plenty good, too. French fries are deliciously spuddy, beans are powerfully sweet, and meringue-topped lemon pie is a local legend.

Sykes is just a few blocks from exit 112 off I-20 and has a drive-through window if you are in a hurry and need barbecue fast.

Bogue's	
3028 Clairmont Ave., Birmingham, AL	$
(205) 254-9780	ß£

For those who enjoy a neighborhood café with attitude, Bogue's is irresistible. Its well-cooled, double-wide dining room with pea-green plaster walls and slick-textured Naugahyde booths has been a three-meals-a-day haunt for Birminghamians since mid-century. It is especially popular among all-night revelers who arrive when it opens, at 6 AM, for kill-or-cure plates of high-powered country ham with biscuits, grits, and peppery cream gravy. Lunch specials include such Dixie standards as country-fried steak, catfish, and Gulf Coast stuffed devil crabs. On the side come legions of vegetables: collard greens, snap peas, sautéed squash, rice and gravy, etc.

Honestly, it is not the food that keeps the clientele so loyal; it is the staff. Even if you are a first-timer, the waitress is likely to call you "Hon," pour your coffee and leave the pot so you have instant access to more, and engage in Ciceronian hash-house repartee. "Aw, take a pill and hush up!" our gal instructs a nearby customer who complains too much about the weather.

"Make me," he says.

She whisks the coffeepot from his table and holds it hostage until he apologizes for his bad attitude.

Veterans recall the days Mr. Bogue ran the place, when his advertising slogan was "It's vogue to eat at Bogue." In a reverse-chic sort of way, it still is.

The Brick Pit	
5456 Old Shell Rd., Mobile, AL	**$**
(334) 343-0001	**LD**

WELCOME TO THE BEST DAMN SMOKED BAR-B-QUE IN THE GREAT STATE OF ALABAMA says a sign on the portal leading to the parking lot of The Brick Pit, a home that has become a barbecue restaurant on the western fringe of Mobile. It is hard to disagree with the boast when you savor pulled pork so tender that it literally melts on your tongue (it is smoked thirty hours), or when you gently touch the meat on a rib and it slides off the bone in bite-size hunks and shreds, edged with good sauce. It is four-star Q without a doubt, essential on the itinerary of all smokehouse pilgrims, served appropriately in a casual dining room on which the walls are covered with exuberant graffiti and where, instead of music, the background sound is mostly groans and moans of joy issued by ecstatic eaters.

The Custard Cottage

1800 Old Shell Road, Mobile, AL	$
(334) 450-0098	LD

Like most of the deep south, Mobile is not a serious ice cream city. But the sundaes, sodas, milk shakes, and concretes (super thick shakes) at The Custard Cottage are world-class. The reason is the custard itself, which you can watch being made and slowly surging out of its silver freezer just behind the order window. It is pure white and soft as sweet cream; and it makes a marvelous foundation for such baroque delights as a bananas Foster sundae with sliced bananas and rugged-textured brown sugar syrup, an apple caramel sundae, or a turtle sundae. But good as all the toppings and mix-ins are, we recommend you have at least one cup or cone of this superb custard plain. It is pure frozen bliss.

Dew Drop Inn

1808 Old Shell Road, Mobile, AL	$
(334) 473-7872	LD

George Widney introduced hot dogs to Mobile when he opened the Dew Drop Inn in 1924. The City on the Bay is now rightfully famous among traveling epicures for all its good seafood, but no one can claim to know its true culinary soul until they have sat in the cool wood-paneled dining room of the Dew Drop Inn and devoured a brace of Dew Drop Dogs, either regular (topped with sauerkraut, chili, mustard, ketchup, and pickles), upside down (the dog atop the condiments), or shaved (without kraut). The chili is an unusual beefy hash with a sweet smack that is also used to top Dew Drop cheeseburgers, which singer Jimmy Buffet credits with generating his burger lust when he was a boy. And don't forget onion rings: these fresh-from-the-fry-kettle hoops are the dogs' and burgers' best friends.

Dreamland Bar-B-Q

5535 15th Ave. E., Tuscaloosa, AL (205) 758-8135	$
also in Birmingham at 1427 14th Ave., S. (205) 933-2133	£D

Ribs, juicy and crusted with sauce, draw crowds to this old smoke-house, which dates back to the 1950s. Service is do-it-yourself, and decor in the utilitarian dining room includes pictures of celebrity clientele, vintage license plates, and stacks of hickory and oak wood all around the pit. White bread, pickle slices, and potato chips are all that is needed to make a pig-perfect meal that will set your tongue aglow for hours. (Dreamland sauce is packaged to go, a precious Alabama souvenir.)

Highlands Bar and Grill

2011 Eleventh Ave., S., Birmingham, AL (205) 939-1400	$$$
(reservations advised) Tues–Sat	D

Highlands Bar and Grill is truly and deeply Alabaman. Ingredients are as indigenous as eggs from free-range chickens on a nearby farm and tomatoes from the proprietor's garden, and you'll find such well-known southernisms as grits and Gulf Coast crab claws on the menu. But there is much more to this delicious kitchen than regional loyalty. Chef Frank Stitt III, an Alabama boy, transcends parochial recipes and makes everything his own, sometimes in the most audacious ways: grilled dayboat swordfish (fresh!) is sauced with a pungent gravy made from porcini mushrooms and salty little tiles of apple-smoked bacon. Did we say fish with pork sauce? Believe us, it works. Grits are baked with wild mushrooms, country ham, and fresh thyme. Spit-roasted duck is accompanied by lacy sweet potato French fries.

We could enumerate many good things we have eaten, but the menu changes, so when you dine at Highlands Bar and Grill, you will have a menu all your own. It is a supremely comfortable restaurant, polite but not stuffy, with a convivial dining room, an even more lively bar, and a joyous marble oyster bar (watch Rod Clark, Alabama's best shucker, at work). The staff is suave and knowledgeable, and fellow diners all seem to have a jolly time tossing raw oysters down the hatch, sipping fresh-squeezed watermelon margaritas, and savoring the extraordinary meals that follow. An evening here is a memorable splurge in a great American restaurant.

Hot and Hot Fish Club	
2180 11th Court, S., Birmingham, AL	*$$$*
(205) 933-5474 Tues–Sat	*D*

In a semisubterranean, semicircular space that used to be a raffish tavern, chef Christopher Hastings has established a premier restaurant of high spirits and creative food. There are handsomely crafted tables and chairs arrayed across the old octagon-tile floor, but socially gregarious and culinarily curious customers sit along the curving counter, where a row of high-backed stools provides a view of the open kitchen in which modern artisans prepare such delights as sweet corn and tomato salad with field peas, the world's tastiest fried okra (fresh from the garden, cooked whole), and downhome barbecued beef short ribs with succotash and hot biscuits. It is a delight to sit and watch the show, exchange gastronomic views with neighbors, and sip Hot and Hot martinis, which are made by muddling Ketyl One vodka with hot peppers.

Named for the nineteenth-century South Carolina epicurean club to which the chef's great-great-grandfather belonged, the Hot and Hot Fish Club serves various meats and poultry (vanilla-cured pork rack, grilled sirloin, roasted quail), but it makes a specialty of seafood, including *fresh* grilled anchovies (soft, warm, and tender) on a romaine salad and gorgeous whole snapper roasted in the brick oven. One of our favorite taste memories is of a glistening pink grilled fillet of salmon, presented on a low platform of little spud pilings described on the menu as "fresh dug potatoes."

Irondale Café

at the train station in downtown Irondale, AL	$
(205) 956-5258 Sun–Fri	£𝔇

The Irondale Café is the Whistle Stop Café made famous in Fannie Flagg's book and the movie made from it, *Fried Green Tomatoes*. In business since the 1930s, and now something of a tourist attraction, it is still as easygoing as a plate of field peas and turnip greens (always on the Sunday menu). Service is cafeteria style, and the menu is different each day of the week. To accompany such stalwart entrees as meat loaf, fried chicken, and country steak, there are about a dozen vegetables from which to choose, *always* including fried green tomatoes. We especially recommend the deliciously starchy crowder peas, on the menu Monday through Thursday, and the supersweet, Marshmallow Fluff–topped sweet potato soufflé Sunday and Wednesday.

Boardinghouse Meals

The Deep South still has a handful of old-fashioned hostelries that serve food family-style at big communal tables. The cuisine is tradition incarnate: fried chicken is the customary entree, always surrounded by phalanxes of well-cooked, powerfully seasoned, and sinfully enriched vegetables. It's great fun to break bread with strangers and, as the motto of the Mendenhall Hotel implores, EAT 'TIL IT OUCHES.

- ☞ Florida House Inn, Fernandina Beach, FL (p. 139)
- ☞ Hopkins Boarding House, Pensacola, FL (p. 141)
- ☞ Buckner Family Restaurant and Music Hall, Jackson, GA (p. 147)
- ☞ Dillard House, Dillard, GA (p. 148)
- ☞ Smith House, Dahlonega, GA (p. 151)
- ☞ The Dinner Bell, McComb, MS (p. 166)
- ☞ Mendenhall Hotel Revolving Tables, Mendenhall, MS (p. 169)

Johnny Ray's

316 Valley Ave., Birmingham, AL	$
(205) 945-7437	£D

A small Alabama chain with one branch in Crestview, Florida, Johnnie Ray's is considered by many connoisseurs to be the best place around for barbecue and pie. The Q includes beef, blonde chicken (white meat) and brunette chicken (dark meat), chopped or sliced pork, and big spareribs crusted with hot-spiced red sauce so tongue-tingling it can seem effervescent. Although pig purists insist on eating nothing but ribs or Johnny Ray's pulverized chopped pork, there are a couple of iconoclastic combo sandwiches we like a lot—double-decker pork and beef, and a pork-beef-chicken combo with baked beans, coleslaw, and French fries on the side.

Now, about those pies: they are pure Dixie, powerfully sweet, piled high with gobs of whipped cream. The lemon pie is cool and just faintly tart on a yummy graham cracker crust; coconut is thicker, on a crumbly crust; chocolate pie, made with good ol' Hershey's syrup, is a chocolate dessert from an age of innocence, not sinfully sweet, but angelically so.

John's

112 21st St., Birmingham, AL	$$
(205) 322-6014 Mon–Sat	£D

A rather regal downtown luncheonette with deluxe foil wallpaper and silverware wrapped in white linen, John's is a bastion of proper southern food with a Greek accent. Alabama's coastal setting and the proprietor's Aegean heritage make seafood the star of the menu. Since 1944, Birminghamians have enjoyed dark, smoky gumbo accompanied by crisp corn sticks, charcoal-broiled snapper in a lemony oregano sauce, and Gulf crabmeat served plain in a cocktail or marinated for the delicious "West Indies salad" unique to the Gulf Coast. Fish frowners can feast on tender pot roast with natural gravy, ham steak with red-eye gravy, or high-seasoned, crisp-skinned Greek chicken with luxuriously cooked southern-style vegetables on the side. One curious not-to-be-missed specialty is John's coleslaw, which arrives at the table as nothing but finely shredded raw cabbage in a bowl. There is a squeeze bottle on the table containing secret-recipe slaw dressing, which each customer squeezes on to taste. It is beguiling opaque orange stuff, vaguely like sweet Russian dressing but with sharp, spicy undertones.

Jus' Gumbo	
2 South Church St., Fairhope, AL	$
(334) 928-4100	£𝔇

We have no kitchen and we have no stove," says Donna Becker, proprietor of Jus' Gumbo, a tiny bar and café in the flower-filled town of Fairhope on Mobile's East Bay. With a cement floor, tin walls, and a scattering of tables arrayed with panoplies of hot sauce, Jus' Gumbo is an eatery stripped down to essentials. But what excellent essentials these are! "The Muffin Man across the street bakes our bread," Donna says to explain the crusty French loaf she slices at the bar to accompany our mid-afternoon lunch; then she points out three assorted Crock Pots behind the bar that are used to hold seafood gumbo, Cajun red beans with rice and sausage, and—on Fridays only—crawfish étouffée.

Our chat with Donna over bowls of deliciously smoky gumbo, loaded with shrimp, crabmeat, and tiny, tasty crab claws, is a sneezy one, for we are sitting at the counter and she is standing behind it mixing dried spices by the cup and spoonful, filling a couple of big plastic tumblers with the peppery blend that is her gumbo's soul. It is a complicated process—we give up trying to take notes—and the air soon fills with a superfine piquancy. Significant as the gumbo is, it is served humbly—in a Styrofoam bowl with a plastic spoon, accompanied by crackers and a couple of slices of that good bread. The beer list is bigger than the food menu—domestics, locals, and premiums—and a large part of the business is gumbo-to-go, sold by the pint, quart, and gallon.

Nan-Sea's Restaurant

4170 Bay Front Rd., Mobile, AL	$$
(334) 479-9132	LD

With its open patio overlooking Mobile Bay, Nan-Sea's provides a beautiful place in which to eat plates of expertly prepared Gulf seafood. We recommend starting with the locally beloved appetizer, a West Indies salad, which is nothing but a pearly heap of marinated crabmeat and sweet onion, then moving on to something fried. The subtle art of fish-frying is here practiced to perfection; and from Nan-Sea's bubbling kettles come huge shrimp, oysters, and meaty crab claws encased in a brittle batter so light that it seems to melt on the tongue. We tend to eat fish 'till we bust at Nan-Sea's, but on those occasions when dessert is needed, a cool slice of Key lime pie puts just the right exclamation point on this meal.

Niki's West

233 Finley Ave., W., Birmingham, AL	$
(205) 252-5751 Mon–Sat	BLD

A weird, wonderful, out-of-the-way dining treasure, Niki's West is located across the road from the Birmingham Food Terminal, a complex of buildings where produce is bought and sold. Although the streets outside rumble with trucks, the cavernous interior of Niki's is cool and secluded, decorated in a Mediterranean seafood motif. Service is cafeteria-style; select from an astonishing array of approximately four dozen vegetables, all direct from the market and cooked southern-style, meaning candied, stewed, and enriched. We adore such indulgences as broccoli-rice-cheese casserole and sweet stewed tomatoes, but simple in-season choices, such as sliced tomatoes, watermelon, and cantaloupe, are farm-fresh and wonderful, too.

Entrees include such cafeteria standbys as fried pork chops and country steak; but there are always a few Greek-accented items available, such as baked chicken, roast lamb, and kabobs, which we highly recommend. Also notable is seafood, which sparkles: broiled mackerel almondine, baked fish Creole, fried shrimp and flounder.

Dessert pies are unremarkable, although a nice little dish of creamy banana pudding—here considered a vegetable!—is an appropriately sybaritic conclusion for a Niki's banquet.

Ollie's	
515 University Blvd., Birmingham, AL	$
(205) 324-9485 Mon–Sat	£D

Entering Ollie's is appetizing, not only for the smell of smoke and sizzling pork but for the display up front—bottled sauce and Bible literature are for sale. That's a combination that almost always signals smokehouse greatness. And the food served on Ollie's thick, unbreakable plates confirms it: this is pork-lover's Q, cut into big chunky slices of both tender inside and crusty outside meat (unless you specify you want more of one or the other) and served sauceless. The pale, flavorful meat, insinuated with the taste of smoke, is elegant stuff. Sauce, available on the side, is a thin, tangy dressing with a vinegar bite that complements the pork but doesn't overwhelm it.

Ollie's menu is simple: pork or chicken, chili in the winter, and a short list of sandwiches. For dessert, you can pick up an Eskimo Pie or Nutty Buddy ice cream cone from a freezer near the cash register.

Roussos	
166 S. Royal St., Mobile, AL	$$
(334) 433-3322	£D

A brick-and-cedar-walled eating hall next to historic Fort Condé, Roussos is THE place to indulge in all of Mobile's seafood bounty. Polite but not fancy, always crowded but fast and efficient, it has a menu that features such locally loved classics as West Indies salad, Creole gumbo, fried crab claws, Gulf shrimp (tails on or off), and soft-shelled crab. Proprietary specialties include oysters on the half shell baked with a zesty red sauce, bacon, and cheese that form a luscious, caramelized mantle over the nugget of moist marine succulence; spectacular Greek salad available in giant sizes to feed a whole table; and the most delicious chicken in town, chicken "George," which is half a well-seasoned bird that is slow-cooked in a pan of butter until it attains maximum succulence. Just about any seafood on the menu is available "Greek style," meaning simply cooked in olive oil and lemon juice and sparkling with Roussos's secret spice mix.

ARKANSAS

☆ ☆ ☆

B&B Bar-B-Q	
230 S. East St., Fayetteville, AR	$
(501) 521-3663	ℒⅅ

B&B is one of a kind. Founded in 1960 by Bill and Betty Bassett, who are still in charge, it is a first-class barbecue restaurant with its own way of doing things. Each booth in the wood-paneled dining room is equipped with an orange telephone. Pick up the handset and tell the voice at the other end what you'd like to eat. In a short while, a light glows atop the phone, signaling your meal is ready. Go to the kitchen window, pay, and pick it up.

Pork and beef are cooked in the classic southern way—ten to twelve hours in a long pit over smoking hickory wood. Featured are "What-a-Meal" sandwiches and rib dinners that put a twist in tradition with their wonderful homemade bread instead of ordinary buns. The hearty bread, which is slightly sweet, sliced thick, buttered and toasted, makes a perfect companion to the tangy sauce that glazes B&B's succulent meats.

Side dishes are something special, too: batter-dipped French fries with pillow-soft insides; mouth-watering fried dill pickle chips with a briney smack encased in a luscious, crunchy coat of batter, and fried

pies for dessert that are cooked to order ("Please allow twelve minutes," the menu warns). The sweet pies are elegant pastries dusted with
cinnamon-sugar, their flaky crusts enveloping warm lodes of peach or
apple preserves.

One of the strange things about B&B is its location in a small
hollow below the road. Townsfolk and University of Alabama students
know it well enough to come like homing pigeons, but strangers traveling along Route 71b might easily miss the small sign that peeks up
from behind the road's shoulder. Look closely and be prepared to ease
down a steep driveway into the B&B parking lot: it is a detour rewarded by an excellent and unique Arkansas smokehouse meal.

The Bean Palace	
11045 War Eagle Road, Rogers, AR	$
(501) 789-5343	BLD

While dining at The Bean Palace, you will feel the earth move and
the floor shake. The good vibrations come from a huge, water-
powered, buhrstone grist mill two floors below, grinding corn and
grain just as it did when it was originally built a few centuries ago. Restored in 1973 by Kentucky riflemaker Jewell Medlin and Zoe Medlin
Caywood (now the miller), The War Eagle Mill offers fifteen different
grain products for sale as well as two stories of rustic kitchenware, locally put-up preserves, and fascinating culinary Ozarkiana, plus a lit-
eral taste of country cooking in The Bean Palace restaurant on the
third floor of the mill.

It's a casual eatery, where big families gather at the long red-
checked tables and plow into such country vittles as buckwheat waffles or wheat germ biscuits with gravy at breakfast, warm yellow corn
bread (oh, what good corn bread!), and pinto beans at lunch. Sodas are
served in glass mason jars; decor is a collection of colorful old flour
sacks and rice bags.

Bubba's	
Hwy. 62 W, Eureka Springs, AR	*$$*
(501) 253-7706 Mon–Sat	*LD*

aby back ribs—the tenderest of pig parts you can barbecue—are a Bubba's delight, cooked long and slow in an earthen-floored pit and basted with sweet sauce. But these tender little bones are available only after 5 PM; earlier in the day, you'll have to settle for excellent pork shoulder, packed into sandwiches with coleslaw or as part of a fine dinner with barbecued beans and slaw. Also notable is the "Bubba link," a smoky hot sausage blanketed with spicy chili and cheddar cheese, served on a sturdy (but not sturdy enough) French roll.

For a barbecue house, Bubba's is quite civilized. There is a written menu, and there are actually nonbarbecued items on the menu to eat, including hamburgers, nachos, and grilled cheese sandwiches.

Catfish 'N'	
Dardanelle Dam Rd., Dardanelle, AR	*$*
(501) 229-3321 Tues–Sun	*D*

atfish 'N' is an eating barn above the Arkansas River where the catfish is succulent, encased in a golden crust, and accompanied by fine, onion-sweet hush puppies. Coleslaw and French fries are also part of the help-yourself, all-you-can-eat deal, as are a good assortment of pickles, onions, hot sauces, peppers, and lemon wedges. The big feed here, an Arkansas custom, is immensely popular among locals as well as travelers along I-40, so beware of long lines and a wait at mealtime.

Coursey's

Hwy. 65 (Rte. 1, Box 42), St. Joe, AR	$$
(870) 439-2503 or 439-2504	BLD

M y father started fifty years ago in that old dirt-floored smoke-house," Mrs. Paula Hale said, pointing to the well-settled log shack in the yard out front of Coursey's modern display room. "He hung each ham from a nail in the wall and wrapped it in a dry-goods box."

Now that the ham business is regulated by the federal government, Coursey's meats are smoked in stainless steel facilities and the wooden cabin is only a reminder of days gone by. But FDA regulations have not tarnished the old-time charm of this roadside smoked-meat shop, now run by the grandchildren of Mr. Coursey. We spent an educational half-hour consulting with Mrs. Hale and her kids about how to best get a ham and a couple of pounds of bacon shipped to us during a summer heat wave (we finally decided to wait until cooler weather), and we discussed the fine points of making tasty red-eye gravy. Mrs. Hale clued us in to the joy of a good ham hock, which should never be thrown away once the ham has been eaten: It makes the perfect pot-companion for long-cooked greens or beans. And she reminded us that when we fried this bacon—corn fed and slow-cured over burning green hickory logs—we should save the delicious drippings to season our hominy or cabbage.

Primarily a mail-order and take-out business, with handsome deep-scarlet hams hanging on a rack in cloth bags flavoring the air with their hickory perfume, an assortment of jerkies in jars, and shelves of interesting local jellies, sorghum, and honey for sale, Coursey's has a small counter in back where you can have a sandwich made of ham, turkey, or peppered beef. Nothing fancy here: just meat (cheese optional) on supermarket bread. The ham is lean, sweet, and tender, with an alluring wood-smoke bouquet but none of the pungency of salt-cured country ham.

Craig's Bar-B-Q

Rte. 70, De Valls Bluff, AR	$
(870) 998-2616	£D

Circle De Valls Bluff, along I-40, on your map of Arkansas. Get off and stop at Craig's for superb Ozark barbecue: pork, slow-cooked to sublime tenderness, sauced mild, medium, hot, or extra hot (and how!), served on a bun with coleslaw, accompanied by silky sweet beans. Craig's is a one-room joint with a handful of tables inside and a lot of take-out business from Q connoisseurs who prefer to dine in the front seats of their pickup trucks. The dining room walls display artistic taxidermy, a portrait of Dr. Martin Luther King, Jr., advertisements for equine studs, and announcements for local concealed weapons classes.

Doe's Eat Place

1023 W. Markham St., Little Rock, AR (501) 376-1195	$$$
£D Mon–Fri, D only Sat; closed Sun	£D

We confess that we have been unreasonable snobs about the *original* Doe's eat place in Mississippi (p. 167), which we have long touted as the best steak in the South, maybe in all America. But after a few dinners at this Little Rock branch, we believe that Doe's excellence does indeed travel, at least across the Mississippi River; and we would stack up the Little Rock Doe's against any T-bone-and-potatoes meal, anywhere.

The steaks are gorgeous: up to three pounds of pillowy porterhouse, sirloin, or T-bone. They are accompanied by hugely flavorful French fries, tamales with spicy chili ladled on top, and an oily, garlicky marinated salad.

The ambience is delicious, a sort of pool-hall chic with a worn linoleum floor, pictures of Delta bluesmen on the wall, and waitresses in blue jean cut-offs and sneakers. Because it is in a less-than-elegant part of town, Doe's keeps a chaperon just outside to escort you to and from your car.

Family Pie Shop

Rte. 70, De Valls Bluff, AR (870) 998-2279	$
About 9 AM–5 PM, Wed–Sun	BL

Not quite a restaurant, the Family Pie Shop is nevertheless a place all hungry travelers need to know about. For more than fifteen years now, Mary Thomas has been attracting locals and travelers to her backyard bakery by selling fantastic pies of every sort: pecan pie to die for, sweet potato pie that sets the standard, fluffy-topped meringues, and small, folded-over fried pies filled with spiced apples or peaches. The latter are individually sized, and Mrs. Thomas recently took to making miniature (two-portion) versions of some of her favorites and a few tables have been installed for those of us who need to eat immediately.

Feltner's Whatta-Burger

1410 N. Arkansas, Russellville, AR	$
(501) 968-1410	LD

There are Whatta-Burgers throughout the southwest, but none like Feltner's. This you know the instant you enter the low-slung brick building and an eager order taker nearly accosts you at the door to find out what you want. You tell him the precise details of your order—from a simple Whatta-burger (that's a quarter-pound patty on a five-inch bun) to a Whatta-burger with double meat and double cheese—including which condiments you want. Then you snake through a short line where you have a view of the most bustling kitchen imaginable: a dozen green-uniformed enthusiasts flipping burgers, frying fries, drawing shakes, and bagging meals with all the joy and earnestness of kids putting on a musical at a summer theater.

At the end of the line, you pay and receive your meal on a tray in a white bag, beverage on the side. Find a booth in the big dining room, where the walls are lined with humorous and inspirational homilies: "The hurrier I go, the behinder I get"; "Cherish yesterday, dream tomorrow, live today." When we recently visited, a sign warned customers, "We'll be closing Monday at 5 PM for our annual employee swimming party." Feltner's is THE town burger joint, a favorite for families, teens on dates, and Arkansas Tech students. We shared the dining room with a happy stampede of approximately three dozen boisterous, fresh-faced six-footers attending basketball camp at the college, each of whom carried a tray with a brace of double-doubles (double meat, double cheese) and a heap of French fries.

The burgers are a beau ideal of fast food—not overly thick, but juicy and high-flavored, nestled in nice spongy buns; the crunch-crusted spuds are a reminder of just how good a log of potato can taste when fried in fresh oil, well-salted, and served immediately; and the milk shakes are too thick to suck up a straw. Available shake flavors include chocolate, strawberry, vanilla, pineapple, orange, cherry, banana, and butterscotch; a large one is at least a quart.

For many years, Feltner's Whatta-Burger has won accolades from the local press as the best hamburger in northwest Arkansas. We'd place it on any nationwide honor roll.

Franke's

300 South University, Little Rock, AR	$
(501) 666-1941; other locations at 400 Broadway and	£D
11121 Rodney Parham in Little Rock	

Arkansas's oldest restaurant started as a Little Rock donut shop in 1919, became a thriving bakery, and is now one (actually, three) of the Deep South's premier cafeterias. It is an eminently civilized place to eat, with plenty of elbow room in the dining area, which is decorated with still life paintings in gilt frames and eighteenth-century equestrian prints. Along the "preview line," where you can study the vast assortment of good foods as you inch towards the trays, a wall displays vintage pictures of Franke's from the old days as well as a framed tribute to Mr. Rufus Whitmore along with a newspaper clipping from the occasion of his celebration of fifty years as a cafeteria employee.

The consummate Franke's dinner tray would start with "marinated springtime" (vegetable salad) or a bowl of fresh fruits (scooped from a hollowed-out watermelon), then move on to a plate of sliced-to-order roast beef swimming in natural gravy or sweet and tender pit-cooked ham accompanied by turnips and greens, escalloped eggplant casserole, candied sweet potatoes, or cheese and macaroni casserole. Grab a few corn pones or triangles of jalapeño corn bread and a plate of balmy egg custard pie or hot banana pudding and a tall glass of ice tea, then find a table and feast—all for well under ten dollars per person.

Fred's Fish House

Just off U.S. 62, Mountain Home, AR	$
(870) 492-5958 Mon–Sat	£D

If you are traveling through northern Arkansas, put Fred's on your eating itinerary. The catfish are exemplary: Arkansas-grown and fried in clean peanut oil so they have a crisp, sandy crust and luscious insides. You can get platters of any size, from small individual filets to all-you-can-eat banquets. (For catfish frowners, there is nice fried shrimp.)

Fred's is fish-camp casual, with picture windows that provide a pleasing view of Lake Norfolk and the Arkansas countryside. We recently received a reassuring note from Ron and Lori Pruett, first cousins of Fred and now proprietors of the restaurant he established. Knowing we have been fans of Fred's for years, they said that all the recipes they use to make catfish, sweet-centered hush puppies, and shredded coleslaw are Fred's originals.

Jones Café

Hwy. 65, Pine Bluff, AR (870) 534-6678	$
B£D Mon–Sat; £ only Sun	B£D

We found Jones Café while on a dessert-eating pilgrimage through Arkansas. The day we stopped in the inconspicuous roadside eatery, the repertoire of pies included chocolate cream, coconut, egg custard, sweet potato, apple, pecan, and lemon pecan, plus bowls of supersweet peach cobbler. Prior to sampling the excellent sweets, we enjoyed lunch of baked pork chops with greens and fried okra, chili mac, and shredded slaw. It was an estimable southern café lunch, but Jones Café lingers in memory as a high point in pie paradise.

McClard's Bar-B-Q

505 Albert Pike, Hot Springs, AR	$
(501) 623-9665 or 624-9586 Tues–Sat	£D

Best in the state since '28" is the truthful motto of McClard's, where exquisitely tender, hickory-cooked beef, pork, and pork ribs are served with stupendously good hot sauce and accompanied by chili-spiked barbecued beans, hand-cut French fries, and exemplary milk shakes or beer. For barbecue believers in search of smokehouse enlightenment, McClard's is a holy place.

Mickey's Bar-B-Que

1522 Park Ave., Hot Springs, AR	$
(501) 624-1247 Tues–Sat	£D

A snug smokehouse on the road into Hot Springs, Mickey's has a drive-through window and two small dining rooms. Customers who eat here get their own food on a tray along a short cafeteria line that is a powerful appetizer. Select from a handsome array of pork rib racks waiting to severed, lengths of plump pink sausage, roasts of beef, pork, and ham all blackened and crusty on the outside by their long, slow sizzle over wood smoke, and also bean pots and pit potatoes. The latter two side dishes are local specialties, the bean pot a small bowl of shreds and chunks and chewy debris off the ham roast combined with vivid red sauce and soft beans. The pit potato, which is slow-cooked over hickory smoke along with the meat, has a dark, leathery skin and cream-soft center. It is available as a side dish or stuffed with chopped beef or pork barbecue.

Mickey, a big man who wields carving knife and fork with the skill of a martial artist, cuts the meat and assembles a plate of whichever one you choose (or a "Taste 'em all" sampler). He also cuts open the hot potato and, as starchy clouds of steam escape, inserts two globes of butter that quickly melt. Available garniture includes pickles, peppers, garlic toast, and sweet little deviled eggs. For dessert there is fried pie—a folded-over, flake-crusted pastry with warm peach or apple filling. "Y'all have enough?" Mickey is fond of asking customers as they tote loaded trays to a table.

There are a few seats in the front room that afford a view of the handsome food in the cafeteria line; or you can choose to dine in the adjoining "Hickory Nut Room," where a half-dozen booths provide a measure of seclusion and the comfort of rustic decor that includes napkin holders and a coat rack carved from tree limbs as well as wood paneling branded with scenes of animals that hunters like to see behind the bead of a shotgun: deer, ducks, pheasants.

Mrs. Miller's Dinners

4723 Central (Hwy. 7 South), Hot Springs, AR	$$
(501) 525-8861 Tues–Sun	D

When Mrs. Miller's opened for business in 1937, it was far out in the quiet countryside, miles beyond Oaklawn race track. Now Hot Springs has grown and the gracious white dinner house is on a busy strip of garish enterprise; but step inside and you find peace. A hostess in a long gown greets you and leads you across thick carpet to a linen-clothed table in a dining room where soft background music provides soothing ambiance and white-uniformed waitresses patrol the tables with the vigilance of sentinels.

"Dinners cooked to order," a menu headline says. This is NOT fast food. So have a cocktail, sit back, and relax. The menu is simple, each meal a familiar ritual that begins with salad and a basket of crunchy toasted half-biscuits served with Mrs. Miller's wonderful purple fruit conserve. Then comes grilled steak, a brace of Arkansas quail, farm-raised catfish, or pan-fried chicken accompanied by a nice baked potato or French fries, soulful green beans, more biscuits (but these are soft and fresh from the oven), and finally a little dish of fruit cobbler. What could be nicer?

Recently an outdoor smoke pit has been added to supplement the menu with barbecued ribs and chicken.

Murry's

Cypress St., De Valls Bluff, AR (870) 998-2247	$
Fri and Sat	D

Catfish, deep fried, accompanied by steamy corn cakes, French fries, and coleslaw: that's the consummate country-style meal in these parts, nowhere better than at Murry's. Housed in a collection of house trailers and serving Arkansans since the 1950s, Mr. Murry's place is the definitive country catfish parlor. His relatives have opened a spruced-up Murry's on Old Route 70 where they also deep-fry shrimp and oysters, and offer steak as well. Whichever place you find, it's those crisp-fried Arkansas mud puppies—sweet and moist and satisfying like no other fish—that draw the crowds (and there are crowds every precious night Murry's is open).

FLORIDA

Bern's Steak House

1208 S. Howard St., Tampa, FL	$$$
(813) 251-2421	D

There isn't a restaurant in the nation more conspicuously opulent than Bern's Steak House. To the tune of a strolling accordionist in plush dining rooms where Louis XIV would have felt at home, you eat what many enthusiastic carnivores consider the best steak in America. It's dry-aged on the premises, available in every known cut and whatever size you like, selected from a menu titled "Art in Steaks," and accompanied by the best of everything else that money can buy and human ingenuity can bring to the dining table.

The Laxer family grow their own organic vegetables, offer the largest wine list in the world, roast their personally selected coffee beans, and blend tea from flowering tips and tops only. To conclude the ultimate in sybaritic meals, customers leave their dinner tables and repair to rooms devoted to nothing but eating dessert and drinking dessert wine and coffee.

Blue Heaven	
729 Thomas St., Key West, FL (305) 296-8666	$
𝕭𝕷𝕯 Wed–Sat; 𝕯 only Mon and Tues; brunch and 𝕯 Sun	𝕭𝕷𝕯

Blue Heaven serves three meals most days, but we like the morning best because of the company: a flock of roosters and hens who scratch about the dirt-floored patio among the tables, crowing and cackling at the sun, chasing one another, and nesting with newborn chicks. Off the beaten path in Key West's Bahama Village, Blue Heaven has been the home of a boxing ring (Ernest Hemingway liked to spar here), a bordello (the tiny rooms upstairs are now part of an art gallery), a bookmaking parlor, and a cockfighting pit (heroic roosters are buried in a little graveyard behind the dining area), as well as the inspiration for Jimmy Buffett's "Blue Heaven Rendezvous." Today, it's a restaurant, artists' studios, a one-dollar shower stall, and a hemp shop.

What a nice experience it is to eat delicious banana pancakes under the ancient shade trees, to drink coffee from miscellaneous souvenir mugs, and to wile away the morning in an ultra-casual setting that makes every meal a picnic. Shrimp and grits are served at Sunday brunch, and dinner specialties include jerk chicken and barbecued shrimp, as well as a delish flamed "Banana heaven" dessert . . . but in the evenings, and especially on weekends, you'll wait in line.

Branch Ranch

Branch-Forbes exit off I-4 in Plant City, FL	$$
(813) 752-1957 Tues–Sun	LD

Farm feasts, served to hungry hordes: that's the Branch Ranch experience, a gourmand's ritual ever since Mary Branch began inviting friends to dinner at her home in the 1950s. The private home has given way to a vast barn of a restaurant; but the family-style meal never changes. Choose your entree—chicken, ham (baked or country-style), or steak—and it comes with a feast that includes pickled beets and bread-and-butter pickles, hot buttermilk biscuits with marmalade and strawberry jam, candied yams, scalloped eggplant, pole beans, baked yellow squash, and dumpling-topped chicken pot pie. Dessert is apple or peach cobbler or coconut cake.

You will wait for a table at busy mealtimes, and the ambiance can be as hectic as a college mess hall. But don't let the commotion dissuade you. A Branch Ranch meal is true and pure country cooking.

Conch Cupboard Luncheonette

in Dennis Pharmacy, 1229 Simonton St., Key West, FL	$
(305) 294-1577	BL

The luncheonette half of Dennis Pharmacy, this merry little eat shop has a double-horseshoe laminate counter and a scattering of tables where Conchs (Key natives) come for espresso and *café con leche* with lengths of buttered Cuban bread in the morning, and where Conchs and everybody else come for cheeseburgers later in the day. They make a nice Cuban sandwich, too (that's a Dagwood of ham, pork, and cheese), as well as hearty picadillo (Spanish sloppy Joe, souped up with a jolt of spice and olives). We even like the conch chowder, which is a non-gourmet version of the local favorite—thin and quite deliciously institutional.

(For you roadside kitsch fans, Dennis boasts of being the *Southernmost Pharmacy, Luncheonette, and Photo Lab* in the continental United States.)

The Crack'd Conch

Mile Marker 105, Ocean Side, Key Largo, FL	$$
(305) 451-0732 (closed Wed)	LD

Heading out the Overseas Highway towards Margaritaville at the end of the Florida Keys, The Crack'd Conch (on the ocean side of the road) makes a fine way station. Started as a fish camp in the 1930s, it has been remodeled over the years, but in no way gentrified. It remains a ramshackle shanty—white clapboard and lattice trimmed in violet and green, with picnic tables on its front porch, a breezy back patio, and a helter-skelter dining room in which wall decor consists of customers' business cards and foreign currency. To call it "casual" only hints at the laid-back beatitude that makes this place such a good taste of Conch Republic style.

Fried gator, steamed shrimp, and house-smoked chicken are all long-time favorites, and the fried shrimp are so startlingly light that you think they have no coating at all until you crunch through a translucent crust, but the essential thing to eat is the house specialty, crack'd conch. Nuggets of sweet and tangy mollusk meat, tender but with mouth-watering tooth resistance, are encased in lush breading and served in a great, tangled heap. On the side, we like oily fried bananas—a soft, supersweet, hedonistic tropical food that has no match in the Northeast where we live.

Who will be your neighbors when you dine at the Crack'd Conch? The fun of the place is that you never really know. During our last visit, we were sided by one table with a pair of white-haired septuagenarians who accompanied their mammoth oyster po' boys with at least a dozen beers from a brew list of a hundred interesting brands. At the table next to them were three leather-clad bikers with three halter-topped biker chicks, all enjoying dainty little plates of conch salad and glasses of iced tea.

Dixie Crossroads

1475 Garden St., Titusville, FL	$$
(407) 268-5000	LD

Rock shrimp are the specialty of the house. Order them by the pound, or as an all-you-can-eat feast, and they arrive grouped in crowded rows, splayed open and in the shell like an army of tiny split rock lobster tails. A cocktail fork is provided to pull the meat out of its hard translucent shell. It comes away easily in one whole, hefty piece. A buttery dunk is provided, but it seems like gilt for the lily, for there is hardly any seafood more inherently buttery than these glistening creatures.

Also on the menu are tiny, briny local scallops hardly bigger than pencil erasers; catfish with a frail, nut-brown crust; and mullet, broiled or smoked. Meals are preceded by can't-stop-eating-'em corn fritters with crunchy red-gold crusts, dusted with powdered sugar.

Just across the river from the John F. Kennedy Space Center, Dixie Crossroads is a popular, sprawling eatery, especially crowded around shuttle launch times, when the clientele include not only tourists but friends and families of astronauts.

El Siboney

900 Catherine St., Key West, FL (305) 296-4184	$$
Mon–Sat	LD

When you consider El Siboney is just ninety miles from Cuba itself—closer to Havana than to Miami, you understand why its Cuban food tastes so right. This is the best place we know in Key West to taste grilled garlic chicken, a half-bird with a crisp skin and meat so tender that it slides off the bone when you try to cut it. Plantains on the side are slightly crusty and caramelized around their edges. And *yuca*, a side dish served with roast pork, beans, and rice, is a revelation not quite like any other vegetable. Soft and glistening white hunks, reminiscent of a well-baked potato, but more luscious and substantial, are served in a bath of heavily garlicked oil and garlanded with onion slices. El Siboney is a clean, pleasant place with red-striped tables topped with easy-wipe plastic and silverware presented in tidy little paper bags. If you don't speak Spanish, the waitresses do their best to help you understand the menu. Ours explained that El Siboney was a Cuban Indian, and that the Indian-themed art on the walls is a tribute to him.

Florida House Inn	
22 S. Third St., Fernandina Beach, FL (904) 261-3300	$
Sun brunch only; Mon lunch only	*LD*

The oldest hotel in Florida, now a quaint bed and breakfast with four-poster beds and a romantic fireplace in most rooms, also serves groaning-board meals to the public. At tables-for-twelve, guests and suppertime visitors help themselves, family-style, to bowls full of collard greens, stewed okra with tomatoes, seasoned rice, green beans, corn bread, fried chicken, and pork chops with gravy (and seafood jambalaya on Friday night). Desserts include banana pudding, chocolate-frosted yellow cake, and apple cobbler. The beverage, naturally, is iced tea, available sweetened or plain. As in any traditional boardinghouse, guests are expected to bus their own plates after they've had enough to eat.

Half Shell Raw Bar	
1 Lands End Village, Key West, FL	$$
(305) 294-7496	*LD*

Conch chowder is a fascinating brew, made from the mollusk by which south Floridians like to label their own distinctly hedonistic ocean culture. There are few better places to taste it than the Half Shell, a breezy joint at the shrimp docks in Key West. There is a blackboard menu that ranges from good hamburgers and deep-fried shark nuggets to deluxe crab-stuffed local lobsters, fine, fresh fish as well as clams and oysters on the half shell. We love the crusty conch fritters as well as the smooth, savory chowder. With an afternoon's worth of

Southernisms

Southern menus contain many wonderful things to eat that non-Southerners might not recognize. Here are a few basics to help you choose wisely and eat well south of the Mason-Dixon line:

Boiled peanuts	A roadside-stand treat, best eaten warm from the kettle
Chess pie	Simple sugar pie, so named perhaps because it's "jes' pie"
Congealed salad	Jell-O
Country captain	Hunter's stew, usually made with curry powder, in Georgia
Frogmore stew	Shrimp, sausage, and corn stew, native to the Carolina coast
Greens	Collard, turnip, or mustard; long cooked with pork till tender
Grits	Hot, creamy corn cereal, especially good with ham and gravy
Hush puppies	Deep-fried cornmeal balls, almost always served with catfish
Perloo	A South Carolina jambalaya, also spelled pilau and pilaf
Pine bark stew	A spicy fish stew indigenous to the Carolinas and Georgia
Pot likker	The porcine soup retrieved when greens are cooked with pork
Red rice	Seasoned rice usually made with peppers, onion, and tomato
Red-eye gravy	Ham drippings, usually mixed with black coffee or water
Sawmill gravy	Thick, creamy white gravy, frequently used to top biscuits
Spoon bread	Cornmeal soufflé

beers on the Half Shell porch, such fare is the basis of great vacation eating.

Hopkins Boarding House

900 N. Spring St., Pensacola, FL (850) 438-3979	$
BL Tues–Sat; BLD Sun	BLD

Eating at the Hopkins Boarding House always feels like a holiday. Share a table, pass the platters, eat until you have to let out your belt a notch, then eat some more. The food is deeply, deliciously southern, with plenty of fresh vegetables, plain and fancy; biscuits and bread-stuffs; plus fried chicken and some other meat as a second choice. Hot cobblers arrive for dessert and, on occasion, there is fine banana pudding to sample.

Located in the old part of Pensacola, Hopkins is a grand landmark of happy eating with a fan club of customers who come from coast to coast.

Joe's Stone Crab

227 Biscayne St., Miami Beach, FL (305) 673-0365	$$$
October 15 through May 15; closed in the summer	LD

You have not tasted Miami Beach until you have eaten a platter of stone crabs at Joe's. Plump and juicy, not cold but not too warm, easy to extract from their coral-pink claws, dipped in Joe's creamy mustard sauce, these beautiful hunks of food are vastly expensive—Damon Runyon once said, "They sell by the karat"—but no other shellfish meat is quite as sweet. There are good side dishes, including creamed spinach and cottage-fried sweet potatoes, and a full menu of local lobsters, shrimp, and oysters. But it's stone crabs on which the reputation of this old place was built.

A grand, rambling landmark with formally attired staff, Joe's itself is a memorable experience. A timeless south Florida eating establishment still in the family of Joe Weiss, who opened for business back in 1913, it is mobbed by Miami Beach natives as well as tourists.

La Teresita	
3248 W. Columbus Dr., Tampa, FL	**$**
(813) 879-4909	**BLD**

Customers sit at the serpentine counter (there are no booths or tables) and eat what are known hereabouts as "Cuban sandwiches"—roast pork heaped into lengths of elegant toasted and buttered bread. With the mighty sandwiches, they gulp down coffee thick as syrup and strong as TNT. At breakfast, the same good bread is warm and buttered with cups of café con leche, and at lunch, the bread accompanies such Caribbean standbys as black beans and rice, carne asada, and roast chicken. Throughout the day, you'll see groups of happy gents gathering in the street after dining at La Teresita. Here they fire up big made-in-Tampa cigars and look like kings who have just enjoyed a royal feast.

Manny and Isa's Kitchen	
Mile Marker 81.6, Islamorada, FL	**$**
(305) 664-5019 Wed–Mon	**LD**

Many locals come to Manny and Isa's for a sandwich or a plate of chicken or to take home chili con carne or conch chowder by the pint. But for those of us on eating tours of the Florida Keys, the one overriding allure of this little café is Key lime pie. Made from limes Manny Ortiz grows in his own orchard, it is an exquisite balance of zesty lime, sweetness, and cream, topped with an honest meringue and set upon a chewy graham cracker crust.

Manny and Isa's pre-pie menu of Spanish/Caribbean specialties is pretty wonderful, too, from succulent conch fritters to classic ropa vieja that has reached a point of maximum tenderness and delirious beefy flavor, accompanied, of course, by a timbale of tasty rice and inky black beans.

Pepe's	
806 Caroline St., Key West, FL	**$$**
(305) 294-7192	**BLD**

Pepe's is a personality-plus eatery where hearty breakfasts are accompanied by a different tropical-tasting bread every day (pray it's coconut!), and where Apalachicola Bay oysters go down the hatch by the dozen—raw on the half shell, baked, or roasted. Every Thursday, you can count on a full-bore Thanksgiving dinner, and every Sunday a mouth-watering barbecue with a choice of Pepe's good sauces.

The place itself is a joy, with an old wood dining room and varnished booths, a huge circular fan overhead, and a patio outside illuminated by a miscellany of fixtures that include a crystal chandelier, green-shaded billiard lamps, and year-round Christmas lights strung among the trees. Out back is the bar where locals congregate.

Vigi's Café	
3880 NW 25 St., Miami, FL	**$**
(305) 871-7581	**BLD**

If you fly into South Florida and need instantly to knock back a shot of strong coffee or to heft a Cuban sandwich, pull up to the order window at Vigi's, a jolly little pink café just yards from the Avis lot adjacent to Miami Airport. Dine at the counter or off oilcloth-covered tables inside, or eat standing in the street with the din of jets overhead and street traffic rumbling past.

The java is thick, black, and strong, served in tiny white plastic cups. Sandwiches are piled thick into lengths of crusty warm bread. The classic *Cubano* is a beaut: multiple layers of ham with roast pork and Swiss cheese, mayo, and mustard. There are steak sandwiches and a Vigi Special sandwich, of steak and eggs, or simpler and delicious combos of bread packed with garlic and tomato or with luscious yucca fritters. To-go sandwiches are encased with a fistful of potato sticks in wax paper tubes twisted tight to limit spillage, then packed in brown paper bags on which the waitress writes the name of the sandwich in ballpoint pen. To slake thirst, there are thick fruit shakes in dreamy tropical flavors—mamey, papaya, banana, orange-carrot—and super-sweet lemonade.

Wakulla Springs Lodge	
1 Springs Dr., Wakulla Springs, FL	**$$**
(850) 224-5950	**BLD**

Surrounded by a thick pine and oak forest, Wakulla Springs Lodge is a Spanish-style retreat for nature lovers, with the added attraction of good southern food served three times a day: fried chicken, country ham, and such Gulf Coast specialties as Apalachicola oysters, deviled crab, and broiled or fried shrimp. Whatever else you order, don't miss the navy bean soup, a legend for decades. To tell the truth, our favorite meal is breakfast, bright and early, when the birds outside the great arched windows of the dining room are busy on their morning errands and provide a spectacular backdrop to a table piled high with sizzled ham steak, hot grits, biscuits, and gravy.

The nearby springs are a true wonder of the world, crystal clear and undisturbed by visitors. Back in the mid-1950s, the primeval setting was used to film location footage for *Creature from the Black Lagoon*.

Wolfie Cohen's Rascal House

17190 Collins Ave., Miami Beach, FL	$
(305) 947-4581	BLD

With pink tile walls, aqua upholstery, and white-uniformed waitresses with big hankies pinned to their chests, Wolfie's is a Miami Beach delicatessen rhapsody. The leitmotif is schmaltz (chicken fat), spread on corned beef sandwiches if the meat isn't fatty enough for you, blended into luscious chopped liver, and infusing crusty potato pancakes. Puckery pickles start the meal—half-sours, green tomatoes—and the bread includes chewy mini–onion rolls and tough-crusted rye and pumpernickel. You can drink a glass of cool flamingo-pink borscht, available with or without a boiled potato, choose from a long list of sandwiches and smoked fish platters, then conclude with berry-topped cheesecake or mile-high lemon meringue pie. It isn't a light meal, but if classic Jewish deli food is what you hanker for, it gets no better than this.

At busy meal times, prepare to wait in a mazelike system of lines, depending on how many are in your party. The people-watching is good, usually including Miami Beach yentas, Cubans, Haitians, and homesick New Yorkers in search of a pastrami fix.

GEORGIA

★ ★ ★

Bilbo's	
Hwy. 78 W, Bremen, GA (770) 537-4180	$
Tues–Sat	LD

Just a few minutes from exit 3 off I-20 near the Alabama border, Bilbo's is a restaurant that hungry travelers need to know about. There are two entrances: one to the dining room, a modest wood-paneled space with leatherette booths, the other to the take-out window. The menu includes steaks and chicken, but aside from hickory-smoked prime rib (a weekend-only special), what's interesting is pork barbecue. It is quite delicious, chopped fine and mixed with a sweet, tangy sauce and served on a bun or on a plate with coleslaw, French fries, and Brunswick stew. The stew, a traditional companion to smoked meat meals in these parts, is a thick pork gravy, laced with meat and vegetables, and positively addictive once you start mopping it with bread or spooning it up from the bowl with crackers crumbled on top.

Blue Willow Inn	
294 N. Cherokee Rd., Social Circle, GA	$$
(770) 464-2131	LD

Come to Social Circle, Georgia, one of the loveliest towns in all the South, find this pillared antebellum mansion, and eat to your heart's delight. The prices are fixed, from $8.95 for a weekday lunch to $14.95 for the Friday night seafood and southern food buffet, and the choices are staggering. "We have two rules here," the waitress warns us at the beginning of a meal. "Rule one is that no one goes home hungry. Rule two is that everybody has to have at least two desserts."

With a minimum of four meats and more than a dozen vegetables on display at the buffet tables, not to mention the umpteen pies, cakes, cookies, brownies, and cobbler, you either aim for a tiny bite of everything you like or you make hard choices: pass up opulent macaroni and cheese in favor of skillet squash; ignore corn bread dressing so you have room on the plate for a heap of fried green tomatoes. If you fancy baked and smothered pork chops, then you likely won't have a chance to savor streak o' lean—thick strips of bacony pork that vary in texture from wickedly crusty to meltaway-lush, blanketed with smooth white gravy. Customers are welcome to return to the buffet for second, third, fourth, and fifth helpings, but the problem is that some dishes (like the fried chicken) are so dang delicious that you want to pile your plate with them again and again, recklessly sacrificing variety for monomaniacal satisfaction.

Buckner Family Restaurant and Music Hall	
Exit 66 off I-75 (State Rte. 36), Jackson, GA	**$**
(770) 775-6150 Wed–Sun	**£D**

It is good to come for lunch any day the Buckner Family Restaurant is open, but it is divine to come for supper on Thursday, Friday, or Saturday night. That is when you will be serenaded by a gospel choir. The food is always glorious: a lazy Susan piled high with fried chicken, braised beef, mashed potatoes, creamed corn, and various vegetable casseroles galore, all accompanied by sweet iced tea and topped off with warm peach cobbler. This is a Dixie meal to remember.

The Colonnade

1879 Cheshire Bridge Rd., Atlanta, GA	$$
(404) 874-5642	LD

Trust the Colonnade's waitstaff of good ol' girls to take good care of you. In this polite place, a bastion of southern food since the 1920s, waitresses speed broad trays of food to tables full of families who have been customers for generations. The specialties, which never change, include excellent fried chicken and crusty catfish, served with plenty of soulful southern-style vegetables (great okra!) and genteel side dishes that include tomato aspic, lovely corn muffins, and yeast rolls.

Dillard House

Hwy. 441, Dillard, GA	$
(706) 746-5349	LD

Bring a mighty big appetite to Dillard House. You'll need it to plow through the extravagant feast that has inscribed this boisterous eating hall onto America's good food registry. Tables may be shared by strangers during peak summer hours, but that doesn't inhibit anybody from having a wildly good time tucking into country ham and fried chicken, yams, biscuits, and peach cobbler, all served family-style in communal bowls that are replenished by the kitchen until all diners have had their fill. Aside from lavish food, Dillard House is a favorite travelers' destination for its location. The north Georgia landscape that includes awe-inspiring waterfalls, enchanting backwoods cabins, hiking trails, and picturesque highways served as scenery in several good ol' boy movies starring Burt Reynolds, whose signed 8 × 10 hangs on the dining room wall.

The GA Pig

Exit 6 off I-95, Brunswick, GA	$
(912) 264-6664	LD

Pork is slow-cooked over hickory wood, basted with sweet sauce, then hacked into juicy chunks that are mixed with another soupçon of sauce. The resulting food is an attraction all hungry travelers along I-95 in Georgia need to know about. It is served on a platter or in a sandwich with delectable barbecue beans on the side. If you are in a hurry, you can get it to gobble in your car, or there are picnic tables, inside and out, that make this pine-shaded rustic shack a pleasant place to linger.

Harold's

171 McDonough Blvd. SE, Atlanta, GA	$
(404) 627-9268 Mon–Sat	LD

Pork, smoked and sliced to mouth-watering succulence, with Brunswick stew and cracklin' corn bread on the side—it is the definitive Georgia smokehouse meal, nowhere tastier than at Harold's, a pit on the wrong side of town (that's the Federal Pen just down the street; Harold's windows have bars on them, too). Good manners prevail in this humble dining room where walls are decorated with religious slogans and no alcohol is served. Established in 1947 by Harold Hembree, now operated by his widow and children, it's a retreat where good food transcends a bad neighborhood.

Melear's

GA 85, Fayetteville, GA	$
(770) 461-7180	BLD

The Melear family has been known for its barbecue skills since Grandpa John Melear started selling pork south of Atlanta in the 1920s. Today's roadside restaurant, with its old wood tables and deeply saturated smoke smell, is a north Georgia pork shrine. Cooked over hickory and oak, the meat is mild and sweet. It is hacked up and served in sandwiches or as part of a platter with the side dish known as Brunswick stew, itself a zesty gallimaufry of sauce, meat, and vegetables. You can also try the meat in an item listed on the menu as a "bowl of pork," which is nothing but meat and sauce, a meal fit for monomaniacs.

Note: Melear's iced tea is a sweet southern paradigm, served in huge tumblers that are refilled on the house. Eat enough of this spicy meat and Brunswick stew, and you'll need it.

Sconyer's Bar-B-Q

2511 Windsor Spring Rd., Augusta, GA	$
(706) 790-5411 Thur–Sat	LD

Sconyer's is huge, impersonal, and way too busy. But its chopped pork sopped with tangy sauce and its racks of meaty ribs are piggy perfection, at once lean and dizzyingly succulent. On the side of whatever you order, you want hash (or you can make a meal of it), a Deep South treat made of all the barbecued meats—ham, chicken, and beef—chopped up with tomatoes, onions, potatoes, and plenty of good sauce.

Silver Skillet

200 14th St., Atlanta, GA	$
(404) 874-1388 𝓑𝓛 Mon–Fri; 𝓑 only Sat and Sun	𝓑𝓛𝓓

We highly recommend you go to the bathroom at the Silver Skillet. The route leads through the kitchen, which is hot as Hades but provides an incredibly appetizing tour of fine food being created by masters in humble surroundings: onion rings pulled from hot oil, country ham drizzled with powerhouse red-eye gravy, great slabs of meat loaf plated alongside sweet yams and butter-tender cabbage and tangy fried green tomatoes.

The dining room itself, where glass windows slant rakishly outward at the angle of 1950s tailfins, is a blast from the past; green-and-orange Naugahyde-upholstered booths frame boomerang-pattern Formica tables. A sign on the wall advises USE A LITTLE SUGAR AND STIR LIKE HELL. WE DON'T MIND THE NOISE. Each table is strewn with pencils. As you peruse the written menu and the long list of daily vegetables and specials posted above the counter, a waitress delivers you a couple of checks on which you write your own order.

Breakfast is especially worthwhile. The skillet-cooked ham is the real thing, strong and salty; biscuits are oven-hot; grits and gravy are pure country. And the people-watching is swell; high and low, rich and poor, the famous, the notorious, and the unknown all make themselves right at home in these old booths.

Smith House

202 S. Chestatee St., Dahlonega, GA	$$
(706) 864-3566 Tues–Sun	𝓛𝓓

Country cooking, served family-style—for a half-century, the Smith House has been luring appetites with its pay-one-price, eat-till-you-drop meals. Fried chicken is always the main attraction, with ham or catfish as alternatives, surrounded by a glorious assortment of such vegetables as candied sweet potatoes, brandied chestnut soufflé, fried okra, and turnip greens and accompanied by a battery of biscuits, rolls, and corn bread. It is a high-spirited feast, with strangers becoming friends as they pass the butter beans and exchange tales of wondrous meals they have eaten in their travels.

The Varsity	
61 North Ave., Atlanta, GA	$
(404) 881-1706	*BLD*

An Atlanta institution since 1928, The Varsity is a huge drive-in with seats inside for some eight hundred customers, plus curb service. It is famous for not just fast food but *lightning-fast* food, garnished with plenty of hash-slinger sass. "What'll ya have?" countermen bellow, calling out to the vast kitchen orders for "Yankee steaks" (hamburgers with yellow mustard), "strings" (French fries), and "FOs" (frosted orange drinks). The aplomb of the staff is of mythic proportions. Senator Phil Gramm recently recalled that when he was at college in Atlanta, the *Journal-Constitution* had a party for its paperboys. The organizer stepped up and ordered *six thousand* steaks, to go. The counterman, without missing a beat, shot back, "Watcha drinkin'?"

Hot dogs are the house specialty, little pink tube steaks served in steamy-soft buns, begging to be dolled up with condiments. The prime adornment is chili, a finely pulverized brew that perfectly complements either dog or burger. Chili dogs are customarily served with stripes of yellow mustard across their tops, accompanied by cardboard boats full of crusty onion rings and/or excellent French fries.

By the way, this is health food, at least according to Varsity founder Frank Gordy, who once proclaimed, "A couple of chili dogs a day keep you young."

Ye Olde Colonial Cafeteria

On the Square, Madison, GA	$
(706) 342-2211 Mon–Sat	BLD

We cannot say what, exactly, is colonial about Ye Olde Colonial Cafeteria, which is located in a former bank building in a town full of antebellum mansions, but we can tell you this for sure: it is a great place to eat true southern cooking, served southern-style in a short cafeteria line. The fried chicken is cooked to crisp succulence, and the shredded pork barbecue is moist and saucy. These tasty entrees are served alongside classic Dixie vegetables that include rutabaga casserole, candied yams, and collard greens drenched in pot likker. Corn sticks have a fetching crunch, apple cobbler is irresistible, and tables are equipped with pitchers full of presweetened iced tea. Ye Olde Colonial, the nice place in town, is a great eating opportunity for anyone on the road between Atlanta and Augusta.

LOUISIANA

Black's Oyster Bar

311 Pere Merget St., Abbeville, LA	$
(318) 893-4266	LD

"Live Longer! Love Longer!" is the promise of Black's menu to all who eat enough oysters. If you do relish oysters, fresh from the Gulf and on the half shell, this is the place to eat them by the dozen, with an assortment of hot sauces to add spice and oyster crackers to cleanse the palate.

If twenty or thirty oysters only pique your appetite, follow them with some delicious fried oysters or fried shrimp, both available on a platter or, the best deal of all, combined and stuffed into a po' boy sandwich with mayo and/or mustard as a garnish. Once you've had this sandwich, you will long to return to Cajun country during oyster season.

Bon Ton Café

401 Magazine, New Orleans, LA	$$
(504) 524-3386 Mon–Fri	£D

Elegant but not snooty, pricey but worthwhile, a vintage city restaurant that is equally good to old-timers and tourists, the Bon Ton Café is the best place we know for a pleasant, classic Creole meal. In starched white outfits, the suave staff will serve you such local delicacies as oyster pan roast, crawfish étouffée in crawfish season (spring), shrimp étouffée in the summer, and not-to-be-missed redfish Bon Ton, served with a delicious crabmeat-laced sauce. There is only one dessert you need to know about: bread pudding with whiskey sauce. There are many food-savvy New Orleaneans who say this thick block of cake is the best bread pudding in town, and in this bread-pudding-crazed city, that is saying plenty.

Boudin King

906 W. Division St., Jennings, LA	$
(318) 824-6593 Mon–Sat	£D

The powerfully spiced pork sausage known as boudin is a hallmark of the Cajun kitchen, and it's the food on which Ellis Cormier's drive-in restaurant has built its reputation since Monsieur Cormier, the Boudin King of swamp country fairs and food festivals, opened for business in 1975. His boudin is sold in large links, mild or spicy, for eating here or to take home. But beware, even the mild boudin packs a punch, so spicy it's sinus-draining. Either kind is porky, powerful food, best enjoyed in the company of other good things served up by his kitchen. They include smoky gumbo, crisp-fried catfish, and fried crawfish, as well as freshly made hog's head cheese. Although the restaurant looks like any modern franchise, it is one of a kind, and one of the reasons it is such a pleasure to eat one's way through Louisiana.

Café du Monde	
800 Decatur St., New Orleans, LA (504) 587-0840	$
always open	*BLD*

No traveling eater is allowed to visit New Orleans without breakfast at Café du Monde, the open-air, open-all-night café where the café au lait is bracing, the beignets (little holeless rectangular donuts sprinkled with sugar) are sweet, and the people-watching is spectacular. Fellow customers early in the morning range from fresh-scrubbed little old ladies off the Dubuque Scenic Tours bus to drag queens and French Quarter kooks finishing a long, hard night.

Camellia Grill	
626 S. Carrollton Ave., New Orleans, LA	$
(504) 866-9573	*BLD*

Cheese and chili omelets, pecan waffles, chocolate milk shakes—what a joy it is to watch the food being prepared as you sit at the counter of this distinguished diner, where the waiters are dressed formally but the meals are cheap and delicious. An only-in-New Orleans eating experience.

Casamento's

4330 Magazine, New Orleans, LA	$$
(504) 895-9761 (closed throughout summer)	£D

asamento's is a shipshape little oyster bar that serves a distinctive
sandwich called an oyster loaf, which is like a po' boy but bigger.
Sweet, freshly fried oysters are piled into an entire loaf of white bread
that is cut lengthwise and scooped out to make a big fried-fish pocket.
There is no easy way to eat it, but that's of no concern, for the contrast
between the cushiony bread and crisp, briny oysters induces a kind of
ravenous ecstasy that makes you want to tear at the food and feel its
textures on your fingertips even before you savor them on your tongue.

The oyster loaf is the signature dish all newcomers must have, but
regular customers patronize the vintage neighborhood spot for other
delicacies, such as raw oysters by the dozen, fried shrimp, the Italian
Creole pot roast known as daube, as well as good old-fashioned
spaghetti.

Central Grocery

923 Decatur St., New Orleans, LA	$
(504) 523-1620 until 5:30 PM	BLD

entral Grocery lays claim to inventing the muffaletta, a New Orleans sandwich on a circular loaf of chewy bread that is sliced hori-
zontally, like a yeasty flying saucer. The cold cuts loaded on the bottom
half include salami, ham, and provolone, topped with a spicy melange
of chopped green and black olives fragrant with anchovies and garlic;
the bread is generously sprinkled with olive oil; and the whole package
is wrapped in paper so you can carry it away. There are no tables or
chairs in the old grocery store, where the air is perfumed by cheese and
sausage; most customers take their sandwich, with a bottle of root beer,
to a bench in Jackson Square at the French Market. The muffaletta, cut
in quarters by the deli man, is a mighty handful, one of the Crescent
City's culinary wonders.

Creole Menu Crib Sheet

First, you should know that the difference between Cajun and Creole is itself a little blurred, the former originally referring to swamp-country folk culture, the latter to the more cosmopolitan ways of city folks. Culinarily, the two are now too mixed up to separate neatly. These are terms from both traditions you need to know to eat well in New Orleans or out in the bayous.

Andouille	Spicy smoked pork sausage, usually grilled
Beignet	A light, holeless donut customarily served with café au lait
Boudin	Country sausage, blanc or rouge (with or without blood)
Court bouillon	A dense, spicy tomato sauce, customarily served on redfish
Dirty rice	White rice cooked with giblets and gravy
Étouffée	"Smothered"
Grillades and grits	Seasoned steak or beef or veal with gravy and grits on the side
Gumbo	A stew built upon long-cooked roux (butter and flour)
Jambalaya	A gallimaufry with almost anything, but usually ham and rice
Muffaletta	A circular Italian-flavored cold-cut sandwich with chopped olives
Pain perdu	French toast, made with French bread
Po' boy	A long loaf of French bread jam-packed with ingredients
Praline	Creamy candy made with pecans
Remoulade	Piquant mayonnaise used for dressing chilled shellfish

Crawdad Variations

In Cajun country, the crawfish is king. The lobstery fresh-water crustacean is generally at its biggest and best in the spring. The simplest way to enjoy it is boiled. Twist the tail from the head, crack the top of the tail, squeeze, and out pops one sweet, succulent mouthful of meat. Then scoop the "butter" (actually crawfish fat) from the head. Four or five pounds make a nice meal.

But of course restless Cajun country cooks aren't satisfied with merely boiling and seasoning anything, so many restaurants in the area offer these ways with the delicacy known to its friends as the mudbug:

Cajun popcorn	Deep-fried crawfish tails
Crawfish bisque	Buttery soup filled with crawfish heads
Crawfish boulettes	Crawfish meatballs
Crawfish gumbo	Thick stew, often including okra
Crawfish étouffée	Tails stirred into a peppery sauce, served over rice
Crawfish pie	Baked with garlic and vegetables in a thin crust

Dean-O's

305 Bertrand Dr., Lafayette, LA	$
(318) 233-5446	£D

Trust us. When you see Dean-O's, you will want to drive right past. It looks about as interesting as a Domino's franchise. In fact, you can order some pretty ordinary pizza in this plasticine place. But if you did, you would then miss the truly sensational pizzas they make that are topped with small, succulent marinated crawfish tails (in season after Mardi Gras), shrimp, or big pieces of fresh Gulf crabmeat.

Eddie's

2119 Law St., New Orleans, LA	$$
(504) 945-2207 £ Mon–Fri; 𝕯 Fri and Sat; brunch Sun	£𝕯

Eddie's is a gumbo shop, and then some. On a forbidding side street near Elysian Fields, it is an insider's haunt that all serious fans of New Orleans soul food need to seek out. The diverse and mouth-watering menu includes luscious fried chicken with powerhouse greens on the side, stuffed pork chops with oyster stuffing more oystery than the law allows, red beans and rice with a garlic wallop, and cold-cut po' boys on fine French bread, as well as a classic oyster loaf loaded with crunchy nuggets of sweet seafood. The gumbo is a Creole paradigm—dark and smoky, loaded with shrimp, oysters, chicken, ham, hot sausage, beef, and pork—so brilliantly spiced it will make you dizzy.

Joe's Dreyfus Store

Hwy. 77 South, Livonia, LA	$$
(504) 637-2625 £𝕯 Tues–Sat; £ Sun	£𝕯

In a general store that his family has run since the 1920s, Joe Major operates a four-star Louisiana kitchen. Having learned to cook as a child, then spending time in many of the better kitchens of New Orleans and Baton Rouge, Joe uses time-honored recipes to make such classic dishes as crawfish étouffée, batter-fried whole catfish, and speckled trout sauté meuniere, as well as to-die-for desserts that include crème brûlée and rum-soaked bread pudding. His homemade white boudin is a tubular miracle, served with good hot pepper jelly; and the Italian salad sets a new high standard for this local favorite. Joe's wife Diane is the dining room hostess, greeting customers with true Cajun charm; and a lovely little B&B is part of the enterprise.

Lagneaux

445 Ridge Rd., Lafayette, LA	$
(318) 984-1415	D

There is a sit-down menu, but who can resist a buffet that features such satisfying swamp country meals as crawfish-stuffed peppers and jambalayas of Gulf seafood, plus crunch-crusted fried chicken and a large selection of well-cooked vegetables on the side, with biscuits or lengths of good bread to mop it all off the plate? At low single-digit prices, these high-spiced everyday feasts are exactly what make an eating trip through Creole country so extraordinary.

Lasyone's Meat Pie Kitchen

622 Second St., Natchitoches, LA	$
(318) 352-3353	BL

Once sold from corner carts all over town, the lusty bayou specialty known as a Cane River meat pie had nearly vanished from Natchitoches when James Lasyone opened up a meat pie kitchen in 1967. His little restaurant on the picturesque cobblestone streets of Natchitoches (where *Steel Magnolias* was filmed) is now a good-eats landmark, and meat pies are back.

Mr. Lasyone's is a beaut, a golden-crusted pastry pocket about the size of a taco, crunchy near the crimp, soft near its mounded center. Inside the flaky sheaf is a heap of seasoned ground beef, moist enough to make gravy irrelevant. Spicy but not fire-hot, complex and succulent, Lasyone's meat pie is an honest piece of food that satisfies in an old-fashioned way. You can get one for breakfast, accompanied by eggs and hash browns; most steady customers come midday to get a pair of them for lunch, with soulful "dirty rice" on the side, darkened with gizzards and topped with zesty gravy. After meat pie, our personal weakness is a dessert Mr. Lasyone invented some years back called Cane River cream pie, which is similar to Boston cream pie but dark and spicy and made from gingerbread.

Mandina's

3800 Canal St., New Orleans, LA	*$$*
(504) 482-9179	*LD*

Not a tourist attraction, but nonetheless mobbed at mealtime (with loyal locals), Mandina's is the sine qua non of any genuine New Orleans eating tour. Nothing fancy, not too expensive, and a bit down-at-the-heels, it is a neighborhood restaurant where the French bread is impeccably fresh, the marinated crab claws are plump and succulent, the seafood po' boys are loaded with crisp oysters and/or shrimp, and the bread pudding with whiskey sauce is heavenly. Like so many of the definitive New Orleans restaurants, Mandina's Creole cuisine has a strong Italian accent. Even the Jambalaya has a soulful Mediterranean twist to its spices, and you can't go wrong ordering spaghetti and meatballs or Italian sausage. Whatever else you taste, begin with turtle au sherry soup.

Middendorf's

U.S. 51 N, Pass Manchac, LA	*$$*
(504) 386-6666 Tues–Sun	*LD*

Oh, how our culinary dreams dance with great, heaping plates of Middendorf's thin-sliced fried catfish! Crisp, sweet, exquisitely seasoned, and impossible to stop eating, catfish has made this Tangipoa Parish restaurant into a favorite destination for big eaters since Louis and Josie Middendorf opened for business in 1934. There are fine thick catfish fillets on the menu, too, juicier than their thin counterparts (but without the irresistibly sinful deep-fried crunch), and there is a whole menu of local seafood, including oysters, crab, crawfish, shrimp, good gumbo, and po' boy sandwiches. As a concession to the fat-obsessed customer, broiled catfish has recently been added to the menu. However, to come to this big, happy barn of a restaurant and not eat something fried would be as dumb as going to a Kansas City steak house for the vegetarian platter.

Mosca's	
4137 U.S. 90, Waggaman, LA	$$
(504) 436-9942 Tues–Sat (closed in August)	D

You will think you are lost on the way to Mosca's, situated in a god-forsaken swamp far outside of town. Even when you find it, you will wonder, Can this ramshackle way station with the blaring jukebox really be the most famous Creole roadhouse in America? Once oil and butter from the spaghetti bordelaise begin dripping down your chin and you inhale the fragrant bouquet of chicken à la grandee or herbed Italian oyster casserole, you will know you have found a culinary epiphany. Rude as it is, roadside food gets no better, or more garlicky, or heartier, than this. Go to Mosca's with friends: the bigger the group, the more different wonders you can sample; and besides, everything is served family-style.

Mother's	
401 Poydras, New Orleans, LA	$
(504) 523-9656 (closed Sun and Mon)	BLD

This only-in-New Orleans proletarian cafeteria has been dishing out biscuit breakfast and hot lunch since 1938, and it remains one of the great Creole eating experiences, regardless of its low-low prices. Red beans and rice, with hefty lengths of sausage, is a definitive rib-sticker, with good corn bread on the side; baked ham, piled into fleecy French bread along with little bits of cracklin' from the outside of the roast, may be the tastiest ham on earth. It is the star attraction in a messy but magnificent po' boy called a Ferdi, where it is combined with roast beef, coleslaw, assorted condiments, and an item known as debris, which is gravy-sopped little shreds and succulent morsels from the roast beef. The debris is so good that you can get a po' boy with nothing but.

Less renowned, but one of the city's culinary wonders, is Mother's breakfast, which includes a crawfish étouffée omelet and an omelet made with green onions and nuggets of crusty sweet ham from the outside of a roast, both served, of course, with oven-warm biscuits and grits.

Old Tyme Grocery

218 W. St. Mary Blvd., Lafayette, LA	$
(318) 235-8165 Mon–Sat	£D

Old Tyme Grocery has some tables, but it is not a sit-down restaurant. Accomodations are irrelevant, for this is an essential stop on the po' boy trail. At the meat counter, yard-long loaves of fresh, fluffy-centered bread are stuffed with whatever ingredients you specify. Connoisseur's choice: crusty fried shrimp, about eight hundred of 'em in a single sandwich. While the man makes your sandwich, you can admire such local favorites in the cold case as hog's head cheese and dark, scary-looking sausages.

Robin's

Hwy. 352, Henderson, LA	$$
(318) 228-7594 £D Tues–Sat; £ only Sun	£D

Crawfish heaven! Lionel Robin's restaurant makes all sorts of wonderful Cajun food, but in the spring at the height of crawfish season, that's all you want to know. Get 'em stewed, fried, boiled, étouffeed, brewed in gumbo, and creamed for bisque. Or have garlicky crawfish pie, in which the butter-rich creatures are accompanied by a handful of vegetables in a paper-thin crust.

Robin's is worth a trip even when it isn't crawfish season. Okra gumbo made with shrimp and even the nonseafood sausage gumbo are outstanding meals. Henderson is a dot on the map, miles from everywhere, but if you want to eat well in southern Louisiana, a visit to Robin's is urgent.

Soops Seafood and Steak House

Maurice, LA	$
(318) 893-2462	LD

Soop Hebert, who started the "Specialty Meats" shop next door, also opened the Cajun eatery that bears his name. Now run by Soop's daughters, it is one of the gumbo beacons of Cajun country. Thick with sausage and chicken or sweet hunks of seafood, Soop's brew is intoxicating just to sniff; eating it—slowly, as rapture builds and taste-buds weep for joy—is a not-to-be-missed culinary experience. Soop's menu is a bonanza of local flavors: crabmeat, crawfish, stuffed rabbit, quail, and alligator, with homemade cherry pie for dessert.

Uglesich's

1238 Baronne, New Orleans, LA	$$
(504) 523-8571 Mon–Fri	£

If you like a restaurant that is immaculate and orderly, serving food that is beautifully arranged on lovely china plates, go somewhere else. But if you are in the market for some of the most delicious fried oysters in a serious fried-oyster town, for crisp-fried trout po' boys, for parchment-brittle soft-shell crabs, and for drippingly juicy hot roast beef po' boys, then be brave and find Uglesich's. The neighborhood stinks, but here you will feast on delicious, blue-collar Creole food. This unceremonious café (that's an understatement!) is the sort of place that makes New Orleans paradise for the adventurous eater.

MISSISSIPPI

Abe's	
616 State St., Clarksdale, MS	$
(601) 624-9947	£𝒟

A winsome pig plays the violin in a mural on the wall of Abe's little dining room, where the smoke-cooked pork is lean, sweet, and tender. It is served sliced, sizzled on the grill, along with sauce-spritzed slaw and beans. Add your own sauce to the meat; you get a choice of mild or lip-searing hot. Barbecue has been Abe's fame since the 1920s; connoisseurs of regional fare will also want to savor tamales, served with or without chili on top, but not available during the sultry summer months.

Bill's Hamburgers	
Main St., Amory, MS (601) 256-2085	$
Mon–Sat (opens at 7 AM, but no breakfast food is served)	ℬ£

D ine on a bar stool with a view of burgers being cooked. The menu at Bill's is simplicity itself: a single or double burger, with or without onions and cheese (but no lettuce or tomatoes are available), with French fries on the side. The fine, old-fashioned burgers—like the kind every drugstore lunch counter once served—are presented wrapped in wax paper. That's the way it is at this culinary relic from seven o'clock every morning (hamburgers for breakfast!), and that's the way it's been, since 1929.

The Blue and White

Hwy. 61, Tunica, MS	$
(601) 363-1371	BLD

Breakfast at the Blue and White truck stop is a Route 61 rite of passage. Since the 1930s, this broad-shouldered roadside restaurant has become a landmark for drivers, farmers, and wanderers who come for huge morning meals of eggs and grits with ham and red-eye gravy, accompanied by bottomless cups of coffee. It is all dished out by a staff of take-no-prisoners waitresses who can fill you in on good local gossip from a hundred-mile radius.

The Dinner Bell

229 Fifth Ave., McComb, MS (601) 684-4883	$
L Tues–Sun; D Fri and Sat only	LD

The Dinner Bell is one of the South's great big feeds. Serve yourself from lazy Susans in the center of the round tables shared by strangers. Vegetables are always outstanding and include such local delights as butter beans, field peas, fried okra, and sweet potato casserole. Chicken and dumplings, ham, and fried chicken are some of the entrees from which to choose, and there is always a good assortment of oven-warm biscuits and corn breads. The fun and the challenge of a communal meal like this is to grab what you want when the lazy Susan spins by. You want to be quick (although platters are replenished throughout the dinner hour), and a boardinghouse reach is perfectly appropriate.

Doe's Eat Place

502 Nelson, Greenville, MS	$$$
(601) 334-3315 Mon–Sat	**D**

Many people believe that the original Doe's Eat Place serves the best steaks in America. It is impressive to see the raw ones paraded out from the cooler for customers' inspection, and even more thrilling when they arrive at the table awhile later, sputtering hot and seeping savory juice onto the plate.

Everything else Doe's serves is terrific, too: French fries are sizzled to tan perfection in a deep iron skillet, spicy hot tamales could be a meal unto themselves, and fresh salads are mixed with lemon juice and olive oil dressing at kitchen tables that share space with dining tables.

The real fun of this place is its extreme informality. Located on a side street in a broken-down building that used to be a grocery store, just getting to it is an adventure. Once inside, eating a meal is like supper at Grandma's. Customers sit in mismatched chairs at assorted tables in a back room kitchen and in other miscellaneous rooms where the proprietors used to live.

The Elite

141 E. Capitol, Jackson, MS	$
(601) 352-5606	**BLD**

Where the elite (and everyone else) in downtown Jackson meet, this 1940s-era three-meals-a-day café is a pleasure for anyone who appreciates quick, home-cooked plates of food at low prices. The dinner rolls are superb and the breakfast biscuits are steamy-hot; the southern vegetables—greens, yams, squash, etc.—are classics; entrees range from a stupendously good enchilada plate to catfish or pork chops and a veal cutlet as crisp and succulent as a good chicken-fried steak.

Lusco's	
722 Carrolton Ave., Greenwood, MS	*$$$*
(601) 453-5365	**D**

The walls of a big, wood-floored vestibule are painted institutional green and festooned with small game trophies. In one corner are some waiting-room chairs and a couch arranged around a television set and an old kiosk with a pay phone inside. In the back, private dining carrels are arranged off dim hallways, so although you can hear other customers, you see no one but your dining companions across a field of luxurious white cotton cloth and thick folded napkins. To summon help, each booth is equipped with a buzzer.

The strangeness of the setting has no doubt enhanced Lusco's reputation in the Delta where eccentricity is treasured, but the main reason for its renown is deluxe food. Founders Mama and Papa Lusco were Italian by way of Louisiana, so the flavors of the kitchen they established are as much Creole as they are southern or Italian. Gumbo, crab, and shrimp are always on the menu, and oysters are a specialty in season, on the half shell or baked with bacon. Because so many regular patrons have always been big spenders from well-to-do cotton families, the menu is best known among them for its high-end items. Lusco's T-bone steaks are some of the finest anywhere; sumptuous cuts are brought raw to the table for your approval, then broiled to pillowy succulence. Pompano has for many years been a house trademark, broiled and served whole, bathed in a magical sauce made of butter, lemon, and secret spices.

Mammy's Cupboard	
555 Hwy. 61 S, Natchez, MS	*$*
(601) 445-8957 Tues–Sat	**£**

Mammy's Cupboard, a restaurant shaped like a woman (you dine under her skirt), has gone through many changes since it was built over fifty years ago. Originally, Mammy was an African-American maid with a black face, and crisp fried chicken was the specialty of the house. Now the cuisine is more ladylike Dixie tearoom fare, with cold vegetables to start the meal, good soup, sandwiches on homemade bread, and one hot lunch special every day—roast pork loin with rice and chicken pot pie with broccoli corn bread are the ones we enjoyed. The restaurant itself has been politically corrected and the face of the woman under whom you eat is European-American.

Mendenhall Hotel Revolving Tables

Old Hwy. 49, Mendenhall, MS	$$
(601) 847-3113 Tues–Sun	£

At the center of each large round table in the Mendenhall Hotel's dining rooms is a big lazy Susan piled with food. Spin it and take what you like from a vast assortment of beautifully prepared Dixie dishes that range from biscuits and cracklin' corn bread to hot peach cobbler for dessert. Entrees include fried chicken, pork chops, and barbecued beef, and there are always way too many vegetable casseroles to ever get a chance to sample all of them—candied yams, buttered squash, creamed spinach, etc. It is a feast to remember, all the more fun for the high spirits that prevail among hungry strangers sharing the fun in a dining room where a needlepoint sampler on the wall advises, EAT 'TIL IT OUCHES.

Phillips Grocery

541-A East Van Dorn Ave., Holly Springs, MS	$
(601) 252-4671 Mon–Sat	£

A two-story wood-frame house by the railroad tracks, Phillips has built its reputation on hamburgers since the 1940s. Many customers buy them to go, but there are seats, too: a short counter with stools, a handful of wooden school desks, and a few odd tables where regulars finish off their meals with a short stack of marshmallowy Moon Pies from the grocery shelf.

Hamburgers are available in various sizes and are wrapped in yellow wax paper inside a bag for easy toting. When you peel back the wrapping, particularly on a half-pound Super-Deluxe, you behold a vision of beauty-in-a-bun. Cooked on a hot grill, it is a thick patty with a luscious crunch to its nearly blackened skin. Inside, the meat is moist enough to ooze juice when you gently squeeze the soft bun wrapped around it. The flavor is fresh, beefy, and sumptuous, an American classic on a par with the esteemed hamburgers of Cassell's in Los Angeles, Louis Lunch in New Haven, and Kincaid's Market in Fort Worth.

Smitty's	
208 S. Lamar, Oxford, MS	$
(601) 234-9111	B L

Oxford's good old town café, patronized by Ole Miss students and townies alike, Smitty's is a fine place to go for biscuits and grits in the morning, served with country ham and red-eye or creamy sawmill gravy. Lunch classics include sandy-crusted whole catfish, fried steak smothered with gravy, and a heap of greens with hog jowl and corn bread. The beverage of choice, naturally, is iced tea.

SOUTH CAROLINA

★ ★ ★

Alice's Fine Foods	
468–470 King St., Charleston, SC	$
(843) 853-9366	L D

An airy, multiroom cafeteria with a television at one end and a freezer with sixteen flavors of ice cream at the other, Alice's is where Charlestonians go to eat low country soul food. Fried shrimp and oysters are served by the dozen, sheathed in melting-crisp crust; deviled crab is plump and spicy; and okra is served in a spicy soup with beans and tomatoes. Side dishes include: collard greens dotted with hunks of salty ham, macaroni thick with cheese, rice laced with chicken and giblets. Desserts include plain and perfect layer cakes.

The Bakers Café

214 King St., Charleston, SC	$
(843) 577-2694	B£

Here are beautiful poached eggs in all configurations. Have 'em southern style on corn bread with country ham, "à la hash" atop a crisp cake of corned beef hash with dark Madeira sauce, with artichokes or bacon and cheese or crabmeat. Plates are handsomely garnished, and portions are demure enough that you might also want one of Bakers' delicious glazed Danish pastries or rugged raspberry scones on the side. This is a quiet, civilized little café, suitable for morning meditation over breakfast coffee, and a nice place for lunch, when the egg menu is supplemented by sandwiches and light entrees.

Beacon Drive-In

225 Reidsville Rd., Spartanburg, SC	$
(864) 585-9387 Mon–Sat	B£D

The Beacon is a huge drive-in with speedy car service. But the connoisseur's way to dine is inside, where you experience the rudest, and most exhilarating, cafeteria service in America. If you are slow choosing between a chili cheeseburger and a pork-a-plenty platter, you'll be yelled at, and likely pushed aside by others who have come into this madhouse knowing exactly what they want. "Move!" counterman J. C. Strobel hollers. "Come on, come on down," he shouts to those who have placed their order and aren't quick enough getting to the cash register. It all happens so fast that novices are left in a daze. But if you survive, you will walk away with a tray of excellent pork barbecue (inside or outside meat can be specified, depending whether you like it creamy soft or crunchy), sided by hash, slaw, and onion rings, or any one of several dozen hamburger variations. The iced tea, served in titanic tumblers, is Beacon barbecue's perfect companion. It is served sweetened to the max. In fact, a counterman here once bragged to us that the Beacon uses two tons of sugar every week, just for tea. Yum!

D&H Bar-B-Que	
412 South Mill, Manning, SC (803) 435-2189	$
Tues–Sun	£D

I t is possible to order from a menu at D&H—you can get chicken by the piece and sandwiches; but it is much more fun to pick your pig plate from the buffet line. Here are the good parts of the pig torn into shreds and chunks, accompanied by hash and gravy, along with rice, slaw, rolls, and hush puppies. To drink: sweet iced tea. This is a simple and inexpensive meal, but a resoundingly delicious one you won't find anywhere outside of pork-happy South Carolina.

Duke's Bar-B-Q	
725 Robertson Blvd., Walterboro, SC (803) 549-1446	$
Thur, Fri, Sat only; also at Hwy. 17 S in Ridgeland	£D
(exit 22 off I-95) (803) 726-3882 Fri and Sat only	

A clean, plain eat-place with picnic table seating and weekend-only hours, Duke's descends from the pig-pickin' fetes that people in these parts have enjoyed for centuries. Service is cafeteria-style. Help yourself to tender, succulent hacked pork with a choice of three sauces, spoon some hash over your rice (hash is a visceral stew made from pork parts), take some bread and pickles and all the sweet iced tea you want. (There is also fried chicken available, and it looks good, but pork wins our vote every time.) Although simple and cheap, this is a grand regional meal to remember.

Jestine's Kitchen

251 Meeting St., Charleston, SC (843) 722-7224	$
Tues–Sun	LD

"Southern food with lots of soul" is the motto of Jestine's, a tidy storefront with a mouth-watering menu of blue-plate specials and a dozen vegetables every day. Named by owner Dana Berlin for Jestine Matthews, the centenarian African-American woman who raised her (and developed many of the kitchen's recipes), Jestine's is a place to feast on classic low country food such as crab cakes on Saturdays, shrimp and grits on Sundays, and okra gumbo every day. Even the simplest foods have a soulful twist: macaroni and cheese is chewy and luscious, mashed potatoes are laced with savory gravy, red rice glows with a kaleidoscope of spice. A sound system that plays old-time jazz quietly in the background completes the pleasant scene.

Field Guide to South Carolina Barbecue

Every region of the country has its own unique way with barbecue, but no place is as diverse as South Carolina, where at least four distinct variations of sauce are served (the meat is invariably pork):

- Northwest South Carolina: tomato-based, with a whisper of sweet relish.
- Northeast South Carolina: vinegar-based marinade, no tomato whatever.
- Central South Carolina: mustard-flavored. To the north, sauces are a mixture of ketchup and mustard, but the closer to the center of the state you get, the more mustard there is. Columbia's best sauces have no tomato or ketchup in them at all.
- Southern South Carolina: vinegar-based sauces, but often flavored with a dash of mustard.

Maurice's Piggy Park

1600 Charleston Hwy., Columbia, SC	$
(803) 796-0220	£D

Acclaimed by traveling trenchermen for its hickory-cooked pork, and known for its huge flag flapping over the parking lot and lightning-fast curb service, the Piggy Park is one tasty chunk of Americana. Pull into one of the tin-covered car slots, peruse the illuminated menu, and call your order in using the intercom provided. Less than three minutes later—guaranteed!—out speeds a carhop, dressed in a crisp uniform of red, white, and blue, carrying your tray of barbecue. Piggie Park Q is tantalizing stuff, infused not only with the taste of smoke but with a dose of Bessinger's eye-opening, cider-sweet, mustard-flavored sauce. On the menu, the sauce is referred to as a "million-dollar heirloom recipe."

Middleton Place

Hwy. 61 (Ashley River Rd.), Charleston, SC	$
(843) 556-6020 £ daily; D Fri and Sat	£D

Not quite an ordinary public dining room (you pay $12 per person to pass through the front gate), Middleton Place Restaurant is part of a grand effort to interpret the low country's cultural heritage on the grounds of the vast old Middleton Plantation. When it opened as a tearoom run by the Junior League in 1928, its specialties were okra soup and sandwiches. In recent years, recipes were developed by chef Edna Lewis, whose expertise in southern foodways resulted in a lunch menu that is a knock-out sampler of low country favorites. Start with creamy she-crab soup, move on to ham biscuits or shrimp gumbo with hoppin' John and sweet corn pudding, and top things off with a gooey-chewy piece of Huguenot torte. On the side, drink iced tea, which, curiously, comes unsweetened. "You have to sweeten it yourself!" griped a southern gentleman sitting next to us, stirring sugar into his glass. "And they call this a plantation!"

Pinckney Café

Motley Lane and Pinckney St., Charleston, SC	$
(843) 577-0961 Tues–Sat	LD

Patronized by artistic Charlestonians, savvy tourists, and many of the city's creative young chefs, the laid-back Pinckney Café is a little jewel in the rough. Place your order at the kitchen and take a seat, indoors or on the piazza. Soon you will be spooning into scrumptious Cajun gumbo thick with seafood, or forking up a copious black bean burrito or such daily specials as San Diego–style fish tacos, vegetarian pizza, or a pasta du jour. Specialty coffees include a dreamy cappuccino float, the beer list is long and distinguished, and do not consider your life complete until you taste the bread pudding. It is one of the great desserts in this universe or any other.

Summerton Diner

Exit 108 off I-95, Summerton, SC	$
(803) 485-6835	BLD

If you are traveling along I-95, this is a good place to enjoy bacon and eggs and grits or hotcakes and sausage for breakfast; or better yet, come for lunch. Our favorite lunch specials are fried chicken with mashed potatoes and gravy (or rice and gravy) and a rich casserole of sausage, potatoes, and cheese. There is always a good choice of vegetables, including sweet yam sticks, collard greens, squash casserole, and an apple salad to remember. For dessert, you want pie, preferably coconut cream.

Sweatman's Bar-B-Q

SC Rte. 453, Holly Hill, SC	$
Fri and Sat only	£D

Bub Sweatman's place is consummate pig-pickin' served in an old country farmhouse shaded by pecan trees. Meat is cooked the old-fashioned way, in an open pit out back, and it is set out on the buffet unsauced so that purists can savor its succulence *au naturel*. If you do want sauce, try the South Carolina stuff, with its mustard base. Alongside the choice chunks of pork, you can also choose ribs, pork hash over rice, and even strips of fried pigskin. Pay one price and pile your plate high, find a seat at an oilcloth-covered table in one of Bub's lovely rustic dining rooms, then tuck into a feast that Carolinians have enjoyed for a couple of centuries.

Note the weekend-only hours.

The Wreck of the Richard & Charlene

106 Haddrell Point, Mount Pleasant, SC	$$
(843) 884-0052 £ Fri, Sat, Sun; D daily	£D

There is no sign, not even an address, outside the ramshackle bait locker tucked between the Wando Seafood Company and Magwood & Sons Seafood on Shem Creek, and you enter through a hallway decorated with stacked-up beer cartons. But at mealtimes, the Wreck (named for a ship hit by Hurricane Hugo) is mobbed. Discriminating locals skip the tourist-oriented eateries on the docks nearby and find a paper-topped table on the breezy porch to feast on fresh fried oysters, shrimp, and flounder, boiled shrimp and stone crab claws by the pound, with beer (served in the bottle) to wash it down.

Midwest

ALL-AMERICAN

ILLINOIS

INDIANA

IOWA

MICHIGAN

MINNESOTA

MISSOURI

OHIO

WISCONSIN

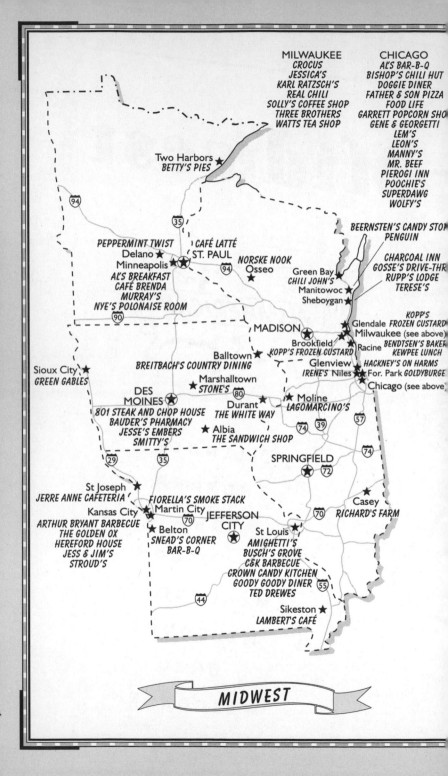

MILWAUKEE
CROCUS
JESSICA'S
KARL RATZSCH'S
REAL CHILI
SOLLY'S COFFEE SHOP
THREE BROTHERS
WATTS TEA SHOP

CHICAGO
AL'S BAR-B-Q
BISHOP'S CHILI HUT
DOGGIE DINER
FATHER & SON PIZZA
FOOD LIFE
GARRETT POPCORN SHO
GENE & GEORGETTI
LEM'S
LEON'S
MANNY'S
MR. BEEF
PIEROGI INN
POOCHIE'S
SUPERDAWG
WOLFY'S

Two Harbors ★
BETTY'S PIES

94

35

PEPPERMINT TWIST
Delano ★
Minneapolis ★
AL'S BREAKFAST
CAFÉ BRENDA
MURRAY'S
NYE'S POLONAISE ROOM

CAFÉ LATTÉ
ST. PAUL ★

94

NORSKE NOOK
Osseo ★

Green Bay ★
CHILI JOHN'S
Manitowoc ★
Sheboygan ★

BEERNSTEN'S CANDY STOR
PENGUIN

CHARCOAL INN
GOSSE'S DRIVE-THR
RUPP'S LODGE
TERESE'S

90

MADISON ★

Balltown ★
BREITBACH'S COUNTRY DINING

KOPP'S
Glendale *FROZEN CUSTARD*
Milwaukee (see above)
Brookfield ★ *BENDTSEN'S BAKER*
KOPP'S FROZEN CUSTARD Racine *KEWPEE LUNCH*
Glenview *HACKNEY'S ON HARMS*
IRENE'S Niles ★ For. Park *GOLDYBURGE*
Chicago (see above)

Sioux City ★
GREEN GABLES

Marshalltown ★
STONE'S

80

Durant ★
THE WHITE WAY

Moline ★
LAGOMARCINO'S

57

DES
MOINES ⊛
801 STEAK AND CHOP HOUSE
BAUDER'S PHARMACY
JESSE'S EMBERS
SMITTY'S

★ Albia
THE SANDWICH SHOP

74
39

SPRINGFIELD ⊛

74

29

35

72

St Joseph ★
JERRE ANNE CAFETERIA

Kansas City ★
ARTHUR BRYANT BARBECUE
THE GOLDEN OX
HEREFORD HOUSE
JESS & JIM'S
STROUD'S

FIORELLA'S SMOKE STACK
★ Martin City
JEFFERSON
CITY ⊛
★ Belton
SNEAD'S CORNER
BAR-B-Q

70

Casey ★
RICHARD'S FARM

St Louis ★
AMIGHETTI'S
BUSCH'S GROVE
C&K BARBECUE
CROWN CANDY KITCHEN
GOODY GOODY DINER
TED DREWES

55

44

Sikeston ★
LAMBERT'S CAFÉ

⟨ MIDWEST ⟩

ILLINOIS

★ ★ ★

Al's Bar-B-Q	
1079 W. Taylor St., Chicago, IL	$
(312) 733-8896 Mon–Sat	£ D

In Chicago's old Little Italy, Al's is a small shop with a tremendous reputation for Italian beef sandwiches. Accomodations are all stand-up counters, and in nice weather, many customers dine off the trunk or roof of their car in the parking lot.

To order sandwiches at Al's, use this handy guide to Italian beef shorthand:

"Big beef, double-dipped": An extra-large sandwich of gravy-sopped beef that, once assembled, is reimmersed for approximately one second in a pan of natural gravy so the bread is soaked through.

"Beef with hot": a request for the relish known as giardiniera, an eye-opening garden melange of finely chopped celery, capers, and spice that is roast beef's perfect complement.

"Dry and sweet": tells the sandwich-maker to pluck a heap of beef from its pan with the serving tongs and let excess juice drip away before inserting it in the bread. "Sweet" is the popular alternative to giardiniera: big, tender shreds of roasted green bell pepper. Some customers order double hot or double sweet; some get their sandwich sweet *and* hot.

Calling for a "Combo" or a "Half and Half" is a request for a sandwich that contains not only beef but also a plump, four-inch length of Italian sausage, retrieved from the appetizing haze that hovers over the hot metal grate just behind the order counter. A charcoal fire gives Al's taut-skinned tubes of peppery, coarse-ground pork a sharp, smokey flavor and makes the sausage itself a major lure for many customers who sidestep beef altogether and order double-sausage sandwiches, hot or sweet, dipped or dry.

After a meal at Al's, we recommend you stroll across the street to Mario's Italian ice shop for the perfect dessert.

Bishop's Chili Hut

9253 W. Cermak Rd., N. Riverside, IL	$
(708) 442-5600	BLD

Chicago is not widely known for chili, but Bishop's Chili Hut has been a shrine for chiliheads since Helen Bishop sold her first bowl of beef here seventy years ago. As her heirs now tell the story, Chicago was rich with chili parlors in the 1920s, and Mrs. Bishop, who worked at the illustrious Ollie's, decided to cut out on her own. Her recipe, still used today, makes a spicy bowl of fine-ground meat with beans, served with pepper sauce for heat and oyster crackers for relief. With noodles, this deliciously plebeian concoction is known as chili mac—the connoisseur's choice, especially flavorsome with a side order of a big Thuringer sausage in a bun and a tall beer (or good draft root beer) to slake inevitable thirst.

Doggie Diner

712 W. Armitage, Chicago, IL	$
(312) 266-2925	LD

Among Chicago's most delicious declasse delights, red hots (hot dogs) are generally served in joints that are—how shall we say it?—not deluxe. Although Doggie Diner does offer the amenity of seats, including a pleasant outdoor patio and some counter stools, it is basically a hole-in-the-wall with a menu limited to things that can be boiled, griddle-cooked, or deep fried, plus gyros sliced from an immense shaft of reconstituted lamb.

We don't know about the rest of the menu, but Doggie Diner's red hots are fine: Vienna all-beef tubes served in tender Rosen-brand poppy seed buns and so expertly assembled that one with the works manages to stay a neat package as you heft it from its wrapper (there are no plates) to your mouth. French fries are also noteworthy: cut into stubby little sticks and fried to order, they are wickedly dark and well salted; and each huge portion is presented in a double bag to protect your car's upholstery from hot, leaking grease.

Father & Son Pizza

2475 N. Milwaukee Ave., Chicago, IL	$$
(773) 252-2620	£Ð

Chicago is known as the home of thick-crust pizza cooked in a pan, but there is another, lesser-known variation that serious eaters need to sample: Father & Son's thin and crispy pizza. In this big, casual restaurant on the Northwest Side, the menu in fact offers four different types of pizza:

1. thin and crispy
2. Chicago-style (thick crusted)
3. New York-style (thicker than thin, but not doughy)
4. classic pan-pizza

It is the thin pie that is unique, an amazing creation. Scarcely thicker than a saltine, it is crisp and crunchy and tough enough to stand up to rafts of topping . . . which is another important decision you'll have to make at Father & Son. We counted twenty-four available topppings, from alfredo sauce to zucchini, including all the usual sausages and peppers plus such curiosities as pineapple, Italian beef, and barbecued chicken.

If you can't find a pizza you like in this restaurant, you don't like pizza!

Food Life

835 N. Michigan Ave., Chicago, IL	$
(312) 335-3663	£Ð

Food Life is to mall food courts what Disney World is to roadside attractions: a spectacle beyond belief. Located in posh Water Tower Place, it is a whole 'nother culinary universe, where all appetites are satisfied. Armed with plastic debit cards inspired by the punch cards used at vintage delicatessen counters, grazers in this vast culinary theme park select what they want from twelve terminals, each with a different theme: burritos and fajitas, seafood, pastas, etc.

The choices are mesmerizing. There is no assembly-line franchised food here; everything is fresh and appealing, and you can eat wholesome fare everywhere you turn. Stuff a potato with al dente steamed broccoli or low-fat yogurt, enjoy luxurious but egg-free Caesar salad dressing, or plow into a casserole of grains and roasted vegetables. There are many rich things to eat (baby back ribs, hefty burgers, flourless chocolate cake), but vegetarians, dieters, and anyone in search of a fast, fit meal will have a field day.

Hot Dog Hall of Fame

This roster of America's wonderful wieners does not include Wisconsin brats, Cajun sausages, Texas hot links, Spanish chorizo of the West, or Portuguese linguica of the Northeast. It is limited strictly to cheap, pink tube steaks dished out in long buns, with or without chili, in eat-places of which your mother would likely disapprove.

- ☛ Camp Washington Chili, Cincinnati, OH (p. 224)
- ☛ Dew Drop Inn, Mobile, AL (p. 116)
- ☛ Doggie Diner, Chicago IL (p. 181)
- ☛ Flo's, Cape Neddick, ME (p. 20)
- ☛ Katz's Deli, New York, NY (p. 67)
- ☛ Lafayette Coney Island, Detroit, MI (p. 207)
- ☛ Nick Tahou, Rochester, NY (p. 69)
- ☛ Pink's Chili Dogs, Los Angeles, CA (p. 345)
- ☛ Poochie's, Skokie, IL (p. 189)
- ☛ Superdawg, Chicago, IL (p. 190)
- ☛ Swanky Franks, Norwalk, CT (p. 11)
- ☛ Ted's Jumbo Red Hots, Tonawanda, NY (p. 72)
- ☛ The Varsity, Atlanta, GA (p. 152)
- ☛ Wolfy's, Chicago, IL (p. 191)

Garrett Popcorn Shop

670 N. Michigan Ave., Chicago, IL (312) 944-2630;	$
Mail-order phone: (312) 944-4730	LD

The warm caramel smell is overwhelming at the Garrett Popcorn Shop on Michigan Avenue. It is a tiny store (one of three Garretts in Chicago), but it bustles with popcorn-eaters calling out orders by the ounce or pound, all day and long into the night.

"Mix!" is the connoisseur's cry—a bag of equal thirds of caramel corn, cheese corn, and buttered popcorn. The cheese corn is thick and rich; the butter corn makes fingers glisten. Caramel corn is simply the world's best, crunchy but not so brittle it has lost the puffy lightness of popped corn. Each kernel is veiled with a buttery sweet coat of dark amber that teeters on tasting burnt and makes taste buds cry for more, more, more.

Gene & Georgetti

500 N. Franklin, Chicago, IL	$$$
(312) 527-3718	D

Because the white-jacketed waiters take care of customers with efficiency instead of obsequiousness, some reviewers have decided that Gene & Georgetti is unfriendly. There is a notorious "Siberia" upstairs where newcomers are sometimes seated; but it is our experience that no matter where you sit, you are treated with respect. More important, the steaks are exquisite. Served unadorned on an oval plate, these sirloin strips and filets mignon are ravishing hunks of prime beef with glistening crust and succulent insides.

Thick cottage-fried potato chips are the customary side dish, and the cornucopic tossed antipasto known as "garbage salad" (a local passion) is definitive: iceberg lettuce, celery, tomato, radish, slivers of cheese and salami, pepperoncini, and big pink shrimp lightly marinated in an Italian vinaigrette.

Culinary anthropologists, take note: Gene & Georgetti is one of the few remaining old-time establishments to offer those curious, garlicky Chicagoland specialties, shrimp de Jonghe (available as an appetizer) and chicken Vesuvio.

Goldyburgers

7316 Circle Ave., Forest Park, IL	$
(708) 366-0750 **D** daily; **L** Thurs–Sun	**LD**

Never a bad one" is the motto of this comfortable vintage-1926 Chicagoland sports bar, referring to the many and wondrous hamburgers that put it on the good-eats map. Of the half-dozen varieties available, we recommend the Royal Bleuburger, a half-pound broiled sirloin patty topped with melted blue cheese and crisp bacon; and the Big Daddy, three quarters of a pound of beef with adornments of your choice. Fried potatoes and vegetables are available on the side.

Hackney's on Harms

1241 Harms Rd., Glenview, IL	$
(847) 724-5577	**LD**

This pleasant suburban restaurant with an outdoor patio under tall silver poplars is one of a small local chain that built its reputation on hamburgers. *Huge* hamburgers: one-half pound of rosy beef, encased in dark crust, arrives at your table on rye bread, the implication being you could eat it like a sandwich. But it is way too big to pick up in your hands, and the juicy red meat tends to fall apart (unless you have it cooked well done and thereby mummified). So you dig in to the mighty mound with knife and fork. A Hackneyburger comes with French fries, coleslaw, and sliced raw onion, but those in the know pay extra for fried onion rings—a glorious stack of them with a devilish crunch.

Hamburgers are Hackney's glory, but we must also tip our hats to dandy daily specials that have been on the menu at least since we became regular customers back in the 1960s: bratwurst on Monday, hot turkey sandwiches with mashed potatoes on Tuesday, meat loaf on Wednesday, corned beef and cabbage on Thursday, and a crunchy fish fry on Friday, when the choice includes midwestern favorites lake perch and walleye pike.

Irene's

6873 N. Milwaukee Ave., Niles, IL	$$
(847) 647-8147	£D

Irene's is a family restaurant across from a big cemetery. Its business card says that funeral lunches are a specialty, but you don't have to be bereaved to enjoy this treasure house of old-world meals, where all the neighborhood comes to eat. It is a snug sort of place, dark and quiet, with deluxe chandeliers and a thick rug. A majority of the clientele, as well as the staff, seem more comfortable speaking Polish than English. Start with soup, accompanied by good rye bread. The red borscht has a healthy vegetable savor, and the czarnina soup is dark brown and mysterious, strangely sweet but not cloying, served with little pasta shells on top.

Blintzes are superb, served three to an order, buttery tender crepes with a filling that is slightly sour, slightly sweet. Pierogi are the works of a dumpling master; and potato pancakes are just coarse enough to savor the little bits of potato of which they are made. There are many glorious things to eat at Irene's, including pork cutlets sautéed in garlic butter, pork shank with sauerkraut, and simple (but unimprovable) boiled beef with horseradish gravy, but the dish we return for every time is roast duck, which is dripping rich and crisp-skinned, succulence incarnate.

Lagomarcino's

1422 Fifth Ave., Moline, IL	$
(309) 764-1814	£D

Known to generations for its high quality hand-dipped chocolates, fancy fruit baskets, and what just might be the best hot fudge sundae on earth, Lagomarcino's (since 1908) is also a wonderful place for a smoked ham sandwich served on good rye bread. With its octagontile floor, dark mahogany booths, and beverages served in paper-cone drinking cups, this main-street institution is an essential stop for all genuine soda fountain connoisseurs.

Lem's

5914 S. State St., Chicago, IL	$$
(773) 684-5007 **D** daily; **L** Mon–Fri	**LD**

Smoky ribs with a crust that envelops strips of indescribably tender pork, Lem's bones are beyond good. Sauce is available, regular or ultrahot, but these perfect hunks of food scarcely require it. Come during daylight hours and plan to dine in your car or at a picnic table somewhere: seating is scarce or nonexistent, and there is no getting around the fact that the neighborhood is marginal. But a meal at Lem's is worth a little worry, for it is a genuine culinary landmark, serving the best ribs in Chicago since 1952.

Leon's

1640 E. 79th St., Chicago, IL	$$
(773) 731-1454	**LD**

Slabs and half-slabs of glistening dark barbecued ribs are piled into cardboard boats with a mess of French fries glazed with sauce and a couple of tiles of white bread that will meld with the sauce and disintegrate before you can eat two ribs. That lustrous sauce, in its hot version, is one of the world's best, an artful balance of pepper's fire, sweet molasses, and an arsenal of spice. There are good hot links on the menu and whole chickens and wings, but it's ribs that have made Leon's a South Side pork-pilgrim mecca for decades.

Manny's

1141 S. Jefferson St., Chicago, IL	$
(312) 939-2855 Mon–Sat	**BL**

You are never really alone at Manny's cafeteria at the edge of the Chicago Loop, even if you don't come with your business associates, attorney, parole officer, alderman, or image consultant. In this old-fashioned urban delicatessen, seating is perforce communal, and regulars hobnob loudly with one another even if they are four tables apart.

Wherever you sit in the double-wide dining room, you will smell corned beef: briny brick red, sliced thin as prosciutto, radiating mouth-watering pickly aroma as flaps of it are piled between slabs of seeded, sour-crusted rye bread. On the side of a Manny's corned beef sandwich, you want a potato pancake or two. They are hard-crusted but moist and tender inside, served hot on the side of sandwiches or with sour cream or applesauce as a meal unto themselves. Other regular items in Manny's resplendent cafeteria line include chicken pot pie (Wednesday), oxtail stew (Thursday), meat-filled knishes, chicken soup with matzoh balls or little kreplach (meaty dumplings), and such lunch counter standards as beef stew, liver and onions, meat loaf, and stuffed cabbage.

Mr. Beef	
666 N. Orleans, Chicago, IL	$
(312) 337-8500 Mon–Sat	BL

Good Italian beef sandwiches are sold throughout the city; Mr. Beef's are extraordinary—thin-sliced yet profoundly beefy, well-spiced and sopped with gravy, more tender than words can say, heaped into a bakery-fresh roll. Order it wet (the counterman soaks the roll in the gravy), sweet (with roasted sweet peppers), or hot (with hellish relish known as giardiniera); or get a combo, which adds a length of superb Italian sausage with a strong fennel kick. Until you have luxuriated in this sandwich, you cannot say you have eaten well in Chicago.

Pierogi Inn

5318 W. Lawrence Ave., Chicago, IL	$
(773) 736-4815	£D

On Lawrence Street, just one half block from Milwaukee Avenue, known as Chicago's "Polish Broadway," The Pierogi Inn is an old-world joy. A small urban storefront with noisy traffic bustling past the front windows, this oasis of home cooking specializes in pierogi—tender, double-bite-size dumplings filled with ingredients that range from potatoes and cheese or sauerkraut and mushrooms to strawberries. There are also luscious potato pancakes and a long list of interesting soups, including baraszcz with uszka (that's beet soup with little meat-filled ravioli) and soups made from cabbage, pickles, or barley.

Service is warm and friendly, although if your Polish is weak, you may have a hard time making yourself understood. In these parts, English is a *second* language.

Poochie's

3832 Dempster, Skokie, IL	$
(847) 673-0100	£D

Stand at the counter or perch on a stool in this rectangular storefront eatery. Choose from a menu limited to red hots, hamburgers, and Italian beef, accompanied by a motley order of delicious French fries with crunchy skins and creamy insides (or, better yet, cheddar fries, gobbed with melted cheese). The red hots are garlicky Vienna all-beef beauties, boiled or charred over coals until they develop an appealing tan. They are cushioned in utterly fresh, steamy soft poppy seed buns and are available, as per local custom, with any or all of a rainbow of condiments including mustard, ketchup, relish, raw onions, grilled onions, fresh tomatoes, pickles, celery salt, and fire-hot little peppers. Such humble elements transcend themselves and are a great meal unique to Chicago.

Richard's Farm

off Rte. 49 in Casey, IL	$$
(217) 932-5300	£D

Eat in a barn at Richard's Farm. Don't worry, though, you don't share the dining room with livestock. This venerable 1930s hip-roof building, with its feedway down the center and butter churns for decor, is actually quite polite, with a truly farmy salad bar and a sophisticated hardwood grill in the kitchen. The specialty of the house is a mighty one-pound pork chop, broiled in a tangy red sauce (available also in half-pound size), and the fried chicken is crisp and moist. Desserts include warm peach cobbler, berry pies all summer long, and persimmon pudding on occasion in the fall.

Superdawg

6363 N. Milwaukee, Chicago, IL	$
(773) 763-0660	£D

Atop Superdawg stand a pair of humanoid hot dog statues—a shapely female in a toga and a musclebound male with electric eyes that flash like a radio tower beacon. These kitsch characters signal a drive-in with the sort of playful come-hither personality all but vanished from roadside America. The hot dogs served here are all-beef lovelies with taut skin and garlicky insides, presented the only-in-Chicago way, impossibly heaped with condiments and good crinkle-cut French fries. Each one comes in a box, the cover of which announces, "Your Superdawg lounges inside contentedly cushioned in Superfries, comfortably attired in mustard, relish, onion, pickle, and hot pepper." This box full of good eats is a high-flavor, low-price joy that has been pleasing dog-hounds since 1948.

Wolfy's

2734 W. Peterson Ave., Chicago, IL	$
(773) 743-0207	LD

Wolfy's all-beef red hots, cushioned in Rosen's poppy-seeded buns, are among Chicago's elite, served singly or in pairs, topped with chili or cheese or "dragged through the garden," which means smothered under yellow mustard, piccalilli, pickle spears, tomato slices, raw or fried onions, and a scattering of incendiary little pepper pods. It is impossible to eat such a piece of food with any decorum. It falls apart, drips, and oozes; but like all great Chicago doggeries, Wolfy's is equipped for such hazards: there are napkins galore, and all fixtures are easy-wipe plastic.

If regular red hots with crisp fries on the side aren't nutritionally wicked enough, try Wolfy's beef and pork Polish sausages—giant tube steaks with crackling crisp skins that spurt juice when bitten.

INDIANA

✫ ✫ ✫

The Chicken Place

State Rd. 56, Ireland, IN (812) 482-7600	$$
(reservations Mon–Thur only)	D

The chicken in this pleasant little place is fried to a golden crisp and served with German-fried potatoes. If you don't make a reservation, or if it's a weekend night, you will wait in line outside for a precious seat where conversation, not surprisingly, tends to revolve around which restaurants serve the best chicken dinners, an Indiana passion.

Dodd's Town House

5694 N. Meridian St., Indianapolis, IN	$$
(317) 257-1872 Tues–Sat	ℒⅅ

Dodd's is a homey restaurant that serves regal beef. Steaks are skillet-fried to crust-enveloped succulence, accompanied by fine baked potatoes, long-cooked green beans, and a wedge of iceberg lettuce with sweet garlic dressing. There are other good things on the menu, including crisp fried chicken (served family-style to parties of six or more) with fixin's that include mashed potatoes and gravy, green beans and corn, and a little dish of ice cream. The only problem with the latter is that ice cream is definitely *not* what you want for dessert. At Dodd's, you want pie. Chocolate cream pie any time of year, blueberry in the summer, buttermilk in the spring. With meat and potatoes, and pie for dessert, Dodd's is heartland Americana to a T.

King Ribs Bar-B-Q

4130 N. Keystone, Indianapolis, IN (317) 543-0841;	$
other locations in Indianapolis are	ℒⅅ
5610 Georgetown Rd. 291-2695; 2660 Lafayette Rd. 488-0223;	
7336 Pendleton Pike 547-5464; 3599 S. East St. 781-8890	

Fourteen big drums are arrayed to smoke meat in the large front lot of this soul-food enterprise that looks like it used to be a drive-in lube shop. There is no dining room; there are no tables or chairs. All business is drive-through, walk-up, or home delivery. The house motto is "Fit for a King."

Ribs are super tender; their meat pulls away from the bone in heavy, succulent strips, barely glazed with sauce. The flavor is pure—long-cooked pork with a faint tingle of the smoke that cooked it. Side dishes include macaroni and cheese that is as thick as pudding, intensely cheesy, with noodles so soft they are almost indistinguishable from the cheese; and baked beans, fine-cut slaw, and white bread for mopping. For dessert, choose chess pie or sweet potato pie.

The Kopper Kettle

135 W. Main St., Morristown, IN	$$
(765) 763-6767	LD

The Kopper Kettle is rapturously retro-feminine, like a set in a 1950s "women's weepie" flick. Pink voile curtains shimmer at the windows, candelabra grace the larger tables, and among the antiques and bric-a-brac in this venerable family restaurant are tasteful *objets d'art* with the female form as subject; a bas-relief nude resides above the fireplace, a statuette shows Aphrodite running so fast that her toga blows away from her shapely body. Waitresses echo the artistic images, dressed in outfits that might be called Early American Milkmaid, with mobcaps and thigh-length skirts and thick petticoats.

People come from miles away to eat succulent skillet-fried chicken accompanied by mashed potatoes and porky green beans cooked until all their fight is gone.

Laughner's

Washington St. E. at I-465, Indianapolis, IN (317) 356-3388;	$$
for other locations call (317) 783-2907	LD

The Laughner family pioneered the self-service restaurant back in the 1880s, and today their six spacious Indianapolis cafeterias serve heavenly square meals to thousands of loyal customers daily. The chicken is as good as any in town, expertly skillet-fried, but who can resist the big pink ham with lustrous glazed sweet potatoes on the side, or the steamship round of beef displayed in the serving line, glowing pink and moist, ready to be lopped into juice-laden slices? Mashed potatoes are simple perfection, stout and veined with butter, and there are some two dozen other vegetables prepared every day, from farm-simple cooked carrots to green beans that are classic Americana—combined with mushroom soup, slivered almonds, and fried onion rings. The dessert display includes cobblers and dumplings, custards and puddings, ambrosias, jiggly meringue pies, and humble sugar-creams.

Aside from the spectacle of bounteous food, Laughner's long-standing appeal is civility. Dining rooms suggest old-world prosperity, outfitted with coats of arms and oil paintings of eighteenth-century European sea captains and saucy wenches in tasteful dishabille.

Mr. Dave's	
102 East Main St., North Manchester, IN (219) 982-4769	**$**
Mon–Sat (closes midafternoon in winter)	**£ D**

Indiana's best-known way station for tenderloins, Mr. Dave's cuts and breads its own pork patties and fries them to a crisp. The tiles of pork are then inserted into buns and dolled up with condiments. One of these is a superb indigenous sandwich, but modest-size enough that it is best eaten in pairs. Or, better yet, get a tenderloin and a burger on the side. Mr. Dave's hamburgers are a delight—not huge or opulent, just a good ol' burger, the kind you want in a good ol' Midwest sandwich shop.

Mr. Dave's has a drive-through window for pork-famished travelers in a hurry and also freezes tenderloins for shipping to homesick Hoosiers anywhere in the U.S.

Phil Smidt & Son	
1205 N. Calumet Ave., Hammond, IN (219) 659-0025;	**$$**
in Chicago (312) 768-6686	**£ D**

Being in Phil Smidt's restaurant is like finding yourself in the parlor of a duchess who is formal but still has the people's touch. There are huge pink roses painted on the wall and all the napery is pretty pink, yet waitresses are battle-ax tough and will likely call you "Hon" or "Dear."

Generations of families have come to this lakeside eatery to roll up their sleeves and eat big plates of delicious lake perch, climaxed by a wedge of warm gooseberry pie à la mode. If the pink roses on the wall aren't your style—that is, if you prefer more muscular ambiance for your perch supper—Phil Smidt's also has seating in a dining room that affords customers a stunning view of Indiana steel mills and freight trains rumbling past.

Red Geranium	
at the New Harmony Inn, North and Brewery,	$$$
New Harmony, IN (812) 682-4431	D

Don't be surprised if dinner and a night's stay at the New Harmony Inn seem too good to be true. The town of New Harmony was designed to be perfect. Founded in 1814 by followers of George Rapp, who wanted to create a utopian society based on the principles of celibacy and communal property, this bucolic little village on the banks of the Wabash River is still a touch of paradise.

The inn's fine restaurant is called the Red Geranium, where there are a dozen good ways with beef on the dinner menu, including big slabs of prime rib that are char-broiled to maximum succulence, and tenderloin medallions marinated in olive oil and garlic known as "Steak Caesar." Potatoes are offered four ways: baked or hash browned, lyonnaise or sautéed. Desserts range from ultrafancy (flaming cherries jubilee and baked Alaska) to one that is quite literally divine, known as "Heaven cake."

Romney Coffee Shop	
Intersection of U.S. 231 and U.S. 28, Lafayette, IN	$
(765) 538-3133	BLD

Breakfast is the big meal of the day in Lafayette's friendly local café, where the coffee starts flowing before dawn and biscuits emerge from the oven shortly after that. The biscuits are a ploughman's delight, served with thick, rib-sticking gravy, and if you are really hungry, with good hash brown potatoes, too. Wednesday and Saturday mornings, huge hot cinnamon rolls perfume the air.

Wendy Johnson-Niblick, who tipped us off to the pleasures of the Romney Coffee Shop, especially recommended the pork tenderloins, a crisp local treat. Other robust lunches we've enjoyed when taking a detour off I-65 include meat loaf (with poor mashed potatoes, alas) and chicken with noodles. Caramel raisin pudding and Amish vanilla pie are two memorable items from a long and appealing dessert menu. We're still aiming to come to Romney on Friday night, when prime rib and whitefish crown the menu.

Shapiro's	
808 S. Meridian, Indianapolis, IN (317) 631-4041;	$
also at 2370 W. 86th St. 872-7255	*BLD*

Although many members of the staff speak with accents more like Clem and Betty Lou than Moishe and Yetta, Shapiro's food is genuinely Jewish. By *genuine,* we mean that the corned beef sandwich is superb. And we don't mean superb *for Indianapolis,* but by strict Lower East Side standards. Cushioned in rugged-cut rye is a mountain of hot corned beef, sliced thick but not cloddish, unctuous without seeming fatty, and with a mouth-watering equilibrium of peppery spice and melting tenderness.

Breakfasts in this modern cafeteria-style eatery include salami omelets, bagels and lox, and mighty good corned beef hash. One morning the server in the cafeteria line suggested turkey hash instead. "It smells soooo good," she said with a looping southern Indiana twang. "By, gol, I like it better 'n corned beef!" It is indeed delicious, with big shreds of turkey among drifts of potato, laced with onions, alternately crusty and moist. Another notable breakfast is eggs and matzoh, aka matzoh brei. Bite-size scraps of matzoh are sheathed in scrambled egg like a kind of jumbled French toast but with a distinctive unleavened munchiness: home cooking, in a broad bowl.

Teibel's

1775 Rte. 41, Schererville, IN	$$
(219) 865-2000	LD

In this huge, institutional-looking eating establishment, the house specialty is perch, served filleted and glistening with butter. You get plenty on the plate—the proper term hereabouts is "a mess of perch"—and if for some crazy reason you don't like the tender sweet little slabs of lake fish, Teibel's offers alternative entrees of fried chicken or the other northern Indiana favorite, frogs legs.

The Village Inn

104 S. Main St., Middlebury, IN	$
(219) 825-2043	BLD

If you really love pie, pie of all kinds and plenty of it, three times a day, you need to visit The Village Inn. In this town café, where Amish farmers congregate after the local horse auction, a typical day's repertoire includes funeral pie (made of raisins), O.F. cream (meaning "old-fashioned" cream, made of brown sugar and cream), cherry, peach, pineapple, banana cream, custard (white sugar and milk), and peanut butter/powdered sugar. We didn't feel at all gluttonous ordering four pieces for the two of us: two giant-size bearded gents in overalls at a nearby table topped off their hearty Tuesday special chicken-and-noodles lunch with an entire raisin pie, split half-and-half between them.

Beyond pie, Village Inn cuisine tends to be, shall we say, extremely hearty. Breakfast on the kitchen's substantial cornmeal mush and head cheese or have lunch of beef stew and mashed potatoes, and you'll be fueled up for a long day of horseshoeing, plowing or—in our case—napping.

Zaharako's

329 Washington St., Columbus, IN	$
(812) 379-9329 Mon–Sat	£

Zaharako's is famous for its gorgeous fixtures, including a mahogany backbar, twin onyx fountains, and an eye-and-ear-boggling self-playing organ that blares out John Phillip Sousa marches from 185 pipes as well as on its drums, triangle, and cymbals. Now preparing to celebrate its centennial in the year 2000, it is also an oasis of anachronous mixology where you can get a fine sarsaparilla, a fireball, a cinnamon Coke, fresh lemonade or orangeade, or a dazzling tutti-fruitti sundae.

But if you are hungry for a good hot meal before your hot fudge sundae, you need to know about Zaharako's cheese-br-ger. Like a cheeseburger, a cheese-br-gr is a beef and cheese combo, but in this case made with spicy beef chili sauce reminiscent of sloppy Joe and gilded with a slab of Velveeta. These ingredients are sandwiched between two slices of white bread that are toasted on a grill. Suggested beverage: a sixteen-ounce chocolate soda served in a green-tinted, bell-shaped glass.

IOWA

★ ★ ★

801 Steak and Chop House

801 Grand, Des Moines, IA	$$$
(515) 288-6000 𝔇 Mon–Sat; £ Mon–Fri	£𝔇

801 is all dark wood and cut-glass partitions, the cushiony seats of its capacious booths occupied by important men in business suits. Table linen is so thick that highball glasses teeter. Each place is equipped with a heavy-handled steak knife. The forthright muscularity is reminiscent of New York's finest steak houses, but decor consists

of breathtaking oil paintings of heroic bulls and of cows on parade at the Fair. In this bovine Louvre, the menu is *demonstrated,* Chicago-style: the waitress wheels up a meat cart with plastic-wrapped examples of raw beef and discusses the pros and cons of each available cut as she shows it around the table. She exhibits a one-pound Iowa pork chop from an impeccable pig raised on a farm in Latimer and apologizes that the thirty-ounce prime rib, already roasted rare and ready to be served au jus or au poivre, is not available for the in-the-raw show-and-tell. The spud roster includes such delights as redskins in a Maytag (Iowa) blue cheese sauce, garlic mashed, hash browns with aged cheddar, and a beautiful one-pound baked potato.

The beef is prime; the Iowa chop is nearly two inches thick, sweet and fine and as succulent as bacon. When your knife glides through such splendid meat, you fully appreciate why Iowans hold their livestock farmers in such high esteem, and why a blue ribbon at the annual August State Fair in Des Moines is the top of the world.

Bauder's Pharmacy

3802 Ingersoll Ave., Des Moines, IA	$
(515) 255-1124	BLD

It's not for the basic menu of sandwiches we recommend a visit to Bauder's; it is for ice cream, preferably Bauder's delicious strawberry ice cream, loaded with chunks of fruit, made fresh in the summer. You can also get a fine turtle sundae (that's caramel, nuts, and hot fudge topping), as well as shakes, malts, sodas, and floats of every stripe, plus a green river (lime soda), a cherry Coke, or an old-fashioned phosphate.

For those of us who grew up in mid-century middle America, the nostalgic reverberations of this old drugstore soda fountain are comfortably familiar, but not antique: colorful octagon-tile floor, blue-upholstered counter stools and a couple of booths back near the prescription counter, a small glass case of warm salted nuts for sale, and a waist-high cooler with pints of ice cream packed and ready to take home. Plus, of course, shelves of all the patent medicines, knickknacks, liniments, and sundries that made pharmacies such convenient neighborhood emporia in the decades before malls and superstores.

Breitbach's Country Dining

563 Balltown Rd., Balltown, IA	$
(319) 552-2220	BLD

Who can resist a restaurant that boasts of being the only one on earth patronized by both Jesse James and Brooke Shields? Iowa's oldest eatery began as a stage stop; today, it is a big, efficient place with a real Midwest salad bar that boasts organic garden produce and a menu featuring Mississippi River catfish. The best time at Breitbach's is breakfast on Sunday, when local farmers come in for plenty of coffee to accompany the Sunday-only cinnamon rolls.

Green Gables

1800 Pierce St., Sioux City, IA	$
(712) 258-4246	LD

The nice place in town, Green Gables is favored by local customers for its fried chicken basket, T-bones and pork chops, and fillets of walleyed pike, all served efficiently and politely from rolling carts pushed by uniformed waitresses. A comfy place to sit and soak up Sioux City ambiance, Green Gables also happens to feature one of Iowa's top soda fountains. You can have an adult supper of meat and potatoes, or even healthfully cooked orange roughy, a special attraction one recent night, and accompany it with a black-and-white ice cream soda, a chocolate malt, or a green river (lime soda), then top things off with a peppermint hot fudge sundae or the *pièce de résistance*, a goshawful gooey (marshmallow sauce atop vanilla ice cream and orange sherbet).

Jesse's Embers

3301 Ingersoll, Des Moines, IA	$$
(515) 255-6011 £ Mon–Fr; 𝒟 Mon–Sat	£𝒟

The Embers is a supper club where steaks are cooked on an open-pit grill.

If it is a bright day, it will take some time for your eyes to adjust when you walk in from the parking lot. No windows allow harsh sunlight to intrude on this cool carnivore's cocoon, which is paneled in wood and decorated with hunting prints.

The thing to eat is beef, which ranges from a handsome half-pound hamburger to aged prime sirloin or center-cut filet mignon wrapped in bacon. The sirloin resonates well-aged flavor, the filet is butterknife-tender. They are seared over the fire to crusty succulence, insides heavy with juice. Side dishes are fundamental: crisp cottage fries or fluffy baked potatoes served with globes of butter and a cup of sour cream with chives; iceberg lettuce salads with creamy dressing, nice thin-crusted onion rings. Waitresses are pros who keep the cocktails coming.

The Sandwich Shop

14 Benton Ave. W., Albia, IA (515) 932-7756	$
Mon–Sat	£

Tenderloin alert! If you are traveling through the Midwest hunting for tenderloin sandwiches (a worthy quest), be sure to stop in Albia and try one of the extremely tasty pan-fried pork patties served by The Sandwich Shop, an Albia institution since 1921. We are not absolutely certain it's the best on earth, but the pork is sliced thick and luscious and served loaded with pickles, onions, mustard, and ketchup. When marooned in the tenderloin-deprived Northeast, we dream of the simple pleasure of this Iowa delight.

Smitty's

1401 SW Army Post Rd., Des Moines, IA	$
(515) 287-4742 Tues–Sat	£𝔇

Smitty's short sandwich menu is topped by a "King Tenderloin"; its royal status is beyond challenge. Since 1952, this friendly little eat-shack south of Des Moines near the airport has built a mighty reputation on its delicious pounded-thin, crisp-fried pork patties. They are served on an ordinary burger bun, but the bun is irrelevant except as a method for keeping ketchup, mustard, onions, and pickles adjacent to the center section of the ten-inch-diameter cutlet. The tenderloin's meat is soft and flavorful—a generous ribbon of pork succulence embedded in breading that is brittle crisp.

"Home of the REAL whopper" says a cartoon on the wall that shows Smitty and his regal piece of pork. All hail!

Stone's

507 S. Third Ave., Marshalltown, IA	$
(515) 753-3626	£𝔇

Hearty, homey meals have lured travelers to Stone's for 110 years, since Ebson Weed Stone converted a disreputable saloon into a civilized restaurant for travelers. In 1910, it moved to its current location near the train tracks, where it became a favorite of railroad workers who telegraphed ahead so lunch would be ready when they pulled in to Marshalltown. Today, locals and tourists travel to the comfy dining parlors in the old building for a roast beef and baked ham buffet every Sunday, and such weekday comforts as chicken and noodles, pork loin, meat loaf, and the ever-popular (no kidding) tender beef heart with dressing. Every day of the week, the main attraction is dessert, lemon chiffon pie in particular, which is tart, fluffy, and amazingly tall.

The White Way

8th Ave., Durant, IA	$
(319) 785-6202	£𝒟

Durant is the heart of the pork belt, where a dry chop or a gristly loin roast is practically a criminal offense. The White Way, which has won innumerable awards from the state's pork producers, is the place to taste it cooked properly. At about six o'clock each evening, the dining room is packed with townsfolk, most of whom seem to be easing their fork into thick Iowa chops smothered in gravy (that's after they have feasted on the cornucopic salad bar). A word to strangers passing through: reserve a slice of your favorite pie as soon as you sit down; by the end of the dinner hour, many of the homemade pies (including the divine sour cream raisin) are gone.

MICHIGAN

★ ★ ★

Caucus Club

150 W. Congress, Detroit, MI (313) 965-4970	$$$
Tues–Fri	£𝒟

The first time we ate at the Caucus Club, we were sent there by a regular customer, who told us exactly what to eat and which waiter to ask for. When we informed the waiter about our mutual acquaintance, he instantly became our best friend and the best waiter we've ever had anywhere—suave, attentive, helpful, charming. The Caucus Club is that kind of place: for friends, and friends of friends, it is luxury incarnate, a classy, clubby restaurant where classy, clubby food is prepared with decades' worth of expertise.

The menu is an honor roll of great old gourmet wonders. There isn't a better Caesar salad anywhere. Steak tartare? The Caucus Club sets the gold standard. Prime steaks, double-thick chops, a mess of perch, corned beef hash: all these grand and hearty dishes are at their finest in this dark, exclusive place where Detroit's high rollers have dined since Cadillacs had tailfins. And honestly, the times we've gone to the Caucus Club as unknowns have been perfectly pleasant, with efficient if not coddling service. Our suggestions: make a reservation in advance, dress up, and tell them Henry Ford sent you.

Cousin Jenny's Cornish Pasties

129 S. Union St., Traverse City, MI (616) 941-7821	$
Mon–Sat	*BLD*

Miners who came from Cornwall to dig ore in Michigan's Upper Peninsula during the last century were known as Cousin Jacks; their wives were Cousin Jennies. These hardworking immigrants brought the Cornish pasty to the Northland, where it became a staple of local cookery. Pasties, which are essentially beef stew inside a flaky pastry crust, were favored by those who worked the mines because they were easy to carry and easy to eat, a hearty pocket meal.

Cousin Jenny's in Traverse City is a spanking-clean restaurant where the culinary theme is pasties, available in two sizes, both of which are big enough to require knife and fork. They are listed on the menu as "Gourmet Pasties," but the steak pasty is the traditional configuration, filled with beef, potatoes, onion, and rutabaga. In addition, you can get a meatless seven-vegetable pasty with cream and cheese; and there are always novelty pasties available, such as Italian (with pizza sauce and pepperoni) or German (Swiss cheese, ham, and sauerkraut in a rye-flavored crust). There are even hand-holdable breakfast pasties, starting at 7:30 AM, filled with eggs, hash browns, and bacon or sausage.

Dale's Donut Factory

3687 South Lakeshore Dr., St. Joseph, MI	$
(616) 429-1033	BL

Cinnamon triangles, whole buttermilk coffee cakes or eat-it-now slices, gooey caramel pecan rolls and cinnamon pecan rolls, fritters, almond hearts, and a full battery of filled and holey donuts are the menu at Dale's, the donut factory of donut fans' dreams. The pastries hit the hot oil every morning at about 3 AM, and the doors open shortly thereafter, making this an ideal stop for famished travelers along I-94 to hop off (exit 23) for a fresh donut fix. By sunup, nearly all the day's varieties are displayed, but not every good thing is made every day. Some Dale loyalists plan their visits for the weekend, when the dark chocolatey twists known as tiger tails are always in the lineup.

Gustafson's Smoked Fish

4321 Rte. 2 W, Brevort, MI	$
(906) 292-5424	BLD

Along Route 2, which hugs Lake Michigan in the Upper Peninsula, every motel offers freezers to guests who have fresh-caught fish to keep until they get home. For those of us needing immediate fish-eating gratification, there is Gustafson's. It is not a restaurant, but this roadside convenience store sells food that is oh-so-ready-to-eat. Even with your eyes closed, you'll find it as you cruise along the shore road (we don't recommend driving this way) because a sugar maple haze from a quartet of smoldering smokers outside the shop perfumes the air with the unbelievably appetizing smell of whitefish, trout, menominee, chub, and salmon turning gorgeous shades of gold. Inside, coolers are arrayed with the firm-fleshed beauties, which you can buy by the piece, wrapped in butcher's paper. A big, moist hunk of freshly smoked freshwater fish, a fifty-cent stack of saltine crackers, a bag of cheese curds, and a beer, plus the scenic beauty of Lake Michigan's northern shore: what's better than that?

Ham Heaven	
70 Cadillac Sq., Detroit, MI	$
(313) 961-8818	*BL*

Baked, fried, sandwiched, folded into an omelet, ground up for hash, or diced for salad, sweet pink ham reigns in this boisterous sandwich shop near the courthouse. The ham is especially good as the flavor agent of split pea or bean soup. The one dish we cannot resist is called a hamlet, similar to a hamburger: ham ground up with vegetables to form a patty that is fried to crisp succulence and served on a bun. Add a squirt of mustard and you truly are in ham heaven.

Ivanhoe Café	
5249 Joseph Campau, Detroit, MI (313) 925-5335	$$
L weekdays; *D* Fri only	*LD*

This vintage family restaurant, patronized by generations of Michiganders who know it by its nickname, the Polish Yacht Club, used to be famous for the greeting Joe the bartender gave all who entered: "Hello, Iiiivanhoe!" We didn't get the salutation last time we visited, and the neighborhood outside has run down at the heels, but everything else about this comfortable old watering hole is exactly as it's always been. It is a place to eat fine corned beef and cabbage or kielbasa and kraut, hamburgers on pumpernickel bread, and perch served family-style, cooked up by the skillet-full and accompanied by crisp-fried potatoes.

Juilleret's

130 State, Harbor Springs, MI (616) 526-2821	$$
(closed late September to mid-May)	£D

Juilleret's is a good-time place, as rowdy as a small-town soda fountain when school lets out, its stamped tin ceiling reverberating with the noise of summering Michiganders sitting down to dinners of planked whitefish—Juilleret's specialty and one of the not-to-be-missed Great Lakes meals.

The snowy-fleshed sweet fish is heaped on the plank, pooled with butter, strewn with sliced tomatoes, parsley, and lemon, all surrounded by a wall of piped-on duchess potatoes. Even amid the commotion of Juilleret's free-for-all booths, there is something undeniably regal about a planked meal such as this, the exalted entree attended by its legions of vegetables and protected on all sides by sturdy spud ramparts.

When you have cleaned your plank, there is only one way to end the feast—with a soda jerker's specialty. You can get a black cow, a tin roof, a Boston cooler, or a bittersweet dusty sundae. Best of all, you can go with one of the Juilleret's doozies that has been popular for generations: a Thundercloud, in which layers of ice cream and bittersweet chocolate are topped with marshmallow and chopped nuts; or a Velvet, in which the same ingredients are whipped smooth like a milk shake, but so thick you have to eat it with a spoon.

Lafayette Coney Island

118 Lafayette St., Detroit, MI (313) 964-8198	$
always open	BLD

If it's three in the morning and the one thing you really crave before you greet the dawn is a brace of raunchy little wieners smothered in chili and raw onions with a cup of bean soup on the side dished out under glaring fluorescents, you better hope you're in Detroit. When it comes to déclassé frankfurters, Lafayette Coney Island—open nearly round the clock—is in a (dé)class by itself.

The Log Cabin

Hwys. 2 and 41, Gladstone, MI	$$
(906) 786-5621	LD

The Log Cabin is a cozy supper club with a small family of plaster lawn deer permanently grazing out front. Between quaffs of sweet manhattans, made with brandy, the Upper Peninsula way, we availed ourselves of the Log Cabin salad bar—an opulent array of composed salads that might give modern nutrition police conniption fits, but to us looked like midwestern Thanksgiving. There was Waldorf salad with big red strawberries, pea and ham salad, long noodles with mayonnaise salad, short noodles with even more mayo salad, and macaroni salad, also with mayo. The great main course hereabouts is whitefish; the Log Cabin's is perfectly broiled to ineffable tenderness, pulling into fragile white flakes when prodded with a fork.

We love the view from the dining room. At the end of one visit, we sipped another round of candied drinks, listened to a muted-horn instrumental version of "My Way" playing low on the Log Cabin sound system, and gazed out across the plaster deer to the tall grass waving in the sapphire shallows of Little Bay De Noc—a Great Lakes epiphany!

Polonia

2934 Yemans St., Detroit, MI (313) 873-8432	$
Mon—Sat	LD

Good Polish food is one of Detroit's primary culinary attractions, and there is no place better to savor it than at Polonia. This ancient tin-ceiling café, staffed by experts with thick accents and kindly dispositions, offers a golden opportunity to tuck into plump pierogi that are butter-slick and filled with seasoned mashed potatoes, hearty plates of kielbasa and kraut, jellied pigs' feet, bowls of pickly cabbage soup, and stuffed cabbage. Prices are low and portions are gigantic. If old-world fare is food for your soul, Polonia is a comfort-food gem!

Rosenthal Orchard

off Rte. 31, Charlevoix, MI (616) 547-4350	$
seasonal hours, closed winter through spring	

This is not a restaurant, but hungry travelers need to know about Rosenthal Orchard, where the motto is "You pick or we pick." If you nab your own apples from the several dozen varieties available, you are rewarded with a refreshing glass of fresh-pressed cider. The orchard store has bushels of apricots, peaches, prunes, plums, and pears; but the main attraction, in late summer, is cherries—big, dark, sweet, plump Michigan beauties. You can pick those yourself, too, or buy bags of just-picked ones, washed and ready to eat.

Zingerman's Deli

422 Detroit St., Ann Arbor, MI	$
(734) 663-3354	BLD

A grandiose deli that serves every kind of sandwich the human race has devised—from Italian salami subs to brisket-and-schmaltz on rye and a pile of hot pastrami parenthesized 'twixt two potato pancakes. We get weak-kneed thinking of Zingerman's smoked whitefish salad, redolent of dill and red onion, piled on slices of freshly made onion-rye bread. The immense menu is a good hour's read, and ranges beyond sandwiches to such traditional old-world specialties as noodle kugel (a sweet pudding), cheese blintzes (cheese-filled crepes), and knishes (heavyweight dumplings). Or you can choose Thai noodle salad, Arkansas peppered ham, or ratatouille with polenta. Brash, crowded, and invariably delicious, this one-of-a-kind place is an essential stop for all traveling eaters.

Zingerman's stocks a tremendous inventory of cheese, smoked fish, meats, breads, coffees, etc., for retail sale.

MINNESOTA

★ ★ ★

Al's Breakfast

413 14th Ave. S.E., Minneapolis, MN	$
(612) 331-9991	B L

Al's Breakfast serves the best morning meal in town. It is a pint-size diner with an ancient counter of worn yellow linoleum and twelve stools permanently attached that form an aisle with the wall that is too small for any good-size person to pass through without turning sideways. In the front window of the restaurant behind the counter is a minuscule grill where the short-order cook flips pancakes, poaches eggs, and maintains a steady dialogue of wisecracks with customers and staff.

The buttermilk pancakes are superb, available with blueberries in the batter, and there are fine whole wheat cakes, too, but Al's fragile, free-form poached eggs have an uncommon savor that is hard to resist. Many customers get them in the classic eggs Benedict configuration, on Canadian bacon and English muffin halves, gilded with freshly made hollandaise sauce. Or you can get the hollandaise served over scrambled eggs and plates of potatoes. Some folks simply order a bowlful and use it as a dip for rye toast.

Tantalizing aromas billow from the grill up front of hash brown potatoes and corned beef hash. The hash has a briny, well-spiced smell and is thickly laced with shreds of potato. How it's served is up to you, either limp and glistening soft or fried to a brittle mahogany crisp.

Al's customers adore this place for its personality as much as for its food. "It is an organism," explained a friend of the house named John Marshall. "Good things happen here; people's lives change. If you want a car, or an apartment, or a sweetheart, come in and sit at the counter. Come in, have coffee, and chat a while. Pretty soon, I promise, you will get what you need. Al's has a life of its own, above and beyond any of us. We truly believe it is a crossroads of the universe."

Betty's Pies

215 Hwy. 61 E, Two Harbors, MN (218) 834-3367	$
(closed November through April; open weekends only in May)	BLD

Betty's serves first-rate sandwiches—ham salad on homemade rye is especially tasty—as well as homemade soup, hearty chili, and walleye pike from the cold waters of Lake Superior. But the main reason this little outfit is crowded all summer long with locals and tourists, dine-in and take-out customers, is dessert. There are crunchy cookies and lemon angel cakes that melt in your mouth, and about a dozen kinds of pie each day, including berries, fruits, creams, and custards. A beacon of delight on Lake Superior's north shore!

Café Brenda

300 1st Ave. N., Minneapolis, MN	$$
(612) 342-9230 L Mon–Fri; D Mon–Sat	LD

Towering windows give this health-conscious dining room theatrical panache; but at table level, where framed botanical prints hang on clean white walls, the setting is serene, the sort of place that encourages a reverent attitude toward food. Tables are set far enough apart to make meals feel like private parties. We once saw a nutritionally compatible foursome toasting one another with glasses of microbrewed beer, then sharing shrimp satay, grain-and-bean croquettes, and plates of Moroccan vegetable couscous drizzled with peppery harissa sauce.

Chef and owner Brenda Langton recalled that when she started cooking in a St. Paul restaurant in 1976, "healthful ingredients took precedence over flavor." Twenty years have passed, and the meals she serves now are healthful but uncompromised. In this modern urban café, good flavors prevail.

How to Spot a Great Small-Town Café

❧

One of the joys of traveling Midwest back roads is eating in a small-town café. Not only are you likely to find terrific cinnamon buns in the morning and state-fair pie at lunch, you will also get a real flavor of life in the town. This is particularly true in the morning, when many cafés are ad hoc social centers for the exchange of news, gossip, political opinions, and amateur weather forecasts. Conversations tend to be communal, and there might be one large table where customers come and go, helping themselves to coffee refills.

Some signs of a great small town café:

- ☛ Police cars and pickup trucks in the parking lot
- ☛ A large round table at the front window, where customers can see the street
- ☛ A bakery case with pies displayed (bonus for any blue ribbons recently won)
- ☛ A pegboard where regular customers keep their coffee cups
- ☛ A collection jar near the cash register to help out a community member in need
- ☛ Place mats with advertising for the local garage, funeral parlor, and portrait studio
- ☛ Newspapers strewn about for customers to read
- ☛ A daily written menu with a long list of vegetables
- ☛ A motto (Flo's of Marseilles, Illinois, has this inscribed on its menu: "If I can't eat it, I won't serve it!")
- ☛ Peek in the kitchen. Old ladies wearing hair nets, up to their elbows in flour, are almost always a good sign.
- ☛ Hours of operation geared to hardworking clientele, such as from 5 AM to 2 PM
- ☛ Roll down the car windows when you drive along Main Street and sniff. Good midwestern smells include cinnamon buns in Iowa, smoked fish in Michigan's Upper Peninsula, five-way chili in Cincinnati, and charcoal-cooked sausages in Wisconsin.

Café Latté

850 Grand Ave., St. Paul, MN	$
(612) 224-5687	£D

Café Latté is an energetic urban cafeteria with many good dishes to recommend it, including glorious tossed-to-order salads, interesting soups (four each day), hearty stews, and a fresh bread selection that ranges from white chocolate scones to ten-grain loaves. The meal you eat will be satisfying and inexpensive, and it can be very healthful, but the thing that lures us with sweet tooths back is the spectacular selection of desserts, cake in particular. If the devil himself made them, they couldn't be more tempting. There is chocolate Kahlúa torte that nearly drips; an English pecan Triple Sec fudge cake so seductive that it ought to be arrested; strawberry-rhubarb cheesecake and orange chocolate chunk cheesecake to swoon over. The *pièce de résistance*, and one of this planet's outstanding desserts, is a sprawling triple-layer "turtle cake," moist devil's food sandwiching gooey caramel studded with pecans, all blanketed with thick chocolate frosting.

Murray's

26 S. 6th St., Minneapolis, MN	$$$
(612) 339-0909 £ Mon–Fri; D daily	£D

Murray's is an old-fashioned dress-for-dinner Midwestern supper club that is renowned for immense "butter-knife" steaks: the silver butter-knife sirloin or golden butter-knife porterhouse, available for two or three people. These roast-sized blackened hunks of beef arrive whole from the kitchen and are sliced tableside into thick cuts that are indeed tender, but substantial enough that you'll want to use the steak knife that is part of each place setting's battery. Because the steak is so immense, sliced pieces offer an appealing textural range from succulent center to seasoned crust.

Alongside the steaks come au gratin potatoes or French fries, an assortment of interesting-shaped dinner rolls, a salad, and a basket of luscious garlic toast. For years, the word around town was that once all your toast was eaten, the basket was replenished only if your waitress liked you. She must have loved us, as our table of six went through three baskets one evening while laying waste to approximately eight pounds of golden butter-knife porterhouse.

Nye's Polonaise Room	
112 E. Hennepin Ave., Minneapolis, MN	$$
(612) 379-2021	£D

Order a Polonaise Plate, and you get a small taste of nearly everything Polish that this kitchen makes: buttery pierogi, long pink sausages and kraut, hefty cabbage rolls, pork hocks, and spareribs.

The meals are good, and the ambiance is rousing. But what thrills us most about this fine old supper club are the booths in the central dining room. They are shiny gold metal-flake vinyl, the kind of stuff that hisses quietly when you ease down on it. Here's the place to eat yourself silly, drink Polish pile drivers (vodka and Krupnik), and tap your toes to the rollicking Ruth Adams Band (Thursday through Saturday), which is billed as "The World's Most Dangerous Polka Band." Nazdrowie!

Peppermint Twist	
Hwy. 12, Delano, MN	$
(612) 972-2572 Tues–Sun	£D

An hour west of Minneapolis is a half-century trip back in time: a genuine, order-from-your-front-seat drive-in with carhop service and trays built to hook on the window. The hamburgers are big and juicy, the French fries are fresh-fried, and the malts and shakes are thick enough to require serious suction up the straw. The house specialty is a Delano Burger (heaped with Swiss cheese, mushrooms, and onions), and there is a peppermint milk shake dotted with little bits of pink candy. For those who choose not to dine off the dashboard, Peppermint Twist offers some lovely picnic tables spread out on an adjacent lawn.

MISSOURI

Amighetti's

5141 Wilson, St. Louis, MO	$
(314) 776-2855	£🄳

Often imitated, never duplicated" says the tape that secures the butcher-paper wrapper in which an Amighetti's Special sandwich is served. Amighetti's bakes the bread, a thick-crusted Italian loaf with sturdy insides, then piles in slices of ham, roast beef, Genoa salami, and cheese, garnishes it with shreds of lettuce, and dresses the interior with a sweet, egg-yellow dressing. There are other sandwiches available, too, including a garlicky Italian hero, roast beef, and a three-cheese veggie sandwich—all recommended because of the bread on which they're served.

A culinary institution on "The Hill," St. Louis's old Italian neighborhood, Amighetti's is casual and fun: place your order and they call your name when it is ready, and if it's summer, find yourself a seat on the sunny patio.

Arthur Bryant Barbeque

1727 Brooklyn Ave., Kansas City, MO	$
(816) 231-1123	£🄳

There was concern when Arthur Bryant died in 1982 that his legendary smokehouse wouldn't survive without him. But it has, and although the floor isn't as slick with grease as it used to be and the beef isn't quite as oozingly moist, it is still a sensational place to eat barbecue. There are good ribs and sliced pork, but it's that beef brisket that makes us swoon—heaped into white-bread sandwiches, slathered with Bryant's hot, grainy opaque sauce, and accompanied by crisp French fries.

Busch's Grove

9160 Clayton Rd., LaDue (St. Louis), MO	$$
(314) 993-0011	£D

There are two seating choices at Busch's grove: inside or outdoors in a gazebo. The interior is cool, dark, and peaceful; and even the tropical-style outside seating has a breezy calm about it . . . unless it is nighttime and partiers in nearby gazebos are on their third round of mint juleps.

They don't make places like this any more, where the ambiance, as well as much of the clientele, exudes old-money. There are hunting pictures on the wall and the tablecloths are soft white linen that feels like it has been washed a thousand times. Waiters work the dining room with deferential antebellum style; and the meals they serve are square and satisfying rather than avant-garde or trendy. Charbroiled aged steak is what we recommend for supper, preceded by that strange and tasty local delight, toasted ravioli, or by the charmingly unfashionable Russ's salad, which is a julienne of iceberg lettuce, crabmeat, Roquefort, and orange American cheese with Thousand Island and Italian dressing. Top this off with a pleasant little bowl of peppermint ice cream, and you will have eaten well indeed, just as St. Louis's privileged classes have been doing since Busch's Grove first opened in 1890.

C&K Barbecue

4390 Jennings Station Rd., St. Louis, MO	$
(314) 385-5740	D

Darryle Brantley, proprietor of C&K, is a little peeved at us because a few years ago we highly recommended his take-out-only restaurant as the best place we know to eat snoots (that's pig snouts baked until crisp and bathed in barbecue sauce) and ears (boiled tender and served between slices of white bread). C&K still has these rather uncommon soul-food specialties, but let us say here and now that there are plenty of perfectly "normal" smokehouse delicacies available, too. Ribs and rib tips are succulent, tender as they can be without just falling off the bone of their own volition, served with C&K's unusually sugary potato salad and bathed in wonderful thick red sauce. This is St. Louis's great barbecue, even if snoots are not your cup of tea. There are no tables or chairs, so be prepared to eat in or on your car or to take the food to a table somewhere else.

Bonus for night owls: C&K stays open until 2 AM Monday through Thursday, until 3 AM Friday and Saturday.

Crown Candy Kitchen

1401 St. Louis Ave., St. Louis, MO	$
(314) 621-9650	£D

Each booth has a jukebox. Up front are cases of chocolates and a nickel scale that predicts your future. Behind the marble counter is a soda fountain where shakes are blended in tall silver carafes and multisauce sundaes are haloed with whipped cream and crowned with pecans, sprinkles, and cherries. This jovial 1913 ice cream parlor will concoct just about any confectionery pleasure you can imagine (and they serve sandwiches and fine chili dogs, too); the house specialty is a malt made with fresh bananas (with options of chocolate or butterscotch flavor). If you consume five malts in thirty minutes, you get them all free.

Fiorella's Smoke Stack

13441 Holmes, Martin City, MO	$$
(816) 942-9141	£D

To say the Smoke Stack is a barbecue joint would be like saying Superman is strong: a gross understatement. Yes, you can get creamsoft, slow-smoked brisket, fall-off-the-bone tender baby back ribs and succulent lamb ribs, as well as crusty chunks of various barbecued meats known as "burnt ends." (Burnt ends are the *grand cru* of barbecue.)

But there is so much more to eat at this insanely popular roadhouse on the southern edge of Kansas City. Onion rings—thick, sweet Vidalias in a sandy batter—are served in a stack at least one foot tall. Trout and salmon, infused with smoke flavor, will convince even a diehard beef eater of seafood's glory. And oh, what side dishes! Cheesy corn bake is comfort food you haven't known since your mommy fed you in a high chair; cowboy beans are laced with delicious shreds of barbecued meat. Even the coleslaw sparkles. And dessert? Triple chocolate suicide cake, anyone?

The Golden Ox

1600 Genessee, Kansas City, MO	$$
(816) 842-2866	LD

The Golden Ox is a stockman's haven with plush chairs designed for gents to rest their cowboy hats just beneath the seat and a brandy-colored rug inscribed with a cattle brand design. Cattle ranchers, truckers who haul "swinging beef," rodeo cowboys, and Future Farmers of America all consider "The Ox" *their* restaurant in Kansas City.

The big filet mignon is lovely; T-bone tends to be the cattleman's choice; and guys on dates go for extra-heavy prime rib; but if you can eat only one thing at the Ox, make it the KC royal cut strip. It is a boneless pound of center-cut sirloin with a thin amber ribbon of wickedly succulent fat along one edge and a pliant center that glistens with juice sealed inside by the fire.

Side dishes are predictable, but the cocktail menu is extraordinary, including a long list of single-malt scotches and small-batch bourbons as well as giant-size versions of those aperitifs classic-minded beef-eaters like: martinis, manhattans, and Rob Roys.

Goody Goody Diner

5900 Natural Bridge, St. Louis, MO	$
(314) 383-3333	BL

A diner that brims with crowds of happy eaters and a brisk take-out crowd from the time it opens at 6 AM through lunch hour, Goody Goody has been Old Reliable for St. Louisians of all types for more than fifty years. The menu is broad, with lots of interesting omelets in the morning and traditional diner fare at noon: chili in a bowl or served atop spaghetti noodles is thick and soulful; meat loaf comes blanketed with stout gravy; and the hamburgers are particularly good. They are quite modest-sized, but they are hand formed and sizzled on a griddle until slightly crusty, then served inside soft, buttered buns. With French fries or onion rings on the side, a Goody Goody double cheeseburger with the works costs about five dollars, but it's a priceless taste of diner excellence.

Breakfast is served all day Wednesday and Saturday only; other days, it ends at 11 AM.

Hereford House

20th and Main, Kansas City, MO (816) 842-1080; also	$$$
5001 Town Center Drive, Leawood, KS (913)327-0800	LD

In Kansas City, a good T-bone now and then is a fundamental right of all citizens. On Saturday night, a big percentage of those citizens gather at the Hereford House. Opened in 1957 but modernized in recent years, this vast, multiroom restaurant attracts meat eaters by twos and by twenties.

Those who face a long wait are given a beeper that vibrates when a table is ready, allowing them to go outside for a smoke or stand in the vestibule with its view of the hickory charcoal fire over which aged steaks are tended by chefs who manage to give each one a picture-perfect grate-brand before it is set on its silver platter. There is also a lounge, mobbed with happy hungries, where we found standing room near the doorway and watched two women try to wedge towards the bar for a drink. As they brushed past one rotund reveler in a farm cap, the old boy exclaimed with glee, "Ladies! You ain't a-vibratin', are you?"

Sirloins, strips, filets, T-bones, and rib eyes are available from six ounces to pound-plus "cowboy cuts," accompanied by such beefy delights as steak soup and meat-laced "cowboy beans" with a sweet chili flavor. For those who lust after the meatiest red meat, Hereford House has a "baseball cut" top sirloin, which is a heavily marbled hunk known also as the coulotte, fairly dripping with tangy mineral juices. Note also the lunch-only hamburger, made from steak cuttings: With the possible exception of the once-a-year Tubby Burgers dished out from a truck behind Kemper Arena in November during the American Royal festival, there isn't a tastier round of chopped beef anywhere in town.

Jerre Anne Cafeteria	
2640 Mitchell Ave., St. Joseph, MO (816) 232-6585	$
Tues–Sat	£ⅅ

A neighborhood corner cafeteria that's been serving baked ham and beef hash for more than sixty years, Jerre Anne is also an excellent bakery. So even if you don't have all of fifteen minutes to load a tray with a hot meal of juicy roast brisket of beef (or any one of more than a half-dozen other entrees), potatoes, vegetables, rolls, salad, and all the trimmings, you could certainly stop by for an afternoon's supply of cookies, cake, and pastries.

Jess & Jim's

517 E. 135th St., Kansas City, MO	$$
(816) 941-9499	LD

"What do vegetarians eat when they come here?" we ask Marilyn, a seasoned waitress at Jess & Jim's, where a statue of a bull stands atop the roof as an ode to animal protein.

She considers the unlikely occurrence, shaking her head in pity and sorrow, then whispering so no other diner can hear the awful words: "Salad, cottage cheese."

A hungry meat-frowner *could* eat nothing but marvelous potatoes: cottage fries, French fries, or one of the astounding bakers on display along with cuts of raw steak in a glass refrigerator case near the front door. But of course none of these alleged vegetables are prepared to please the culinary prig. Even if you demur on sour cream, bacon, and shredded cheese condiments, the pound-plus baked potato will be served split open and twice-baked, with a scoop of butter that looks to be nearly one-eighth of a pound melting into it.

Yes, broiled fish is on the menu; chicken, too (fine fried chicken!); but who cares when there's great Kansas City beef to be eaten? All around Jess & Jim's every evening, the air is perfumed by the mouth-watering smell of cooking beef; several parking lots are full and streets are crowded with customers eager to savor hand-cut T-bones, filets, porterhouses, and strips. (The management offers a "call ahead" system in lieu of reservations: phone an hour before you expect to arrive, and chances are good you won't have to wait too long.)

A former dance hall on the city's fringe, Jess & Jim's has recently planted plastic ivy in pots above some tables, but its ambiance remains quintessential American roadhouse. In the entryway, Naugahyde couches are arrayed for waiting parties and a twenty-five cent candy machine holds mints for after dinner. Waitresses wear name tags and orthopedic shoes. Dinner begins with a basket of saltine packets and a silver dish of pickled beets. Most customers leave with a Styrofoam container holding the meat they could not finish.

Steaks arrive from the kitchen exuberantly sputtering, crusty from an iron griddle. The top-of-the-line twenty-five ounce "KC Playboy Strip" is a full two inches thick, and unlike the super-tender bacon-wrapped filets, it demands some serious chewing. Not that it is tough; but neither is it a cut of meat for Milquetoasts. Dense and intense, this is steak-lover's steak with a rapturous savor no other food can equal.

Lambert's Café

2109 E. Malone, Sikeston, MO	$
(573) 471-4261	LD

Billboards for Lambert's Café boast that it is home of the throwed roll. From outside, it looks ordinary. Walk in the door and hot rolls are sailing through the air across the dining room, tossed by waiters from the kitchen to customers at tables, who gingerly split them open to let steam escape, then dip them into puddles of sweet sorghum molasses oozing on the tablecloths. Other eaters pop nubbins of fried okra down the hatch, spoon up heaps of beans and pepper relish, and drink iced tea from one-quart mason jars. Lambert's is one of a kind, and not just because its rolls are thrown and by the end of the meal everybody's table is a delicious mess of spilled and dripped food. Like the rest of the chow that emerges from the kitchen, those rolls are good—warm and fluffy—and Lambert's country ham with white beans and turnip greens is Ozark country cooking at its most toothsome.

Snead's Corner Bar-B-Q

1001 E. 171st St., Belton, MO	$$
(816) 331-9858 Wed–Sun	LD

When we are in Kansas City with time for only one barbecue meal, we go to Snead's, a sprawling roadhouse beyond the edge of town. Handsome ribs, lean and juicy beef, ham that is sweet, and turkey that is tender—everything from the smoke pit glows with hickory flavor. The French fries are fresh and the beans have a nice tingle. We especially like Snead's "brownies," which are plates piled high with unbelievably savory burnt ends from the beef and/or ham; and the "log meat" sandwiches, a diced hash of all the hickory-smoked meats on a bun. Someday, we are going to order Snead's fried chicken. The menu warns that it takes forty-five minutes to prepare. Based on the excellence of everything else this kitchen produces, we suspect the chicken is on a par with KC's best.

Complimentary ice cream cones are provided at the end of each meal.

Stroud's

1015 E. 85th St., Kansas City, MO (816) 333-2132	*$$*
also at 5410 Northeast Oak Ridge Road, Kansas City	*D*
(816) 454-9600	

This dilapidated roadhouse on a bleak street south of the city serves four-star fried chicken—our choice as the best on earth. Dark or light, each piece of pan-fried meat is tightly enveloped in a red-gold crust imbued with the succulence of chicken fat exactly the way a crisp strip of bacon is charged with the nectarous goodness of pig fat. When you heft it in your hands (only oddballs use knife and fork) and penetrate the tender wrapping with your teeth, the flavor of sizzled skin is so profound that you might suddenly think you have never really tasted fried chicken before. With it come exquisite mashed potatoes, real pan gravy, and country-style green beans cooked to a fare-thee-well.

Note: the Oak Ridge Stroud's, in a lovely old house furnished with antiques, has a menu almost identical to that of the original except that fry-frowners can get a skinless broiled chicken breast.

Ted Drewes

6726 Chippewa, St. Louis, MO	*$*
(314) 481-2652	*LD*

From its own freshly made custard, Ted Drewes concocts one of the world's greatest milk shakes, known as a "concrete" for its incredible *avoirdupois*. Forget using a straw, suction has no effect on this mighty substance. You practically could use a knife and fork. Customers who come on dates tend to use a spoon; guys in groups pour it down the hatch. Cones and cups of the first-rate custard are also available.

OHIO

☆ ☆ ☆

Bun's	
6 Winter St., Delaware, OH (614) 363-3731	$
closed Mon	BLD

A nice, homey, town dining room, Bun's descends from a family bakery that opened in Delaware in 1863. It still features dandy baked goods at a take-out counter (pecan loaves, butterscotch twists, Danish pullaparts, fudge cake, and breads and buns of all shapes and sizes), as well as a daily printed menu of heartland favorites, from ham salad sandwiches on Bun's-baked bread to meat loaf with escalloped corn and dark rye rolls. Prices are low, waitresses are friendly, meals are fresh and wholesome. Gee, it's great to eat American!

Camp Washington Chili	
Hopple and Colerain, Cincinnati, OH (513) 541-0061	$
always open, except Sun	BLD

For more than half a century, round the clock, Camp Washington has been a prime source of Cincinnati-style chili, which means thick, spicy meat sauce atop a bed of plump spaghetti, garnished with beans, shredded cheese, and chopped onions. Such a configuration is known as five-way chili; subtract the onions, cheese, and/or beans and you get three- or four-way. It is a wild, tasty meal, all the more pleasurable for the classic beanery surroundings: baseball trophies on display, ghastly fluorescent lights, worn (but clean) blue-and-white tile floor.

Beyond chili, Camp Washington is also a good place to have an archetypal Coney Island (a little wiener heaped with chili, cheese, and onions), as well as one of the tall double-decker sandwiches featured in all fine Cincinnati chili parlors.

Note: Camp Washington will be changing location some time late in 1999.

Clark's Dining Room	
Rtes. 40 and 13, Jacksontown, OH (614) 323-3874	**$$**
Tues–Sun	**LD**

On the old National Highway, Clark's is nearing its eightieth year in business. The vintage hostelry (rebuilt after a fire in the 1950s) has established its reputation on iron-skillet-fried chicken dinners with mashed potatoes and gravy, salad with great house dressing, all the vegetables you can eat, and Grandma Clark's homemade pie. In the few decades we've been customers, nothing has changed. Now run by a third generation of the family, Clark's has the same familiar, and familial, menu (with steak and ham added), and still employs personnel who have been part of the place for as long as anyone can remember.

Expect a considerable wait for a table, especially on weekends and holidays.

Doc's	
18625 Main, Tontogany, OH	**$**
(419) 823-4081	**LD**

The only bar/restaurant in town that just recently acquired a gas pump" is how our northern Ohio tipsters, Jennifer Kinney and Michael Nagy, described the fine and funky short-order hash house known as Doc's. Customers come for a lunch of slim hamburgers sided by wicked cheese fries; roast beef with potatoes and gravy on the side; or just big plates of nothing but potatoes and gravy. "Real comfort food," the KinNagys advised, an assessment with which we wholeheartedly agree. They also recommended Doc's Saturday-night Mexican-food specials and its dartboard, which, as officers in the Bowling Green Dart Association, they lauded as "the real bristle-board kind."

Edgewood Inn

U.S. 6 E and State Rte. 1, Pemberville, OH	$
(419) 287-4775	BLD

Thanks to the KinNagys of Bowling Green State University for tipping us off to the Edgewood Inn, which they described as an ideal eatery for anyone with a large appetite and a small budget. It is a meat-and-potatoes roadhouse, with both a lounge and a somewhat more civilized dining room where customers consume great platters of prime ribs (on weekend nights), corned beef, ham steaks, chicken, and gigantic "burritos supremo." The meal includes a shot at a copious, albeit predictable, soup and salad bar.

Flat Iron Café

1114 Center St., Cleveland, OH	$$
(216) 696-6968	LD

Going upscale can be a bad thing for a restaurant, especially one like the Flat Iron Café which earned its reputation as a blue-collar Irish pub in the Cleveland Flats. Although the neighborhood has spruced up and the bar's clientele has gone with it (you'll see more suspenders and designer shirts than work boots and dungarees), this is still a must-eat place as long as the day's supply of fresh-fried lake perch hasn't been exhausted. Sweet, crunchy, and addictive, these fillets are one of the Great Lakes' treasures, and a raucous pub like the Flat Iron is an ideal place to devour them.

Cincinnati's Ways with Chili

Cincinnati chili is a complex brew made with finely ground meat. It is served in chili parlors (preferably open-all-night ones) and bears little resemblance to the chili of Texas or New Mexico. When you order it, you must specify what "way" you want it:

- ☞ <u>Two-Way Chili</u> Chili on top of noodles, aka "chili spaghetti"
- ☞ <u>Three-Way Chili</u> Spaghetti topped with chili and grated cheddar cheese
- ☞ <u>Four-Way Chili</u> Spaghetti with chili, cheese, chopped onions
- ☞ <u>Five-Way Chili</u> Spaghetti with chili, cheese, chopped onions, and kidney beans

According to Timothy Charles Lloyd's treatise on the subject in *Western Folklore* several years ago, "the correspondence between the order of additional ingredients and higher-numbered ways follows a strict rule of cheese-three, onions-four, and beans-five." In other words, if you want spaghetti, chili, and onions *but no cheese,* you would never order a three-way with onions instead of cheese or a two-way plus onions. You would order a "four-way without cheese."

An exception to the rule is the combination of chili, beans, and spaghetti, which is known simply as "chili bean" rather than "five-way, no cheese, no onions."

Three-way chili is sometimes called a "haywagon."

Henry's

6275 Hwy. 40, West Jefferson, OH	$
(614) 879-9321	BLD

With state fair pie and a pine-paneled dining room in a former gas station on an old road that the interstate has made obsolete, Henry's charms are abundant. Regular customers come to eat ploughman's lunch of ham and beans with corn bread on the side, or meat loaf and mashed potatoes, or roast beef with dressing and stewed tomatoes; but for most travelers, the great lure to this lonesome way station is dessert. It is quite literally blue-ribbon pie, having won top prizes at the state fair for years, and while the fillings are exemplary— whether fruit or cream—it is the crust that makes us swoon. Flaky and tender, ineffably flavorful, it is a truly elegant foodstuff. What a joy it is to be seated in one of Henry's weathered old Naugahyde booths and have a good American meal followed by such world-class dessert.

Warning: by late in the day, Henry's often runs out of pie. If you know you will be dining here, call ahead and reserve a piece.

Nancy's Home Cooking

3133 North High St., Columbus, OH (614) 265-9012	$
BLD Mon–Thur; B£ Fri; B only Sat and Sun	BLD

Thanks to eater extraordinaire Mindy Pennington for tipping us off to this jim-dandy home café in her former hometown and advising us that the must-eat meal day is Thursday. That's when golden chicken-and-noodle stew gets ladled over mashed potatoes with green beans on the side. "C&N" is so locally famous that at noon one Thursday during the summer, we spent a good half hour waiting outside with scores of others eager to cozy up to supreme comfort food.

Another great Mindy tip was breakfast at Nancy's, where we started our day with a heap of sizzled-gold home fries and what's known hereabouts as the garbage omelet—green peppers, tomatoes, onions, ham, and cheese. Bravo!

Saywell's

160 N. Main St., Hudson, OH	$
(330) 653-5411 BLD Mon–Fri; B£ only Sat and Sun	BLD

It is possible to have a light breakfast in this Main-Street meeting spot where many citizens of Hudson come to share news and opinions early in the morning, but Saywell's siren song is ice cream. Veteran soda clerk Mary Ann Howe explained that chocolate sodas are especially popular because the chocolate syrup itself is so good—made on-premises, like all Saywell's flavorings and ice creams. Ms. Howe also explained that a phosphate hereabouts is simply soda water and the syrup flavor of choice; an egg cream is the same formula, but with a shot of cream added. With expertise honed fine by experience, she demonstrated the exact technique of making an egg cream. First, flavoring and cream are swirled in the bottom of the glass. Then the glass is held under the fountain nozzle, the paddle of which is pushed back so a furious pinpoint stream of soda squirts down and mixes the cream and flavoring in a great fizzy burst. When the glass is half-full, the paddle is pulled forward, allowing a leisurely flow of seltzer to fill the glass.

Tony Packo's Café	
1902 Front St., Toledo, OH	$
(419) 691-6054	£𝔇

Taut little tube steaks are sliced lengthwise and heaped with fine-ground hot-spiced chili sauce. These infamous longitudinal sandwiches, eaten by most Tony Packo's habitués in bunches of three or four a shot, are wanton and wonderful foodstuffs, the perfect meal when only the raunchiest hot dog will do. They are what Buckeye-state homeboy Klinger of M*A*S*H (Jamie Farr) wanted to get discharged from the army for.

WISCONSIN

★ ★ ★

Beernsten's Candy Store

108 N. 8th St., Manitowoc, WI	$
(920) 684-9616	£D

A seat in one of the beautiful black walnut booths at the back of Beernsten's is a time machine. The town sweet shop since 1932, this charming little confectionery also serves such lunch-counter sandwiches as grilled cheese, egg salad, or peanut butter and jelly, as well as franks and beans or macaroni. But the main attractions are old-fashioned soda fountain specialties. Here is the place to indulge in a Sweetheart (caramel, vanilla ice cream, marshmallow, crushed nuts), a Teddy Bear (chocolate ice cream topped with marshmallow), or a Sunset (strawberry and vanilla ice cream, pineapple, marshmallow, crushed nuts). We love the way fudge for hot fudge sundaes is served—in a separate shot glass so you can pour it on the ice cream yourself, measuring out just the right amount. The sundae comes with small, toasty pecans with just a hint of salt that perfectly balances the sweetness they adorn.

Up front, Beernsten's sells more than a hundred different kinds of hand-dipped candy including a chocolate cosmetology set (brush, mirror, hair dryer), smoochies (like Hershey's kisses, but bigger and more moist), raspberry and vanilla seafoam dainties, and a bon bon known as fairy food, which is a two-inch square of brittle spun sugar molasses enveloped in a sheath of deep, dark chocolate.

Bendtsen's Bakery

3200 Washington Ave., Racine, WI	$
(414) 633-0365 Mon–Sat	BL

Kringle, the delicate Danish pastry ring that has become a specialty of Racine, is not really restaurant food. Most townies buy it at a West Side bakery then eat it at home, where they butter it and consume it with a pot of coffee alongside. Still, it's a swell car snack (if you don't mind crumbs), and Bendtsen's is a good place to pick up one for the road. Flaky, sweet, and laced with your choice of nut or fruit filling, kringle is addictive food. We especially like this particular shop because it always seems to have a little plate of bite-size kringle pieces on the counter for munching while you place an order. Also, Bendtsen's bakers are responsible for the World's Largest Kringle (photo evidence is posted on the wall).

Charcoal Inn

1313 S. 8th St., Sheboygan, WI (920) 458-6988;	$
also at 1637 Geele Ave. in Sheboygan 458-1147	LD

Nothing but a simple town sandwich shop, the Charcoal Inn is a leading source of the great Wisconsin sausage known as a brat. (Rhyme brat with hot; it's short for bratwurst.) It is served in a sandwich, and connoisseurs order a double. A Charcoal Inn double brat is brought to the table without a plate. It is wrapped in wax paper, which you unfold and use as a dropcloth to catch dripping condiments. Each brat is slit and flattened before getting grilled, which makes for easy stacking in the bun. These are brats from Henry Poth, the esteemed butcher shop just down 8th Street, and they are deeply perfumed with spices that burst into blossom when they sizzle over a smoky charcoal fire. Thick and resilient but thoroughly tooth-tender, they are as savory as sausage can be, oozing a delectable blend of meat juice and the pure melted butter with which they are basted when they come off the grill.

For dessert after a brat, you need a torte. The Charcoal Inn's lemonade torte is a square about four by four inches wide and two inches high. It is white and smooth, sitting on a pallet of graham cracker crumbs, and it tastes like a pint of cream that has been reduced, thickened, and sweetened. It is similar in texture to a cheesecake, but it is so pure and rich you want to call it cream cake.

Chili John's	
519 S. Military Ave., Green Bay, WI	**$**
(920) 494-4624 Mon–Sat	**£Đ**

reen Bay chili, a bowl full of spaghetti noodles, beans, meat sauce, and flavored oil, was invented by "Chili John" Isaac, who opened a diner in downtown Green Bay in 1913. Although several restaurants in Wisconsin now serve their own variation of Chili John's spicy concoction, the best place to eat it is at Chili John's, now operated by his descendants. Hereabouts they call it "Texas style," referring to the fact that it's peppery; but in fact, it's unique. Made from ground round and a kaleidoscope of secret spices, the meat sauce would be unbearably hot by itself. But with noodles and beans, cheese and oyster crackers and maybe a dab or two of sour cream to cushion the blow, it is irresistibly delicious. The recommended beverage to accompany a bowl of Chili John's brew is milk.

Crocus	
1801 S. Muskego, Milwaukee, WI (414) 643-6383	**$**
£ Mon–Fri; Đ Fri and Sat (hours vary seasonally)	**£**

hite barszcz is a safe bet," the Crocus waitress says as we consider which of the day's five soups to have with our meal. "If you haven't been raised on czarnina, you might not like it." Czarnina is indeed a strange brew—syrup-brown and sweet, thick with little dumplings, beans, shreds of duck, and plump raisins—the hallmark of every neighborhood Polish restaurant in Milwaukee. Barszcz is a smoky harvest of sausage, ham, potato, and pieces of hard-cooked egg. We also like the aromatic dill pickle soup, which is pale porcelain green with little potatoes, and the red barszcz, a thin broth loaded with beets and onions.

After soup, this neighborhood tavern offers many fine Polish specialties, including braised beef roll-ups filled with a tangy bacon-mushroom mix, and pierogi stuffed with meat, cheese, or kraut and mushrooms. The potato pancakes are the star of the menu, with a refined, lacy texture and a fetching sour taste like something an expert grandmother would make—a fine companion to the fish fry Crocus has every Friday night.

Gosse's Drive-Thru

2928 N. 13th St., Sheboygan, WI	$
(920) 457-7784	£D

Gosse's lets you enjoy Sheboygan bratwurst without leaving your vehicle. Just like at a franchise, you sit behind the wheel and holler into a microphone, then drive forward, pay, and pick up your sandwiches. (There are a handful of picnic tables outside the shack, which is hardly bigger than an ATM booth.) The brats are delectable porky patties, bathed in butter and adorned with pickle slices, raw onion, and mustard. It is also worth noting that perch is always on the menu. Nearly every restaurant around here serves it, but most do so only as part of the ritual Friday fish fry. It is remarkable fish for a fast-food type of operation, sweet and delicate, sheathed in a chewy golden crust.

Jessica's

524 E. Layton Ave., Milwaukee, WI	$
(414) 744-1119	£D

Jessica's is a 1950s-theme burger-and-malt shop with pink walls, a free jukebox, an Elvis clock, and an impressive soda fountain menu. Made with gorgeous creamy frozen custard, the shakes and malts are too thick for a straw; a "heavy" version adds an extra scoop of luxurious custard. We especially recommend the turtle sundaes—custard topped with hot fudge, caramel, toasted pecans, whipped cream, and a cherry—available in four sizes, ranging from Junior to Special, the latter big enough for two (or four) to share. Jessica's hamburgers come the Milwaukee way, with butter melting on top of the patty and sopping the top half of the bun.

Karl Ratzsch's

320 E. Mason St., Milwaukee, WI (414) 276-2720	$$$
(an early dining menu, from 4 PM to 6 PM, is under $15 per person)	D

This grand restaurant has been justly famous since 1904 for its German food, served by a staff of consummate professionals in a civilized dining room of dark woodwork, antique steins, and romantic murals. The old-world menu includes such stalwart classics as liver-dumpling soup, roast goose shank, beef rouladen, and sauerbraten with gingersnap gravy. There are five German beers on tap and a whole array of kümmel, Kirschwasser, and Rumpleminze liqueurs for after dinner. Meals start with wonderful anisette and fennel rolls, and there isn't a more beautiful roast duck in the state of Wisconsin. But here's a secret: the non-German food is grand, too. Steaks and prime rib are utterly regal (get Ratzsch's thick, crusty potato pancakes on the side), and the whitefish is a Great Lakes treasure—tender, sweet, and juicy—served on a wood plank in a ring of mashed potatoes.

Kewpee Lunch

520 Wisconsin Ave., Racine, WI (414) 634-9601	$
Mon–Sat (closes at 6 PM)	BLD

America's least-known hamburger chain has two shops in Lima, Ohio, two in Lansing, Michigan, and this one in downtown Racine, which is almost completely engulfed by a modern parking lot. Despite its modern Formica and clean orange Naugahyde decor, there is a nice antiquated vintage feel about this old burger shop, where a case along one wall is filled with Kewpee dolls. The root beer is homemade; the hamburgers are slim, lunch-counter classics (we recommend a double); and the house motto, inscribed on the paper napery, is inspired: "Hamburger, pickle on top, makes your heart go flippety-flop."

Kopp's Frozen Custard	
Three locations: 5373 N. Port Washington Rd., Glendale, WI	$
(414) 961-3288; 18880 W. Bluemound Rd., Brookfield	£D
(414) 789-9490; and 7631 W. Layton Ave., Greenfield (414) 282-4312	

Kopp's, a joyful place with butter-basted burgers and merry eaters chowing down wherever they can find a place to lean, inside or out, is always mobbed. Sundaes are the specialty of the house.

The sundaes Kopp's makes are so elaborate that there is a brochure at the order counter with diagrams pointing out various ingredients and their place in the architecture of each concoction. The blueprint for the staggering Kopp's Special details pineapple and raspberry sauces, sliced bananas, hot fudge, toasted pecans, and a cherry on top.

The sauces are excellent and the toasted nuts are a revelation, but the foundation is the important part, and at Kopp's it is ivory-white custard made from pure, high-butterfat ingredients with none of the thickeners and stabilizers that gunk up ordinary ice cream. Custard like this is a Wisconsin passion. It is hypnotic to watch it ooze from great silver machines behind the counter. To taste it is to know why Kopp's has been a beloved Milwaukee institution since Elsie Kopp opened her first stand in 1950. Vanilla is superb—the true custard-head's choice—but Kopp's makes a new and different flavor every single day of the year. Last visit we had wonderful Palermo lemon, but it cannot surpass the glorious caramel apple with mixed nuts that was the featured attraction August 31, 1995.

Norske Nook	
207 W. 7th St., Osseo, WI	$
(715) 597-3069	BLD

Although the Norske Nook is a full-menu, meat-and-potatoes town café that even cooks up such Norwegian specialties as lutefisk and lefse at Christmas, most passersby hop off I-94 at Osseo for one reason only: to eat pie. There are always at least a dozen kinds on display, including sweet, buttery rhubarb, berries of all kinds, and mincemeat with rum sauce. Sour cream raisin pie is our personal favorite, cut into titanic slices, cream-sweet ivory custard full of plump raisins, heaped high with ethereal meringue, and piled into a wafer-crisp crust. With a cup of good coffee, this exhilarating pastry has become the Holy Grail for many traveling gastronomes.

Penguin	
3900 Calumet Ave., Manitowoc, WI	$
(920) 684-6403	LD

At this snazzy drive-in, Badger State burger hounds dine in the comfort of their vehicles, on little wire trays that hook onto the window brought to them by uniformed carhops. (There is also counter service inside.)

"Charco grilled" sandwiches are the specialty of the house, including deliciously spiced bratwurst, available as a single link or, in the locally preferred configuration, as a double sandwich. For the latter, two four-inchers with wicked char marks on their crackling crisp skin are split and stuffed into a rugged-crusted (but tender inside) hard roll. Order a double brat with everything and the sausages are smothered with ketchup, diced onions, and a couple of pickle slices.

On the side, good onion rings and French fries can be had, but many customers, whose loyalty to Dairy State foods is inbred, choose cheese nuggets in their place. These are bite-size curds of buttery orange cheese enveloped in glistening golden coats of batter. Like charcoal-cooked brats, they are a local passion.

The other true Wisconsin taste at the Penguin is custard, which is as different from ordinary ice cream as champagne is from jug wine. Made fresh daily at the Penguin, it is an elegant off-white color, smooth as ivory, and richer than top cream. Get it plain in a bowl, atop a piece of pie, as the foundation for a sundae or a jumbo milk shake, or by the pint to savor for miles.

Real Chili

419 E. Wells, Milwaukee, WI	$
(414) 271-4042	£D

Wisconsin has its own way with chili. Here at Real Chili in Milwaukee, they pile spiced ground beef atop limp spaghetti noodles and beans and call it a Marquette. You specify if you want the chili mild, medium, or hot and if you want an extra dollop of spicy grease from the pot ladled on top. The grease makes it all the more luscious. In this fine old parlor in downtown Milwaukee, you can also garnish the meal with a choice of sour cream, cheese, and/or onions, and accompany it with a bowl of crunchy oyster crackers to cleanse the palate.

Rupp's Lodge

925 N. 8th St., Sheboygan, WI	$$
(920) 459-8155	£D

A plump grilled steak, bathed in butter, is what has drawn customers to this supper club in downtown Sheboygan for well over half a century. Start with a trip to the salad bar, which includes bean salads, pasta salads, pickled herring, cheese and sausage, slaw, corn niblets, and even little bowls of butterscotch pudding if you cannot wait for dessert. On the side, have a stack of crisp hash browns. Beyond steak, there is excellent charcoal-cooked bratwurst, roast duck is featured Saturday, perch and walleye fish fries on Friday, and sauerbraten Wednesday. These hearty meals are served in a comfortable dining room with snug booths and a beautiful glassed-in kitchen along one side, and on weekend evenings, Don Van serenades from the piano bar. It is all very

Great American Steak Houses

We admire these places not just because they serve juicy steaks, good potatoes, and icy martinis, but also because they have ambiance well suited to eating red meat in abundance. That ambiance can vary dramatically—Doe's is downhome, Del Frisco's Double Eagle is superswank, Gene & Georgetti's is old-neighborhood comfortable, the Far Western is cowboy-casual—but every one, in its own way, will make you proud to be a carnivore.

- 801 Steak and Chop House, Des Moines, IA (p. 198)
- Buckhorn Exchange, Denver, CO (p. 281)
- Cattlemen's Steak House, Fort Worth, TX (p. 307)
- Cattlemen's, Oklahoma City, OK (p. 297)
- Club El Toro, Hudson, WY (p. 265)
- Del Frisco's Double Eagle Steak House, Dallas, TX (p. 308)
- Dodd's Town House, Indianapolis, IN (p. 192)
- Doe's Eat Place, Little Rock, AR (p. 128)
- Doe's Eat Place, Greenville, MS (p. 167)
- Dreisbach's, Grand Island, NE (p. 259)
- Eddie's, Great Falls, MT (p. 250)
- Far Western Tavern, Guadalupe, CA (p. 339)
- Gene & Georgetti, Chicago, IL (p. 184)
- Golden Ox, Kansas City, MO (p. 218)
- Hereford House, Kansas City, MO (p. 219)
- Jess & Jim's, Kansas City, MO (p. 221)
- Jesse's Embers, Des Moines, IA (p. 201)
- Murray's, Minneapolis, MN (p. 213)
- Peter Luger, Brooklyn, NY (p. 70)
- Ponder Steak House, Ponder, TX (p. 318)
- Rainwater's, San Diego, CA (p. 346)
- Svilar's, Hudson, WY (p. 270)
- Tea Steak House, Tea, SD (p. 264)
- Wolf Lodge Inn, Coeur d'Alene, ID (p. 249)

decent and midwestern, a place Rotarians in Sansabelt slacks take their wives on Friday night.

Solly's Coffee Shop	
4629 North Port Washington Rd., Milwaukee, WI	$
(414) 332-8808 Tues–Sat	BLD

Solly's motto goes over big in Wisconsin, if not with today's nutrition police: "Food should be cooked with lots of love and lots of butter." The waitresses, who handle their chores without a pad and pencil, are pretty darn lovable, and there is butter in abundance on Solly's hamburgers, which fans refer to as sliders for their slippery, can't-stop-eatin'-'em unctuousness. They are itty-bitty burgers, topped with aromatic stewed onions and literally dripping with butter—a genuine taste of Wisconsin, especially when accompanied by one of Solly's thick malts, served in its silver mixing beaker.

Terese's	
1034 Michigan Ave., Sheboygan, WI	$
(920) 458-2551	LD

It seems like there is a tavern on every corner in Sheboygan, a city particularly well endowed with Wisconsin's fundamental Three Bs: beer, bratwurst, and bowling. Our search for the quintessential corner tavern took us to Tiny's, where the ambiance is flawless and the charcoal-cooked brats are delish. Tiny's has since become Terese's but the dining experience is still a Wisconsin classic.

Perch on a stool at a bar that has a shaggy rug to cushion your knees, drink Pabst from the tap, and admire the big softball trophy on display. The brats are massive sausages, blushing pink with crackling crisp casing that bursts apart at first bite. They are generally sold in pairs, the twin tubes sticking out from both sides of a fresh hard roll, and unless you say otherwise, you get the works: pickle, mustard, ketchup, and a big raw onion slice. Presented in paper held around the sandwich by a single toothpick, this double brat is one of the best packages in a brat-crazed town—an impeccable combination of sausage and roll, with the added attraction of the exemplary taproom setting.

Three Brothers	
2414 S. St. Clair St., Milwaukee, WI	*$$*
(414) 481-7530 Tues–Sun	*D*

A handsome corner tavern that was once a Schlitz brewery, Three Brothers is the sort of place that makes eating in Milwaukee such a tasty trip around the world. Established by a trio of refugees in 1956, it serves Serbian cuisine; its main specialty is the *burek*, which is an Eastern European cognate of the burrito, in this case wrapped in filo dough and containing a spicy beef or spinach/cheese filling. Meals start with a wonderful chopped green salad strewn with creamy crumbles of goat cheese; and if you don't order a *burek*, the other great thing to eat is lamb, slow-roasted until you can easily separate a bite-size piece with the edge of a fork.

Watt's Tea Shop	
761 N. Jefferson St., Milwaukee, WI	*$*
(414) 291-5120	*£*

Oh, what demure culinary charms there are to savor in the lunch-room on the second floor of George Watt & Son, a century-old shop that sells fine china and crystal, where the menu is a paean to the art of ladies' lunch. In Watt's tea room you can sip a Waterford spritzer (lemonade, lime, sparkling water) or a cold Russian (coffee, chocolate, whipped cream), munch a lovely little sandwich of minced chicken or ripe olives and nuts on tender-crumbed, freshly baked bread, and indulge in a slice of filled sunshine cake, made using the same good recipe that Watt's cooks have used for decades.

How polite is this ladies-lunch oasis? During one recent visit we picked up a brochure for "Etiquette Classes for Children" being given nearby, promising instruction in social skills for polite society: eye contact, "the personality of a handshake," enunciation, telephone manners, chewing gum (not!), and a list of theater-goers' no-no's that includes such controversial topics as "talking, humming, tapping fingers or toes, and opening cellophane-wrapped candies."

Great Plains

ALL-AMERICAN

IDAHO

MONTANA

NEBRASKA

NORTH DAKOTA

SOUTH DAKOTA

WYOMING

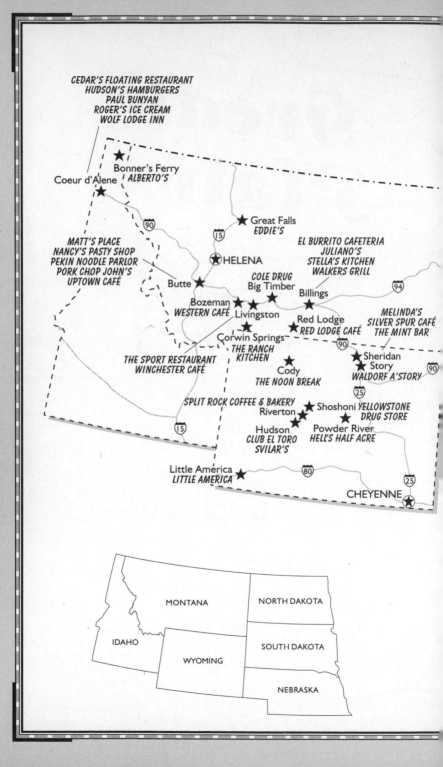

CEDAR'S FLOATING RESTAURANT
HUDSON'S HAMBURGERS
PAUL BUNYAN
ROGER'S ICE CREAM
WOLF LODGE INN

Bonner's Ferry
ALBERTO'S

Coeur d'Alene

Great Falls
EDDIE'S

90

15

HELENA

EL BURRITO CAFETERIA
JULIANO'S
STELLA'S KITCHEN
WALKERS GRILL

MATT'S PLACE
NANCY'S PASTY SHOP
PEKIN NOODLE PARLOR
PORK CHOP JOHN'S
UPTOWN CAFÉ

Butte

COLE DRUG
Big Timber

Billings

94

Bozeman
WESTERN CAFÉ Livingston

Red Lodge
RED LODGE CAFÉ

MELINDA'S
SILVER SPUR CAFÉ
THE MINT BAR

Corwin Springs
THE RANCH
KITCHEN

90

THE SPORT RESTAURANT
WINCHESTER CAFÉ

Cody
THE NOON BREAK

Sheridan
Story
WALDORF A'STORY

90

25

SPLIT ROCK COFFEE & BAKERY
Riverton

Shoshoni *YELLOWSTONE*
DRUG STORE

Hudson
CLUB EL TORO
SVILAR'S

Powder River
HELL'S HALF ACRE

Little America
LITTLE AMERICA

80

15

25

CHEYENNE

MONTANA

NORTH DAKOTA

IDAHO

SOUTH DAKOTA

WYOMING

NEBRASKA

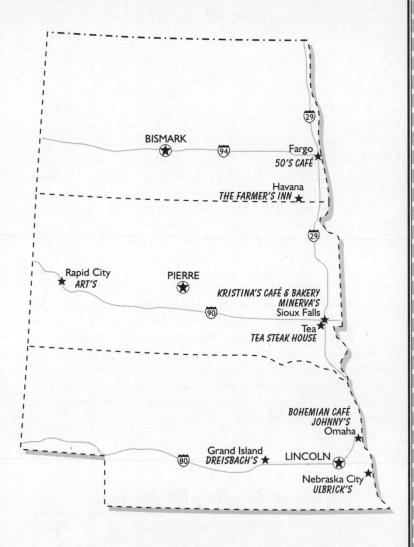

BISMARK ★ 94

Fargo ★
50'S CAFÉ

29

Havana
THE FARMER'S INN ★

29

Rapid City
ART'S ★

PIERRE ★

KRISTINA'S CAFÉ & BAKERY
MINERVA'S
Sioux Falls ★

90

Tea ★
TEA STEAK HOUSE

BOHEMIAN CAFÉ
JOHNNY'S
Omaha ★

80   Grand Island   LINCOLN ★
DREISBACH'S ★

Nebraska City ★
ULBRICK'S

GREAT PLAINS

IDAHO

Alberto's

6536 S. Main, Bonners Ferry ID	$$
(208) 267-7493	LD

An hour north of Coeur d' Alene, just short of the Canadian border, is a log cabin restaurant with a surprise inside. "Welcome to Mexico!" Alberto Mier y Teran says to newcomers who are stunned to find the heavy-timbered dining room gaily decorated with Mexican folk art, masks, ceramics, and a beautiful pinata. With his wife Concepcion, Alberto has created a citadel of exciting south-of-the-border fare that bears no resemblance to the franchised tacos that proliferate along highways. The Mier y Terans are artists from Mexico City, and their menu reflects the cosmopolitan traditions of their birthplace as well as a harvest from Northwest farmers markets, local gardens, and chili-growing friends. Here you can eat a meal called Azteca—corn tortillas layered with chicken and cheese and blanketed with a dark poblano molé redolent of herbs and Mexican chocolate, rich with almonds and spiced with seven different chilies. Tostadas are served with shredded beef so succulent it seems to melt on the tongue; beans "ranchero" sparkle with an infusion of fresh-tomato salsa; dessert cheesecake is gilded with local huckleberries.

Cedars Floating Restaurant

1 Marine Dr., just off Hwy. 95 S. of Coeur d'Alene, ID	$$
(208) 664-2922	D

Have you walked on water lately? You will to reach Cedars Floating Restaurant, a seafood house that has been moored about a hundred yards out on Lake Coeur d'Alene at the head of the Spokane River since 1965. Down a wooden walkway from the parking lot, arriving diners pass ducks looking for a handout and seagulls on pilings ready to swoop down and steal things from the ducks. Now permanently berthed on 300 tons of concrete, Cedars does not bob with the waves (as the original structure did!); but the window tables are virtually on the waterline. We happened to visit on a drizzly autumn day when the lake was steel gray, reflecting stormy skies and low clouds creeping down over a forested horizon.

A crackling fire and the lively sounds of an open kitchen provide cozy ambiance to the spacious circular dining room, where every seat looks out over magnificent scenery. The multipage menu has something for everyone, but the blackboard in the entryway tells what's special: fresh fish. Salmon, ahi, sea bass, halibut, shark, and mahimahi are some of the frequently available choices; they are cut into thick filets and charcoal broiled, served with a choice of clear lemon butter caper sauce, tropical fruit salsa, or cucumber dill sauce. Our Hawaiian wahoo was a gorgeous piece of meat, well over an inch thick, firm and sweet-fleshed with a savory crust from the grill. It came with a handsome baked potato with tawny skin and creamy insides. Followed by fresh raspberry crème brûlée for dessert, it was an exemplary meal.

Hudson's Hamburgers

207 Sherman Ave., Coeur d' Alene, ID (208) 664-5444	$
Mon—Sat	LD

Hudson's, which began as a Coeur d'Alene lunch tent in 1907, is a burger joint that locals adore. On the main street of town with a long row of sixteen stools facing the grill, it serves no French fries or potato chips, in fact no side dishes whatsoever. Just drinks to wash the burgers down and pies for dessert. But who needs frills? These griddle-cooked, hand-formed hamburgers, dressed with a thin slice of raw onion and eight sliced-to-order pickle chips, then crowned with a squirt of Hudson's hot ketchup, are American classics. Do not visit the Idaho panhandle without enjoying a meal in this beef-eater's paradise—preferably a double burger, with a glass of cold buttermilk on the side.

Paul Bunyan	
602 Northwest Blvd., Coeur d'Alene, Idaho (208) 664-2725;	$
also at N. 700 Idaho St. in Post Falls (773-6714) and 8625	£D
Government Way in Hayden (762-2320)	

A good stop any time of year for twin-patty Paul Bunyan burgers or Lumber Jack Burgers (with, ham, cheese, and bacon), or dogs and burgers smothered with Coney Island sauce, this trio of fast-food huts is especially noteworthy from July through September: huckleberry season. The one problem with Bunyan's huckleberry milk shakes is that they simply will not go up a straw. Aside from the fact that the shakes are super-thick, the dark sweet berries are only partially pulverized, so bits and pieces of them inevitably get stuck, forcing you to constantly lift the bottom of the straw from the foamy drink and suck out chunks of purple fruit.

Hamburgers and huckleberry shakes have been a happy late summer ritual in Idaho's panhandle since the first Paul Bunyan opened in 1958.

Roger's Ice Cream	
1224 Sherman Ave., Coeur d'Alene, ID (208) 765-5419	$
(closed in winter)	£D

A Coeur d'Alene delectation since 1940, Roger's has moved from the heart of downtown towards the eastern end of Sherman Ave., where it now inhabits a little red hut with green picnic tables on the side. Burgers and ice cream are its main attractions, especially the ice cream, which is homemade. As long as huckleberries are available (usually from mid-summer through September), dark purple huckleberry ice cream is the connoisseur's choice. Like all the flavors, it is a friendly sort of custard quite unlike the overpowering superrich (and superexpensive) premium brands. This is the sort of sweet you don't mind having in a bowl at lunch after a couple of hamburgers with the works, then again in a cone after dinner, for strolling in the evening air.

Wolf Lodge Inn

Exit 22 off I-90, Coeur d' Alene, ID	*$$*
(208) 664-6665	*D*

A red barn-board roadhouse just yards from the highway with a cow-bell that clangs when the front door opens, the Wolf Lodge Inn is a sprawling wild-west eatery with miscellaneous booths and dining nooks in several rooms. At the back of the rearmost dining area is a stone barbecue pit where tamarack and cherrywood burn a few feet below the grate. On this grate sizzle handsome slabs of beef ranging from sixteen-ounce sirloins and demure filets mignon to porterhouses well over two pounds.

You can start with a plate of "swinging steak"—sliced and deep-fried bull testicles, served with cocktail sauce and lemon wedges—or a pleasant salad or good homemade soup. Dinners come with saucy buckaroo beans, a twist of krebel (fried bread), and either a baked potato or steak fries, each of which is one-eighth of a good-size potato that has been sliced end-to-end and fried so that it develops a light, crisp skin and creamy insides. The beef is delicious, not too crusty but loaded with juice, well-seasoned with salt and pepper and redolent of the burning wood over which it was cooked.

MONTANA

Cole Drug

136 McLeod, Big Timber, MT (406) 932-5316	*$*
Mon–Sat 9AM–5PM	*BL*

There is a swell restaurant for epicures in the unspoiled community of Big Timber at the old Grand Hotel, and there is a jim-dandy tavern called the Timber Bar, where the American cheese poppers go great with a night's worth of beers or brandies. But the place that wins our heart is the soda fountain at Cole Drug. The food menu is limited to microwaved hot dogs, Polish sausages, cheeseburgers, and soup with crackers, but the ice cream special menu is spectacular. Sidle up to the bar and plow into a Sweetheart (chocolate ice cream topped with caramel, marshmallow, peanuts, and whipped cream), or a Montana milk shake (made with ice cream, syrup, and peanut butter), or, if you're really hungry, a Big Timber. That's nine scoops of ice cream, six different sauces, whipped cream, and nuts.

Eddie's	
3725 2nd Ave., Great Falls, MT	*$$*
(406) 453-1616	*LD*

Eddie's menu features many Italian specialties, including homemade ravioli that regular customers extol, and nice-looking chicken and fish and even salad, but there is one spectacularly good reason to come to Great Falls (other than the Charles M. Russell Museum): Eddie's campfire steak. "Campfire" means marinated, which they'll do to any size steak. Our preference is the king tenderloin: big and juicy and easy to slice (but not *too* easy), one of these beauties is just what an appetite demands in Big Sky country. It is all the tastier for Eddie's impeccable supper-club ambiance, which includes slick upholstery in gold metal–flaked red vinyl.

El Burrito Cafeteria	
310 N. 29th, Billings, MT (406) 256-5234	*$*
Mon–Sat; *BL* Sat; closed Sun	*BLD*

El Burrito is a cheap, quick cafeteria that bills its food as "California Style Mexican." Whatever style it is, it's the best for miles around. We favor the hefty burritos filled with a choice of pork chunks, Mexican sausage, or *machaca* (shredded beef) and smothered with green or red chili. We also love the soft-shell tacos piled high with beef, the simple bowl of spicy chili beans, and the tamale plate with rice and fresh red salsa. And although we don't necessarily *love* it, menudo is on the menu, too; so if you are a tripe fancier, here ya go.

El Burrito is a small one-room storefront that is very cramped. Place your order at the kitchen window in back, pile your tray with tortilla chips, hot sauce, and diced pickled jalapéño peppers, then search for a seat. When your food is ready, a woman calls from the kitchen—not by your name or a number, but by what you have ordered. So it's important to remember exactly what you picked from the menu. The meal is presented on a flimsy, disposable plate that is piled so high, edge to edge, that carrying it back to your seat in this crowded dining room can be a precarious operation.

All sorts of citizens of Billings dine here, including well-dressed executives apparently from downtown businesses despite the boast atop the El Burrito menu that it is "The Working Person's Eating Place."

Juliano's

2912 7th Ave. N., Billings, MT (406) 248-6400	$$
£ Mon–Fri; 𝔇 Wed–Sat	£𝔇

Juliano's outdoor patio is one of the nicest places in Montana to enjoy a civilized summer meal, perfumed by the breeze, under umbrellas outside the old stone house that was once a livery stable. Any time of year, chef Carl Kurokawa's interesting menu is a joy for anyone in search of sophisticated New American meals. We have savored such hors d'oeuvres as battered chicken and grapefruit salad, pan roasted portobello mushroom with summer vegetable broth, and seared peppered ostrich on field greens with cranberry vinaigrette. Memorable beefy dinner entrees include a gorgeous garlicked strip steak served with corn fritters, as well as a most unusual lobster-rich fried rice topped with steak. One day at lunch, we swooned over the freshwater savor in a grilled slab of flathead whitefish and also enjoyed an impeccably fine hamburger on a fresh baked bun.

Matt's Place

Montana St. and Rowe Rd., Butte, MT (406) 782-8049	$
Tues–Sat	£𝔇

Pristine and painted white, Matt's is a vest-pocket drive-in restaurant over a half century old. It is tiny, without room for tables, just a short curved counter and a bright red, waist-high Coke machine, the kind in which the bottles tinkle when you pry open the top to fetch one.

No jukebox plays; your serenade comes from the back kitchen— the sound of hamburgers sizzling slowly on a grill—and from the low chatter of other customers. One afternoon we were entranced by a quartet of elderly Butte ladies, with immaculately coiffed white hair in tidy permanent waves, who came in for pork chop sandwiches with heaps of honeytone French fries and pink strawberry milk shakes.

The soda fountain behind the counter is fully equipped with six wands for blending shakes, dispensers for syrup, and three tall seltzer spouts; the menu lists root beer floats, ice cream sodas, malted milks, and nut sundaes. The hot food menu features chili con carne and all sorts of hamburgers, including a Wimpy special (two patties on one bun) and a hamburger with an egg on top.

Nancy's Pasty Shop

2810 Pine, Butte, MT (406) 782-7410	$
Mon–Sat	£𝔇

Nancy's is an eat shack that sells mighty fine pocket meals at a short counter inside or at a take-out window for workers on the go. Pasties were originally brought to America from Cornwall; miners carried them down to the mines and ate them for lunch. They became a staple here in Butte and are now one of the Treasure State's signature dishes. There are several reputable places in town to eat them, including Joe's and Gamer's, but we like Nancy's best of all. Huge, with a lush crust that cleaves into see-through flakes if you rub it in your fingers, each pasty weighs at least a couple pounds and is loaded with a mouth-watering, onion-flavored melange of coarse-cut beef and little chunks of potato. Not only are they simple and delicious food, easily eaten out of hand, these pasties are an edible tradition, an authentic taste of a culture brought West by those who worked the mines.

Pekin Noodle Parlor

117 S. Main, Butte, MT (406) 782-2217	$
Wed—Mon	D

Pekin Noodle Parlor is a relic of Butte's boom days as a mining town, when the small street out back was known as China Alley. An ancient sign on the wall says *famous since 1916*.

Climb a small dark staircase to the second floor of the antique building and you will be escorted to your own curtained dining cubicle. The setting suggests exotic intrigue, like an old Montana version of the Shanghai Express. When the food comes from the kitchen, it is announced by the rumble of the waitress's rolling trolley along the wood-plank floor; the curtain whisks aside, and behold! Here is a vista of foreign food the likes of which most devotees of Asian cookery forgot about forty years ago. Chop suey and chow mein are mild, thick, and harmless; fried shrimp are girdled by a pad of breading and served on leaves of lettuce with French fried potatoes as a garnish; sweet and sour ribs drip pineapple-flavored syrup; and the house specialty, noodles, comes in a shimmering clear broth with scallions chopped on top. Get the noodles plain or accompanied by strips of pork, beef, or chicken served on the side in a little bowl with half a hard-boiled egg.

The after-dinner drink menu-that-time-forgot includes separators, stingers, White Russians, and pink squirrels. The thing to drink before a meal is a ditch—Montanese for whiskey and water.

Pork Chop John's

8 Mercury St., Butte, MT (406) 782-0812	$
Mon–Sat	£𝒟

ork chop sandwiches are now sold in many Montana restaurants, but the place they were invented, and the cognoscenti's choice, is a hole in the wall on Mercury Street known as Pork Chop John's. Although minuscule, John's is easy to spot by the sign hanging out over the street, which portrays three smiling pork chops named Wholesome, Healthful, and Delicious.

The sandwiches are patties of ground pork, breaded and fried to a crisp and served "loaded," which means topped with pickle chips, mustard, and onions. (Mayo, cheese, and ketchup are also available, but must be specified.) They are a savory splurge—crunch-crusted and luscious inside. Enjoy them at John's small counter or at one of three alfresco tables on the sidewalk, from which you have a view of the cramped back street that was the heart of Butte's once-thriving (but now extinct) Chinatown.

The Ranch Kitchen

Hwy. 89, Corwin Springs, MT (406) 848-7891	$
£𝒟 daily; 𝓑 Sun	𝓑£𝒟

his rustic, family-style restaurant serves healthful fare—sandwiches on tweedy whole grain bread, fruit-sweetened sweet rolls, hearty soups, pastas, stir fries, and fresh berry pies. One day at breakfast, we delighted in hot peach muffins and bowls of warm oatmeal topped with puckery-sweet berry syrup. Such nutritionally enlightened fare is rare in restaurants in this part of the world, the sign of an unusual culinary consciousness. Only if you stop next door at the Cinnabar General Store and browse through the religious books for sale does it become apparent that the Ranch Kitchen does indeed have a different slant on life. Like everything for miles around in Paradise Valley, it is owned and operated by Elizabeth Claire Prophet's Church Universal and Triumphant, which apparently believes in eating well right up until the forthcoming apocalypse.

Red Lodge Café

16–18 South Broadway, Red Lodge, MT	$
(406) 446-1619	BLD

Where the locals eat (and tourists, too), the Red Lodge Café is a comfy old-fashioned lunchroom with a stamped tin ceiling, wagon wheel chandeliers, and painted murals of local scenery (white water, the Beartooth Mountains) separated by varnished wooden totem poles. It is a good place to eat a buffalo burger or a regular cow burger, and a midday special we like is tuna noodle casserole (a classic, with pale canned peas on the side). On one occasion, we were surprised and delighted by mighty tasty chicken stir-fry on rice.

The time that's best in this place is just after six in the morning, when the clientele is mostly working Montanans, the whole wheat, blueberry, buckwheat, or sourdough pancakes are piled high, and table-to-table gabfests are conducted about the hot topics of the day.

The Sport Restaurant

114 S. Main, Livingston, MT	$
(406) 222-3533	LD

A real western café/bar known in rowdier times simply as the Beer Hall, the Sport now makes a specialty of burger toppings, which range from beefy chili to a slice of pineapple for the marinated teriyaki burger, plus a long list of "NYO" (name your own) hamburger adornments that include hot or mild peppers, salsa, salad dressing, and assorted cheeses. Proprietor Suzanne Schneider also offers a fine pork chop sandwich ("John's original" her menu says, referring to Pork Chop John's of Butte, where it was invented) and delicious malts and shakes dispensed in tall silver beakers. For dessert, there's apple or peach pie, made from Suzanne's grandmother's recipe. The pie is cut in big homey squares, like shortcake, and demands a scoop of ice cream as its companion.

The Sport's dining room decor is a hoot: there are mounted animal heads and an extraordinarily long rattlesnake skin, a couple of old shotguns hanging in nooses from the ceiling, and stacks of vintage magazines and newspapers for customers to browse.

Stella's Kitchen

110 N. 29th St., Billings, MT	$
(406) 248-3060	BLD

Stella's is a modern lunchroom with a bakery in back. Its glass cases are filled with homey loaves of sunflower wheat bread, sticky fritters and dumplings, and sour cream coffee cake.

Stella's serves three meals a day; the best one is breakfast, especially if you like warm cinnamon rolls. Stella's offers two sizes: regular, made with whole wheat flour, packed with raisins and cinnamon-sugar, with sugar frosting glistening on top; and large, which is the size of a cake for six. Caramel rolls are similarly immense, made with white flour and enveloped in sticky, mahogany-colored glaze.

"Monster cakes"—twelve-inch flapjacks—were put on the menu, Stella says, when "I had a cook who simply could not make a small pancake. So we gave up and raised the price." You have your choice of buttermilk, wheat, applesauce and cinnamon, blueberry, or blueberry wheat; portions range from one to four, and if you eat four in a single sitting, you get a free cinnamon roll.

Uptown Café

47 E. Broadway, Butte, MT (406) 723-4735	$$
L Mon–Fri; D daily	LD

Started in the mid-1980s by Susan Phillips, Barbara Kornet, and Guy Graham, this friendly bistro is now known far and wide for such fashionable dishes as grilled citrus-marinated halibut and chicken Arthur with artichoke hearts and sun-dried tomatoes. Such sophisticated food is rare in Montana; to find it prepared so well is a bonanza.

When we stopped in, Susan was busy making pesto because she had just gotten a batch of good basil, Guy was planning nightly specials that included seared tuna with mango and ginger salsa, and salmon on a julienne of summer vegetables, and Barbara guided us through the café's monthly lunch calendar, which ranges from chicken pot pie and stromboli to pasta puttanesca and Thai beef stir-fry. We delighted in a grandmotherly sausage onion soup, turkey Devonshire with zesty twice-baked potato casserole, and desserts that included a drop-dead delicious chocolate rum pound cake, creamy Bavarian apple tart, and intensely fresh black raspberry pie. It is easy to understand why, even in the winter when it's fifty degrees below zero, customers drive to the Uptown Café from as far as Red Lodge, 227 miles away (actually, not too long a trip by Montana standards).

Walkers Grill

301 N. 27th St., Billings, MT (406) 245-9291	$$
Mon–Sat	D

As soon as you tear into the breadbasket at Walkers, you know a good meal is coming your way. Crusty, faintly sour, and with a soulful chew, this is bread that is pure and simple yet an emblem of real culinary expertise. You cannot watch the bread being baked, but you can see the young masters at work in Walkers' exhibition kitchen at one end of the handsome subterranean dining room, where the modern meals are prepared in a whirl of activity.

From the comfort of "James Beard's meat loaf" with shiitake mushroom gravy and creamy mashed potatoes to Thai rock shrimp pasta sauced with a blend of cilantro and coconut milk, the far-reaching menu is a joy to browse. Pizzas, cooked on quarry tiles, have true Mediterranean character; half-pound hamburgers, accompanied by French fries and homemade ketchup, are flawlessly all-American.

Walkers is the kind of place where some people come to splurge and celebrate; others eat supper here several times a week, simply because it is the best dining room in eastern Montana.

Western Café

443 E. Main St., Bozeman, MT	$
(406) 587-0436	BLD

A cowboy hash house once known as Eat-A-Bite, the Western has been operated for the last twenty years by Dick and Alice Mierva, who inherited its prized recipe for cinnamon rolls from the former owner. The summer morning we stopped in the counter was packed, its surface worn bare at uniform intervals on either side of each stool where customers have rested their elbows for years.

Besides superb cinnamon rolls, the thing to eat is pie. In a state where pies are the pride of every town café, the Western's are outstanding. Timed by baker Annie Robinson to be carried from the kitchen at the end of the lunch hour, there are magnificent meringues, dense fruit pies, Dutch apple, and egg custard. The custard, when it is still slightly warm at one o'clock, jiggles precariously and is nursery sweet—food fit for a toothless god.

Winchester Café	
in the Murray Hotel, 201 W. Park, Livingston, MT	*$$*
(406) 222-2708	*BLD*

Montana celebrities have gravitated to the Murray Hotel for decades. Movie director Sam Peckinpah lived upstairs (and was reputed to fire his six-gun through the ceiling when on drinking binges); Calamity Jane stayed here. Today's clientele is a motley mix of residents, pilgrims, and local literary lights. In the bar, kids play electronic games and adults drink the Montana favorite, a ditch—whiskey and water. Late at night, it is not uncommon for the barroom philosophizers to raise a little hell.

The Winchester Café, located off the lobby, has a flowered rug on the floor, a wine list that fills two sides of a piece of parchment paper limp from handling, and a menu that offers turkey Oscar, shrimp scampi, and penne, as well as a range of hamburgers, sandwiches, and salads at lunch. At suppertime, a trout special is everything it ought to be in angler's paradise—chunky-fleshed, sweet and moist, gilded with maître d'hôtel butter. One late summer special, rack of lamb, came under a rich cordovan-colored sauce made from local huckleberries. Wine was served in brandy goblets. "The hotel took all our wineglasses for a function," the waiter apologized.

NEBRASKA

☆ ☆ ☆

Bohemian Café

1406 South 13th St., Omaha, NE	$$
(402) 342-9838	LD

Several years ago, while traveling through eastern Nebraska, a radio jingle lured us to the ethnic enclave of south Omaha. "It's dumplings and kraut today at the Bohemian Café," the appetizing advertisement said; and sure enough, that night in this unpretentious old-world eatery, we savored not only dumplings and kraut, but also mighty platters of tender boiled beef with dill gravy and masterfully cooked, crisp-skinned duck.

Dreisbach's

1137 S. Locust, Grand Island, NE	$$
(308) 382-5450	LD

Well-marbled, dry-aged beef has been earning Dreisbach's a loyal clientele since 1932. The restaurant has been transformed from a farmhouse into a roadhouse with all the charm of a truck stop, but no one comes for atmosphere. They come for meat. Tenderloins, T-bones, filets mignon, sirloins, and New York strips are all available, served with hot baking-powder biscuits and honey, salad with killer-garlic dressing, and lengthwise-thin-sliced potatoes topped with cheese (known as sunflowers). All-you-can-eat fried chicken is also on the menu, as is rabbit (a legacy of beef shortages during World War II), but if you are a traveler with an appetite along I-80 anywhere near Grand Island, it is steak you want.

Johnny's

4702 S. 27th St., Omaha, NE (402) 731-4774	$$
Mon–Sat	£Ð

Johnny's has been Omaha's stockyards steakhouse for three-quarters of a century. Once a café for cowboys and cow shippers, it is now a grandiose restaurant with well-upholstered chairs, broadloom carpets, and modernistic chandeliers. We love the baronial ambiance, especially because it is balanced by service that is as folksy as in any small town café, courtesy of waitresses unafraid to call you "Hon" and to scold you if you don't finish your T-bone but then want dessert. Beef, of course, is what to eat: Johnny's has every cut of steak you've ever heard of, plus liver, tongue, oxtail, and the like, all nicely cooked with decent accompaniments (except the mashed potatoes, which we don't like). Dessert is corny and ingratiating: crème de menthe sundaes, gooey turtle pie, and clear blocks of Chuckles-colored Jell-O.

Ulbrick's

Rte. 75, Nebraska City, NE (402) 873-5458	$
(reservation advised)	Ð

What road wanderer doesn't have a soft spot for restaurants located in former gas stations? Ulbrick's is one of the best, a decrepit-looking but utterly upright culinary mecca in the midlands. Its divey looks make it all the more fun for the crowds of boisterous fans who gather around the oilcloth-covered tables lined up in the back room to gaily plow through platters of crisp-fried chicken. The delicious bird is preceded by a battery of heartland "salads," served family-style, most of which could double as dessert crowded as they are with marshmallows and mandarin orange pieces; one, called "frog eye salad," is made of tapioca pudding and bite-size Funmallows in all the colors of the rainbow. Alongside the superb chicken come platters of creamed corn, creamed cabbage, ultracreamed chicken and noodles, and green beans cooked the country way—until tooth resistance is but a memory.

NORTH DAKOTA

50's Café

13 S. Eighth St., Fargo, ND (701) 298-0347	$
Mon–Sat	ℬℒ

Unable to find a truly compelling meal in Fargo, we were delighted to eat tasty half-pound hamburgers at the 50's Café. They are hand-formed jumbos, available with all the fixin's imaginable from chili and cheese to pizza sauce or avocados. The configuration we like best is called the Big Bopper, with bacon, cheese, tomato, lettuce, onion, and salad dressing, plus French fries and coleslaw on the side. Available beverages include real malts, and there is a short list of sundaes, sodas, and banana splits available from the 1950s soda fountain. (However, our recommendation for dessert is to sneak a few doors up Eighth Street to Widman's Candy Shop, where the "hot air" candy—spun molasses sheathed in chocolate—is celestial and where you can enjoy such health food Great Plains confections as chocolate-covered wheat, chocolate-covered sunflower seeds, and chocolate-covered potato chips.)

The Farmers' Inn

Havana, ND	$
(701) 724-3849	ℬℒ

Across from the grain elevators in the tiny town of Havana, the Farmers' Inn is owned and operated by a consortium of local farmers. The ladies of the town, and some of the men, take turns flipping flapjacks and cooking eggs in the morning, then making a hearty meal in the middle of the day. The menu changes according to who's on duty. We can speak highly of Murdean Gulsvig's sausage patties and pancakes in the morning, and the pork roast with mashed potatoes, dressing, and gravy that his wife, Doris, cooks for dinner. And don't forget to sign the guest register: it's an event when someone from out of town stops by. And for those of us who make the trip, it's no less an event to sit down for a meal elbow-to-elbow with the good people of Havana, North Dakota.

South Dakota

⭐ ⭐ ⭐

Art's	
1109 Omaha St., Rapid City, SD	$
(605) 355-9490	*LD*

After she and her husband took a driving/eating tour of the West two years ago, Lisa Lauterbach Laskin of Cambridge, Mass., wrote to alert us to a discovery in South Dakota: Art's. "In a strip mall and short on atmosphere," she wrote, "but the barbecue is the real stuff." It sure is! Art's meaty pork ribs are crusted with sauce and his pulled pork is butter-tender. Top it off with warm peach cobbler for dessert, and you will have enjoyed a grand taste of genuine Georgia (Art's original home state) in the shadow of Mount Rushmore.

Kristina's Café & Bakery	
334 S. Phillips Ave., Sioux Falls, SD (605) 331-4860	$
BL; BLD Wed–Sat	*BLD*

Kristina's serves the best coffee in Sioux Falls, strong and spicy. Although it tastes European (or at least Seattlean) in character, cups of it are refilled generously while you dine, service reminiscent of a good mid-American café. Downtowners occupy Kristina's bare wood tables to read the daily paper (spread out for the taking on the counter) and to savor their morning cup accompanied by toasted Italian bread, maple-frosted wheat-cinnamon rolls hot from the oven, or flaky scones. Heartier breakfasts include omelets, baked egg casserole with smoked turkey and melted cheese, and delightful buttermilk pancakes with soft, sautéed apples in the batter and maple butter on top.

Minerva's	
301 Phillips Ave., Sioux Falls, SD (605) 334-0386	*$$*
Mon–Sat	*LD*

L ike many growing cities, Sioux Falls is ringed with franchised restaurants, but the food you want to eat, served in human-scale surroundings, is downtown. In business since 1977, yet with a handsome patina that feels way older than that, Minerva's is a wood-and-tile floor establishment with white-clothed tables, ample booths, and a friendly staff that aims to please. It is *the* fine-dining place in town, where customers come for deluxe rib eye steak—aged and cut on premises—or fresh walleye pike, pan-fried or broiled. Atlantic salmon is always on the menu, and Copper River salmon from Alaska is often available in May and June. While high rollers may feast on a half a honey-glazed roast duck or Cajun fettucine, many regulars come to avail themselves only of the salad bar. It is a sparkling heartland buffet of composed salads that range from ham or pasta to creamy pink Jell-O, plus fresh fruit, and Maytag blue cheese dressing for the lettuce.

A statue of Minerva, the Roman goddess of wisdom and war, presides over the bar. The same people who run this place also operate Minerva's Market Café at 1716 Western Avenue, an upscale market that serves three meals a day and has a large selection of fancy foods and meals to go.

Tea Steak House

Tea, SD (605) 368-9667	$$
Mon—Sat	LD

Off the interstate in the tiny town of Tea, steak-lovers congregate at tables covered with seafoam green oilcloth to slice into handsome T-bones, sirloins, and filets mignon. The Tea Steak House, a low-slung, wood-paneled restaurant that shares a building with O'Toole's Bar, is one of the top beef dens of the Great Plains. Dress-up clothes are not required, but it is a weekend-splurge kind of place. On Friday nights (when fried perch joins the meaty menu), the dining room is packed with couples, families, and star-crossed carnivores on big dates.

Service, by women in nylon uniform blouses, is instantaneous. Iceberg lettuce salad arrives in a little wood-grain plastic bowl along with a silver server with three dressings you ladle on at will. The steaks are tender and juicy, available charbroiled over coals or grilled in a pan. Of the three types of potatoes, French fried and baked are nothing notable, but the hash browns, soft inside with a hard-crusted surface, are delicious. Every table is outfitted with ketchup and Heinz 57 Steak Sauce.

It is a midlands meal of the highest order. And who can resist a restaurant with this motto printed on its menu: "We're Glad You Brought Your Sugar to Tea."

WYOMING

★ ★ ★

Club El Toro

132 S. Main, Hudson, WY	$$
(307) 332-4627	D

Club El Toro is a wonderful restaurant in the tiny town of Hudson that is a destination for beef eaters from miles around. Every evening, this commodious supper club teams with happy families and friends who come to glide their knives into gorgeous rib eyes, sirloins, and filets mignon, as well as some of the largest and tastiest prime ribs anywhere. The red meat is served as part of a full-course feast that includes relish tray, salad, a plate of ravioli, and Serbian stuffed cabbage known as sarma, plus cowboy potatoes (spicy French fries). A delicious, only-in-America experience!

Hell's Half Acre

Hwy. 20–26, 5 miles west of Powder River, WY	$
(307) 472-0018	BLD

You won't have a big choice of places to eat between Casper and Riverton. In fact, you'll have none. But may we suggest that rather than starve along the way you stop at Hell's Half Acre for a snack? We make this suggestion because you will likely want to drive right past. This ramshackle tourist attraction, built around a geological anomaly that spews hot vapors, frankly looks like a rather scary roadkill café. And the day we walked in, the steam-table spaghetti that had been basking in the open for God-knows-how-long didn't do a lot to reassure us. However, the hamburgers we ordered were very tasty. In particular we enjoyed the devil burger, topped with melted Swiss cheese and chopped mild green peppers, served on a nearly elegant toasted and buttered bun, with excellent French fries on the side, and a genuine milk shake, blended as we watched, to wash it down.

We must admit that it wasn't only the devil burger that won our hearts. Decor at Hell's Half Acre includes jaw-droppingly tacky velveteen wall rugs showing bulldogs shooting billiards and brave matadors fighting bulls. The attached souvenir shop is one of the last places in America that still sells original, linen-finish postcards (of interesting nearby rock formations), not to mention rubber tomahawks and toy guns for the little 'uns.

Little America	
Exit 68 off I-80, Little America, WY (307) 875-2400	*$*
always open	*BLD*

It was late-night turkey dinner that made us like Little America: real roasted turkey, sliced thick and served with good mashed potatoes and fresh dinner rolls soft enough to mop up all the gravy. And a bowl of good chili, chock-a-bloc with hunks of beef big as meatballs. Such honest meals can be scarce along I-80 in the West. We stayed the night at this travelers' oasis, which has a clean motel attached, then had breakfast of freshly made corned beef hash and biscuits with thick sausage gravy, gooey pecan rolls on the side, and hit the road feeling fine.

Little America is not the typical sort of folksy town café we generally recommend. It's got billboards up and down the highway and a few branches elsewhere in the West. But if you are hungry in southwest Wyoming, it's a beacon.

Melinda's

57 N. Main; Sheridan, WY (307) 674-9188	$$
ℬℒ Tues–Sat; 𝒟 Wed–Sat	ℬℒ𝒟

Melinda's is a friendly, brick-wall café with many things to recommend it, including drippy-sweet caramel rolls in the morning, clever pastas at suppertime, and a repertoire of afternoon (3 PM to 5 PM) snacks, soups, and salads. What we like best is a bowlful of comfort Melinda calls the TLC Special: a heap of lumpy mashed potatoes topped with chicken noodle soup, accompanied by a few slices of fresh-baked bread. Supper can be as traditional as a grilled steak or stuffed pork chops, or you can eat more adventurously and start with whole roasted garlic bulbs (squeeze the tender cloves onto Melinda's fresh-baked bread) or grilled shrimp marinated in basil and lime, and then move on to an honest plate of fresh, grilled halibut, moist and savory, served with spicy hash brown potatoes on the side.

The Mint Bar

151 N. Main, Sheridan, WY (307) 674-9696	$
(but not really)	ℬℒ𝒟

We cannot tell a lie: The Mint Bar is no place to go if you are hungry. But if you find yourself in Sheridan, Wyoming, and hanker for a drink, or even if you don't want a drink, you must visit The Mint. Outside, its multicolored neon sign shows a wrangler mid-air on a bucking bronc with neon cattle brands like sparks around the hooves. The interior is lined entirely in cedar wood and gnarled pine burls, with rough-hewn log booths and shingle walls that gleam like slick leather. Panoramic photographs of ranch life, circa. 1941, hang alongside portraits of rodeo stars, trick riders, and Western celebrities of every stripe who consider this rugged woody grotto the *ne plus ultra* of cowboy bars.

The food menu is a short one of potato chips, nuts, and three flavors of beef jerky; and when bartender Joann Kunsman asks, "What're you having sweetie?" we advise not asking her for a brandy Alexander or a frozen frou-frou margarita. Gents and ladies sit at this bar to drink beer and/or whiskey, or a "ditch," which is the local term for whiskey and water. (A sign overhead says *Hangovers Installed And Serviced.*)

Many customers come to transact business. Sheridan has been the outfitting center of the region since before The Mint Bar opened in 1907, and its residents include leather workers, gunsmiths, cowboy haberdashers, and wilderness guides. These pros use The Mint as their office, and it is not at all unusual to see a local artisan sharing beers in a booth with a client as they go over hides or silver conchos for a saddle-in-progress.

"Nobody goes to anybody's house in this town," Ms. Kunsman explained. "Everyone meets at The Mint."

The Noon Break	
927 12th St., Cody, WY	$
(307) 587-9720	BL

It's laid back and far enough off the beaten path for few tourists to find it, but the main reason to come to The Noon Break is green chile. There are two kinds available, regular and "Code 10," the latter a hot jalapeño soup made with little chunks of pork sausage, available in a cup or bowl or as the topping of a tasty burrito in a bowl. There are a few more excellent reasons to find this small café. One is the happy breakfast hour, when regulars sip endless amounts of coffee with platters of huevos rancheros, buckwheat pancakes, or biscuits and gravy. Another is the fact that many of the zesty Mexican dishes on the short menu are in fact heart-healthy, such as the red and green chilies, posole topped with yogurt rather than sour cream, and burritos stuffed with beans or potatoes.

One last reason we like this kooky place, which is strewn with newspapers and magazines and decorated with old Wyoming license plates, is a lunchtime item listed as "Louie's Ethnic Plate." It's a Spam sandwich, grilled to order, with potato chips on the side.

Silver Spur Café

832 N. Main St., Sheridan, WY	$
(307) 672-2749	BL

The counter and back-room tables of this elbow-to-elbow little diner are where good citizens of Sheridan gather every morning starting at 6 AM. They come for hearty muffins, griddle cakes, and eggs, accompanied by cups of coffee that get topped off or refilled approximately every thirty seconds by the staff of highly opinionated waitresses who took over the old café when former owner Jan Drake passed away last year. The staff and steady customers welcome strangers into cross-counter colloquies about local news and politics, weather and sports, and all the other subjects that a good dose of morning caffeine brings to mind.

Split Rock Coffee & Bakery

108 S. 3rd East, Riverton, WY (307) 856-4334	$
Mon–Sat	BL

Culinarily speaking, Wyoming's raison d'être is beef. Although it is great to be a carnivore in the Cowboy State, here's a little tip in case you need a respite from animal protein: whole grain meals at the Split Rock Bakery. This little shop, which happens also to be an outpost of espresso, cappuccino, and all manner of modern caffeinated potions, has wheaty cinnamon rolls, healthful muffins, and oat-bran bagels in the morning, as well as noontime sandwiches that range from bizarre meatless garden burgers and tempeh reubens to perfectly tasty egg or tuna salad, cheese, or avocado. For dessert, there is a different low-fat yogurt flavor every day. It's an odd experience, but we have to admit we find it a pleasant diversion from an all-cow diet.

Svilar's

173 Main, Hudson, WY (307) 332-4516	$$
Mon—Sat, but closed alternate Mondays	D

If it's genuine cattle-country meat-and-potatoes you're after, look no further than Svilar's, a favorite high plains supper club since the 1940s. Couples, families, and hungry cowboys all come for the full-course dinner that starts with relish tray and salad, then moves on to a hot-appetizer course of ravioli and stuffed cabbage (Serbian-style). Although chicken, shrimp, and lobster tails are available, the only appropriate main course is beef—steak or prime rib, available in cuts from wee filet to multi-pound rib eye. Maybe there's dessert, maybe not. We've never even bothered to inquire, figuring that if we have any appetite for it at the end of the meal, we simply didn't order a large-enough cut of red meat.

Waldorf A'Story

at the Piney Creek Grocery, 19 North Piney Rd., Story, WY	$
(307) 683-2400 (until 7:30 PM)	BLD

The small community of Story, between Sheridan and Buffalo, has a few destination dining spots, including The Wagonbox for big slabs of succulent prime rib; but our favorite culinary attraction is the crowded, quirky log building called the Piney Creek Grocery. It is an all-purpose convenience store with everything from groceries to rental videotapes, including an inspired selection of barbeque sauces and salsas. Snugged to one side of the retail commotion is a little dining room with mismatched tables where locals come to greet the day with biscuits and gravy, fresh-baked coffee cake, or a superb breakfast sandwich of bacon, eggs, cheese, tomatoes, and onions on French bread crisped on the grill. There are handsome sandwiches at lunch, such ambitious daily specials as fry bread tacos with caramelized apples, and a Saturday night barbeque of ribs and brisket.

    Take-out meals are also available, and the menu lists the Waldorf's phone number as 683-2400-I-AIN'T-COOKIN'.

Yellowstone Drug Store

127 Main St., Shoshoni, WY	$
(307) 876-2539	LD

Since 1909, this Main Street treasure has boasted of "The best malts and shakes in the state." Made with a triple-wand shake maker behind the long counter, they are impressive—served with a spoon because their thickness defies a straw. There are fifty-nine flavors available, from Almond to Wild Cherry, and you can mix any two, allowing a connoisseur to taste a different shake every Sunday from now until the mid-twenty-first century. Yellowstone made 55,146 shakes in 1997, setting a one-day record of 624 on July 6.

Great shakes and a double bacon cheeseburger are just part of Yellowstone Drug's appeal. The store is filled with interesting merchandise, including bookends and gun racks that proprietor Ted Surrency makes from horseshoes and spurs, horsehair bridles made by an inmate at the state prison in Rawlins, and bumper stickers that say "Christian Cowboys Have More Fun."

So if you think America has become all the same and franchised, come to Shoshoni, and experience this one-of-a-kind enterprise . . . while spooning up a fine huckleberry malt.

South- west

ALL-AMERICAN

ARIZONA

COLORADO

KANSAS

NEVADA

NEW MEXICO

OKLAHOMA

TEXAS

UTAH

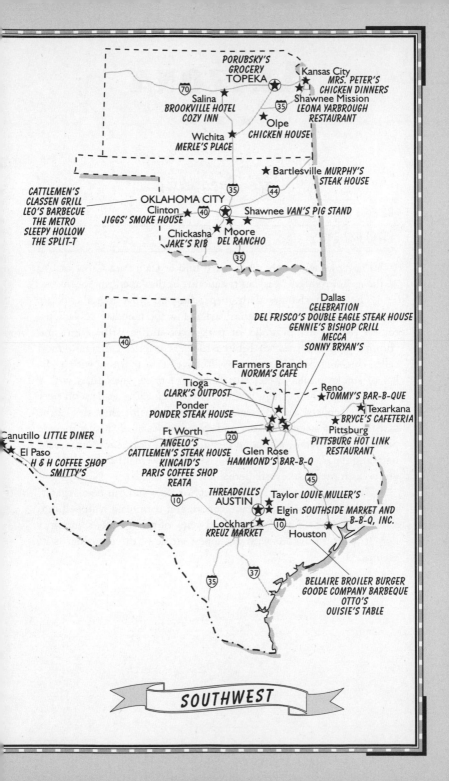

PORUBSKY'S GROCERY
TOPEKA ★

Kansas City ★
MRS. PETER'S CHICKEN DINNERS

Salina ★
BROOKVILLE HOTEL COZY INN

Shawnee Mission
LEONA YARBROUGH RESTAURANT

Olpe ★
CHICKEN HOUSE

Wichita ★
MERLE'S PLACE

★ Bartlesville **MURPHY'S STEAK HOUSE**

CATTLEMEN'S CLASSEN GRILL LEO'S BARBECUE THE METRO SLEEPY HOLLOW THE SPLIT-T

OKLAHOMA CITY ★
Clinton ★
JIGGS' SMOKE HOUSE

Shawnee **VAN'S PIG STAND**

Chickasha
JAKE'S RIB

Moore
DEL RANCHO

Dallas
CELEBRATION DEL FRISCO'S DOUBLE EAGLE STEAK HOUSE GENNIE'S BISHOP GRILL MECCA SONNY BRYAN'S

Farmers Branch
NORMA'S CAFE

Tioga
CLARK'S OUTPOST

Reno
★ **TOMMY'S BAR-B-QUE**

★ Texarkana
★ **BRYCE'S CAFETERIA**

Ponder
PONDER STEAK HOUSE

Ft Worth
ANGELO'S CATTLEMEN'S STEAK HOUSE KINCAID'S PARIS COFFEE SHOP REATA

Pittsburg
PITTSBURG HOT LINK RESTAURANT

Canutillo **LITTLE DINER**
★ El Paso
H & H COFFEE SHOP SMITTY'S

Glen Rose
HAMMOND'S BAR-B-Q

THREADGILL'S
AUSTIN ★

Taylor **LOUIE MULLER'S**

Elgin **SOUTHSIDE MARKET AND B-B-Q, INC.**

Lockhart ★
KREUZ MARKET

Houston

BELLAIRE BROILER BURGER GOODE COMPANY BARBEQUE OTTO'S OUISIE'S TABLE

SOUTHWEST

ARIZONA

Café Poca Cosa	
88 East Broadway, Tucson, AZ	$$
(520) 622-6400	£D

You never know exactly what you'll find at Café Poca Cosa, one of the most inventive Mexican restaurants in the American Southwest.

The menu changes daily, depending on what ingredients are available and what chef Suzana Davila is in the mood to cook. Customers request her picadillo or pork roast stuffed with plums and chipotle chilies; a stash of hibiscus flowers inspires a fragrant meal called chicken tropicale; a farmer will arrive in the morning with a basket of smoky pasilla chilies she can use to make quesadillas with a breathtaking wallop. There is much good beef: carne asada with fiery habanero peppers; grilled steak strips flavored with chipotles; carne asada barbacoa steeped in beer and spiced with chilies. Molés include pollo en molé negro, a strange blend of chili's heat, chocolate's richness, and the zip of cinnamon. Molé verde is as verdant as the molé negro is earthy, with an exotic herbal hue.

Tamale pie is prepared in a variety of ways and can be a vegetarian's delight. It is made of cream, cheese, and corn masa whipped into a tender custard—sometimes around veins of green chile, sometimes not. It is luxurious, but with an honest virtue of the corn that is its essence.

Dot's Diner

at the Traffic Circle on Rt. 80, South of Bisbee, AZ	$
(520) 432-2046 Tues–Sat	B L

Dot's is a silver beanery adjoining Shady Dell Trailer Park, a motel composed of impeccably restored vintage trailers. It is a tiny place, moved from its original home in Los Angeles two years ago and now exquisitely restored to fit right in to the hippest trailer park in the west.

Frequented by local Arizonians as well as overnight guests, Dot's offers a retro-priced workman's special every day: meat loaf and mashed potatoes Tuesday, pork chops and stuffing or spaghetti and meatballs Wednesday, chicken 'n' dumplings with corn bread Thursday, catfish Friday. Dot Bozeman, whose previous restaurant was a three-stool diner with a single table, is a gifted cuisinier. "I just do home cooking," she says, "I'm no chef." Whatever Dot's correct job description, her hot roast beef sandwich with pan gravy and mashed potatoes is simply the best we've ever eaten, with a spicy savor to the meat and gravy that reminds us of the Creole roast beef po' boys of New Orleans. In fact, Dot is from Louisiana; lunchtime hot plates include a wickedly tasty red beans with rice. Her hand-crimped sweet potato pie is a tender wonder.

El Charro

311 N. Court, Tucson, AZ	$
(520) 622-5465	L D

El Charro—since 1922—is a fortress of Mexican-American food, much of it built around delirious tasty carne seca (air-dried beef), a specialty of Mexican cattle country. This beef, which is dried out back in a cage that hangs in the Arizona air above the patio, fills fabulous burritos, chimichangas, tacos, and enchiladas.

One of the most unusual things about El Charro is its emphasis on nutritionally enlightened fare. Even items on the menu that don't seem like they are diet food are made with an eye toward good nutrition: chili sauce is made without oil; almendrado (Mexican custard) is cholesterol-free. If you are serious about eating healthy, you can order tasty frijoles enteros (whole beans) in lieu of frijoles refritos (beans that are mashed and fried with lard); nonfat yogurt can be had instead of sour cream. Vegetarians come for enchiladas made with mushrooms instead of meat.

Still, most customers come to El Charro to indulge appetites and to party hearty. It is noisy and sociable, almost always packed with tourists, Tucsonians, health nuts, and burrito hounds who spoon up fiery salsa picante with corn chips and drink Tecate beer served in the can with a wedge of lime on top. Its wall decor is legendary—a kaleidoscope of straw sombreros and rawhide bullwhips, and years' worth of El Charro calendars, many of which feature melodramatic scenes of Mexican horsemen (known as charros), proud steeds, and pretty maidens all making flirty eyes at each other amidst stormy landscapes.

The Grand Café	
1119 G Ave., Douglas, AZ (520) 364-2344	*$$*
(breakfast starting late in the morning)	*BLD*

A beacon of bordertown hospitality, the Grand Café serves such Sonoran-style dishes as broad flour tortillas with melted cheese on top and limp grilled green onions on the side, steamy husk-enveloped green-corn tamales, and red or green chili beef, plus shrimp scampi and an off-the-menu dark molé that attracts devoted fans from miles away.

There is a small dance floor at the back of this main street café, which is the sort of festive place that encourages you to punctuate the moment between your appetizer of queso fundito (a hot skillet full of melted cheese) and the carne asada (a broad chuck steak served with four-alarm pico de gallo) with a quick twirl with your partner. On especially festive days, proprietor Vanessa Quintana will add to the merriment by dressing up as Marilyn Monroe, a woman she deeply admires and impersonates in local parades.

Jack's Original Barbeque

5250 E. 22nd St., Tucson, AZ	$
(520) 750-1280	£Đ

On the whitewashed walls of Jack's dining room is a snapshot history of this eatery, from its birth in June 1950 at its first location to its current incarnation as a serve-yourself smokehouse, where the motto is "Taste the Wisdom." Despite its fame, Jack's remains a modest place, where food is presented on throwaway plates and a sign implores, IF YOUR TRAY FALLS IN THE TRASH BIN, PLEASE TELL US.

We especially like the hot links with taut skin and spicy insides served with cumin-flavored chili beans. An order of sliced pork provides tremendous variety—some pieces as wickedly luscious as bacon, others like a tender slice from the middle of a loin. And the sloppy joe, a Thursday special, is glorious, like the best school lunch anyone ever imagined: dark, long-cooked shreds of beef in zesty barbecue sauce. Whatever you eat, follow it with sweet potato pie that is super sweet and spiced like Christmas.

Little Café Poca Cosa

20 South Scott Ave., Tucson, AZ	$
	ßL

Eight oilcloth-covered tables are packed in this closet-size café, which brims with sombreros and serapes and is presided over by Luis Dávila, who makes each meal a party. "Musica, musica!" he cries when the mariachi music on his tape machine runs out. Ask to see his kitchen and he shows you the chili colorado and chili verde bubbling on his little cookstove in back. Ask him what's good for breakfast and he will suggest such Sonoran fundamentals as huevos rancheros puddled with salsa, huevos Mexicanos scrambled with tomatoes, onions, and chilies, and machaca con huevo, which is moist shreds of beef with bits of green chili in a thin veil of scrambled egg.

At lunch, Señor Dávila makes smoky sweet beef shreds in pepper sauce known as barbacoa, pollo ranchero (a hearty stew with tomatoes, peppers, potatoes, and onions), and pollo Acapulco (a gallimaufry of broccoli, cauliflower, peas, carrots, and onions). The beverage selection is outstanding: lemonade made the Mexican way, with fresh limes, jugo de durazno (peach juice), and the south-of-the-border cooler called horchata. It looks like milk, but it's nondairy (it is made from rice) and has a refreshing perfumy sweetness.

Old Smoky's Pancake House	
624 West Bill Williams Ave., Williams, AZ	$
(520) 635-2091	BLD

We thank Diane Lanctot for directing us to this fine pancake house on former Route 66 in the town that has long billed itself as the Gateway to the Grand Canyon. Diane recommended not only the buckwheat and buttermilk pancakes but also the French toast made from thick-sliced bread. The bread is homemade, and there are up to eight varieties every day. A small place with knotty pine walls and gingham curtains on the windows, Old Smoky's is a genuine blast from the past. It's the sort of honest town café that helped Americans fall in love with travel on the open road a half a century ago.

Tuba City Truck Stop	
Junction of Rtes. 160 and 264, Tuba City, AZ	$
(520) 283-4975	BLD

Housed in a cinderblock building with the words LET'S EAT on its outside wall, the Tuba City Truck Stop is a reservation café frequented by Native Americans who linger at the tables sipping coffee and reading the *Navajo Times*. Many wear Levi's and T-shirts, but a surprising number are dressed traditionally—women in velvet blouses and turquoise-nugget necklaces; men with long hair wrapped in the traditional Navajo bun. It is possible to eat authentic Native American specialties in this old joint—mutton and hominy stew, for example, or chewy fried bread that makes good munching with coffee—but the best dish in the house is the Navajo taco. A café staple throughout the region, it is a late-twentieth-century melting-pot combination of meat-and-bean chili, melted cheese, lettuce, and tomato chunks atop a puffy pedestal of Indian fry bread.

COLORADO

☆ ☆ ☆

Buckhorn Exchange	
1000 Osage, Denver, CO	**$$$**
(303) 534-9505 £ Mon–Fri; 𝔇 daily	**£𝔇**

Holder of Colorado Liquor License #1 (issued in 1893), outfitted with a museum's worth of antique firearms and furniture, and decorated with a dazzling menagerie of some five hundred game animal trophies shot by former owner Shorty Zietz, the Buckhorn Exchange is no mere frontier-themed restaurant or historical relic. It happens to be a fine place to eat.

At lunch, hamburgers, salads, and sandwiches are consumed without ado by a cadre of regular customers inured to the stare of a thousand glass eyes and the creak of wood floors where Buffalo Bill once trod. Tourists like us cannot help but gape and wonder, and then tuck into a serious ranch meal. We like to start with hearty ham and bean soup or an order of Rocky Mountain oysters (sliced, fried calf testicles), move on to beef steak or buffalo prime rib or savory trout with crunchy cottage-fried potatoes on the side. Top it all off with crumb-topped apple pie and cinnamon hard sauce, and you have eaten a true-West meal.

Conway's Red Top

1520 S. Nevada, Colorado Springs, CO (719) 633-2444;	$
other locations are 3589 N. Carefree and 390 N. Circle Dr.	£D

Hamburger heaven: six-inch-wide patties are sandwiched in high-topped buns, plain or with Velveeta cheese, or with chopped onions and barbecue sauce. Relatively thin, so much so that the degree of doneness is simply not an issue; these are nothing like the plush "gourmet" burgers that sell for near double-digit prices in swankier restaurants. They are wide-load versions of old-time lunch-counter hamburgers, offered at Conway's on a menu that also includes good navy bean soup, beef stew, and, of course, shoestring French fried potatoes.

Daddy Bruce's Bar-B-Q

20th & Arapahoe, Boulder, CO	$
(303) 449-8890	£D

When daddy Bruce Randolph came to Colorado, he hailed from Arkansas, via Texas and Arizona, so the barbecue that is his legacy is fundamentally southern-style, meaning sweet and sloppy and impossible to stop eating. Now in Boulder (the original Denver storefront is history), the restaurant that bears his name offers a classic repertoire of ribs, chicken, and brisket, all infused with a peppery, garlicky red sauce with his unmistakable Dixie panache.

Durango Diner

970 Main Ave., Durango, CO	$
(970) 247-9889	BL

A tip of the Stetson to Gail Zweigenthal, editor-in-chief of *Gourmet* magazine, for alerting us to the Durango Diner, where—according to the menu—"locals have been gathering to eat and talk for decades." Supper in this big, comfortable café includes unalloyed diner fare like fine hot roast beef dinners and hefty French dips, as well as food with a Southwest regional twist (the wild turkey sandwich is available with mashed potatoes and green chili). But the grand meal of the day is breakfast. One huge pancake, made with or without blueberries, blankets a plate and tastes great. There are classic huevos rancheros and breakfast burritos as well as awesome omelets, including one called the "kitchen sink," heaped with green chili. That good green chili is also available to take home, by the pint, quart, or gallon.

The Fort

Hwys. 8 and 285, Morrison, CO	$$$
(303) 697-4771	**D**

In the atmospheric adobe-walled Fort, with an inspiring view of Denver's lights in the distance, you eat old-time frontier vittles prepared in a sophisticated modern kitchen. Buffalo steaks and sausages, Rocky Mountain oysters, and local trout are all found on a fascinating, deluxe menu that serves up a large portion of culinary history as the side dish to every meal. For all its prairie ambiance, the Fort is an eminently civilized theme restaurant and a good place to splurge for anyone whose appetite for big beef steaks is whetted by the storybook romance of the American West.

Juniper Valley Ranch

Hwy. 115, about 15 miles south of Colorado Springs, CO	$$
(719) 576-0741 Wed–Sun	**D**
(limited hours in fall, closed January–March, reservations advised)	

Juniper Valley Ranch has not changed since 1951. New generations of the same family have taken over since the early days of Grandma Ethel and Aunt Evelyn's reign, but the menu has remained precisely the one they instituted: family-style dinners of skillet-fried chicken or baked ham en casserole, accompanied by hot biscuits and apple butter, stewed okra, and riced potatoes. You start with spiced cider or consommé, and finish with cake or cobbler. It is a homey, civilized meal, served at mismatched tables in an ancient red-mud house hidden by juniper and skunk brush.

M & D's Barbecue and Fish Palace	
2004 E. 28th Ave., Denver, CO	**$**
(303) 296-1760	**LD**

Despite its name, M & D's is not palatial; but the soulful fish that attracts customers from near and far is fit for royalty. Dine here in plain but comfortable surroundings, or get the satisfying meals packed to go: sliced barbecued pork, succulent barbecued chicken (weekends only), crusty fried fish. The pork is served in an unwieldy sandwich or as part of a platter with all the fixin's.

KANSAS
★ ★ ★

Brookville Hotel	
KS 140 15 miles west of Salina, KS (913) 225-6666	**$$**
D daily; **L** Sun; closed Mon	**DL**

People drive for hours, from as far away as Wichita and Kansas City, to eat at the Brookville Hotel, which has been serving celebration-size meals in the Kansas prairie since 1897, when Brookville was the roundhouse town for the Central Pacific Rail Line. The fancy old Victorian dining room is crowded every Sunday with families and friends passing and grabbing serving platters heaped with skillet-fried chicken, mashed potatoes, creamed corn, baking powder biscuits, and gravy. It's an eat-till-you-drop affair: whenever serving platters start looking empty, they are filled again.

Chicken House

Hwy. 99, Olpe, KS	$
(316) 475-3386	£ D

Off the Kansas Turnpike south of Emporia in the small cattle country town of Olpe, Leonard and Theresa Coble built a restaurant some forty years ago. It burned to the ground in the mid-1970s, and the new, modern eat-place was constructed, but the Cobles' reputation for good fried chicken has never wavered. The crunchy pieces of bird are accompanied by fried onion rings and honey wheat-nut bread, followed by creamy pies. It's a Kansas meal that packs the capacious new restaurant almost every night, most especially for Sunday lunch.

Cozy Inn

108 N. 7th, Salina, KS	$
(913) 825-9407	£ D

A hamburger landmark, the Cozy Inn started selling sliders—America's original itsy-bitsy wimpies—in 1922. Each tiny tile of meat is grilled with onions, then served inside a steamed bun with a dill pickle slice and a blob of mustard. Six or eight make a meal-size portion. Most customers buy them by the sack to take home, but it is a mesmerizing sight to sit at the minuscule counter, where you can see the grill man flip and garnish patties with supreme finesse, and where the oniony aroma of the grill adds an indescribable *je ne sais quoi* to the dining experience.

Leona Yarbrough Restaurant

2800 W. 53rd St., Shawnee Mission, KS	$
(913) 722-4800 Tues–Sun	£Ð

Emily Post would have felt comfortable lunching off floral-trimmed dinner plates in this gentle establishment, a longtime bastion of heartland cooking with a feminine touch. Leona Yarbrough's kitchen cuts no corners; from homey chicken noodle soup and fresh-baked bread to old-fashioned lattice-top apple pie, the food served here is honest, inexpensive, and delicious. The menu is printed daily; our fond memories include dinners of braised lamb shank, turkey divan, and excellent fried chicken, and for lunch impeccable egg salad sandwiches on toasted whole wheat bread with potato soup on the side and blackberry cobbler for dessert.

Merle's Place

440 N. Seneca, Wichita, KS	$
(316) 263-0444 Mon–Sat	£Ð

We slice our meat thin and pile it high!" boasts the menu at Merle's, a vintage-1935 beer bar that was turned into a civil little eatery about a decade ago. Nothing exotic about the sandwiches served here: just good ham, roast beef, pastrami, or turkey on thick-sliced white, wheat, or rye, served hot or cold, with a full array of condiments, potato chips, and a robust dill pickle. Put a tall, cold beer on the side and you will see just how pleasant life can be.

Mrs. Peter's Chicken Dinners

4960 State Ave., Kansas City, KS	$
(913) 287-7711 £𝔇 Tues–Fri; 𝔇 Sat	£𝔇

M rs. Peter's is known for a ritual Kansas City meal: creamy coleslaw and marinated vegetables followed by heaps of fried chicken, mashed potatoes, gravy, long-cooked green beans, biscuits with honey butter and strawberry-rhubarb sauce, and pie or a sundae for dessert.

The ambiance is country-craftsy. Waitresses wear granny dresses and frilly bonnets; a dainty gift shop up front is tended by a little old lady who folds white cloth napkins when not waiting on customers. When we left two pieces of chicken on our serving platter at the end of a big supper, our waitress, Nell, said, "Whenever I go on a bus trip with the church choir, I stop here first and get chicken to bring along. Please, take these pieces with you for a midnight snack." Such a nice place!

Porubsky's Grocery

508 N.E. Sardou, Topeka, KS	$
(913) 234-5788	£

I f you are lucky enough to be in Topeka between October and March, take the opportunity to taste Charlie Porubsky's chili. This seasonal brew, a specialty since Charlie and his wife, Lydia, opened the store in 1947, has inspired cadres of loyalists, including Kansas governors and senators whose pictures and encomia line the walls. Any time of year, the thing to eat in this friendly old tavern is a sandwich—whatever cold cut you want, accompanied by fire-hot pickles that Charlie makes himself with a blend of horseradish, pepper, and mustard.

NEVADA

☆ ☆ ☆

The Green Shack

2504 E. Fremont, Las Vegas, NV (702) 383-0007	$$
(reservations advised)	D

oover Dam workers were the original customers of The Green Shack, one of the rare Las Vegas landmarks where nothing changes. It is still the humble supper club it always was, and it is still known for country cooking. Fried chicken is the meal on which the Shack's reputation rides: skillet-cooked to crusty succulence and accompanied by genuine mashed potatoes and hot biscuits with a pitcher of honey. In a city of pageantry and excess, such a meal—or the excellent grilled chicken livers or gizzards—makes a convincing reality check. The clientele is almost exclusively locals, who crowd the old saloon in such numbers that getting a seat on a weekend night or around the holidays can be a problem.

Louis' Basque Corner

301 E. Fourth St., Reno, NV	$
(702) 323-7203	LD

ust a few blocks from the casinos' glitter, Louis and Lorraine Ereguible's high-spirited dining room provides customers with a taste of Pyrenees cuisine as developed by Basque cooks and chuckwagon chefs in the American West. A twist of French style (crusty bread), a jot of Spanish spice (in the paella or tripe stew), and a whole lot of garlic are the fundamental elements of the hearty meals spread across Louis's bright-clothed tables. From barley soup to garlicked salad to exotica like chicken Basquaise or shepherd's stew to hefty steaks or pork chops, the tasty meals seem to go on forever. To wash them down, you want hearty red wine; the only thing Louis does not provide is a goatskin flask to squirt it from.

Nevada Dinner House

351 Silver St., Elko, NV	$
(702) 738-8485 Tues–Sun	D

Frontier culture west of the Rockies was enriched by Basque shepherds, cowboys, and chuckwagon cooks. On Silver Street in Elko's old downtown, a few good restaurants express that heritage by serving cordial family-style meals (help yourself from the serving bowl).

The Star Hotel and Biltoki are both good places, but after a wonderful week of trying them all (at the Cowboy Poetry Gathering, which is held here every January), we decided we like the Nevada Dinner House best. It is a casual eat-place with a spacious bar and speedy waitresses, where the food is basically western and the seasoning is Basque. Simply put, that means nearly everything but the liquor and ice cream is shot through with garlic. Meals start with powerhouse salads—no exotic greens or any such wussy ingredients, just good ol' iceberg lettuce—glistening with a delicious lemony vinaigrette. From that, you move on to old-world casseroles and steaks or chops or falling-off-the-bone garlic chicken accompanied by mouth-watering mashed potatoes (are they garlicked, too?!). Start the meal, or finish it, or accompany it with Picon punch, the high-octane Basque digestif made of brandy, Picon liqueur, and a twist of lemon.

The Venetian

3713 W. Sahara Ave., Las Vegas, NV	$$
(702) 871-4190	D

No sybarite should visit Las Vegas without sampling an appetizer called neckbones à la Venetian, a great, messy bowl of inelegant scraps long simmered in pungent wine marinade. It is finger food: pick your way through the heap of pork parts, worry each piece in your mouth, finding tender nuggets of succulent meat and licking bones clean, and use good, fresh bread to mop up the pungent sauce. Another irresistible Venetian exclusive is sautéed spinach and broccoli greens with lots of garlic and oil. Such earthy fare, which is just the beginning of a vast menu of old Italian favorites from honest pastas to scampi fra diavolo and a grand grilled veal chop (with cannoli for dessert, of course!), has made this comfy roadside grotto a beloved haunt of native Las Vegans and visitors for more than forty years. It is a homey place, about as close as this city gets to a neighborhood eatery: waitresses are fast and friendly; brick and stucco and a Venetian mural on the wall create a charming ambiance reminiscent not of Italy but of America circa 1950, when going out to eat Italian food was a romantic adventure.

New Mexico

☆ ☆ ☆

Angelina's	
1226 N. Railroad Ave., Española, NM	$
(505) 753-8543	ℒ𝒟

Angelina's has relocated to a new, clean location, but the menu of classic northern New Mexican fare, prepared with easy authority is unchanged: zesty huevos rancheros, bowls of pure red and green chile (this is the land of chile with an "e"), and fiery carne adovada. On the side come the golden-crisp fried bread puffs known as sopaipillas, perfect for mopping a plate.

Bobcat Bite

Old Las Vegas Hwy., Santa Fe, NM (505) 983-5319	$$
Wed–Sat	£D

You can spend nearly fifteen dollars for a beefsteak in this ancient but utterly pristine roadhouse restaurant, and a swell steak it is, with excellent spuds on the side. There are pork chops and a ham steak, too, but we like to come to Bobcat Bite for a cheap bowl of chile (in the winter only) or a sandwich. There isn't a tastier green chile cheeseburger for miles: high-class meat, mild but tasty chile, plenty of cheese, and potato chips all served in a plastic basket lined with wax paper.

The honest food is all the tastier for the nostalgic (but in no way preciously so) ambiance of the tiny dining room, which is like a set from *They Drive by Night*. If Bogie came in for a cup of java and a ham sandwich, no one would look twice.

Chope's

Hwy. 28, La Mesa, NM	$
(505) 233-9976	£D

A boisterous café-bar favored by planters, horticulturists, and chile-heads, Chope's is surrounded by fields of peppers on the vine. All the specialties star the hot pod—complex blue-corn enchiladas, bowls of pure red or green chile, steamy stuffed cornmeal pockets known as gorditas—but the dish that speaks most eloquently of the local crop is chiles rellenos, which features whole stuffed chiles with stems still attached. They come as a trio on a plate, filled with balmy cheese, breaded, and fried crisp. If you have only thought of chile as a spice to use with caution, these rellenos will convert you. They are a celebration of chile's profound flavor, which is even more remarkable than its heat.

Coyote Café

132 W. Water St., Santa Fe, NM	$$$
(505) 983-1615	D

By elevating vernacular southwestern fare to gourmet status (duck tamales; red chile onion rings; blackened tomato salsa), Mark Miller has made the Coyote Café a beacon of high-fashion food in America. Some locals resent him and his immensely successful restaurant as an invasion of West Coast show-biz sensibility. He argues that the inspiration for his imaginative dishes is ancient Pueblo food that might have been enjoyed by twelfth-century cliff-dwelling Indians. Unless you are a culinary anthropologist, the ego-clash is a silly debate, because the fact is that there are many wonderful things to eat at Coyote Café, from delectable sea bass tacos to tenderloin of pork with red chile chutney. The noise level in the fanciful high-desert-decor dining room is deafening or convivial, depending on your mood, and the clientele is an interesting mix of local high rollers, serious foodie pilgrims, and hapless tourists gasping for air when they taste just how hot the (delicious) chiles rellenos are.

Note: The Rooftop Cantina at Coyote Café serves similar fare at somewhat lower prices and is open for lunch from April through October. On the first floor, there is a great retail store specializing in chiles and related products.

El Norteño

6415 Zuni SE, Albuquerque, NM	$
(505) 256-1431	LD

Soft taco heaven! The menu in this pleasant family-run restaurant lists well over a dozen things you can wrap in the big wheaty rounds of flatbread, including not-for-the-squeamish cabrito (goat) and lengua (tongue), as well as the tastiest barbacoa (charcoaled meat) anywhere. Get two or three different kinds, top them with exhilarating pico de gallo, and have the waiter keep a few cold bottles of beer in an ice bucket by your booth. It all adds up to an authentic taste of northern Mexico, and one of the great bargain meals in Albuquerque.

Horseman's Haven Café

6500 Cerrillos Rd., Santa Fe, NM (505) 471-5420	$
Mon–Sat; **BL** Sun	**BLD**

Situated in a gas station near the interstate, this extremely humble café serves some of the tastiest New Mexican food anywhere, and at rock-bottom prices. At the counter or in one of the half-dozen little booths, customers are surrounded by equine art: statuettes, paintings, and wall plaques of horses, as well as horsemen ranging from Mexico's vaqueros to Hollywood's John Wayne.

Breakfasts are splendid arrays of food: colossal burritos loaded with eggs and bacon and topped with cheese and chile; fiery carne adovada (tender chunks of chile-marinated pork) with eggs, potatoes, and a warm homemade tortilla on the side. The lunch and dinner menu features enchilada pies of beef, chicken, carne adovada, or cheese; tacos on blue corn tortillas; and one of the finest—and hottest!—green chile cheeseburgers anywhere.

M & J Restaurant

403 Second SW, Albuquerque, NM	$
(505) 242-4890	**LD**

Also known as the M & J Sanitary Tortilla Factory, this airy lunch-room across from the bus station is one of the most memorable cheap-eats experiences in Albuquerque. The boisterous dining rooms are outfitted with spacious booths and rough-textured walls covered with love letters to the restaurant written by satisfied customers from around the world. The carne adovada just may be the best in the West, especially when loaded into a burrito; the chiles rellenos and stuffed sopaipillas are exemplary; and the blue corn enchiladas are magnifico! Even old-fashioned ordinary looking tacos, in firm corn shells, are ex-traordinarily tasty, and the chips (made here) and hot salsa that begin the meal are impossible to stop eating.

Nellie's Café

1226 W. Hadley, Las Cruces, NM (505) 524-9982;	$
a spin-off restaurant, Little Nellie's Chile Factory,	BLD
is located at 600 E. Amador, 523-9911	

The motto is "Chile with Attitude," which is what you get at Nellie's and Little Nellie's, a pair of cheeky urban chile parlors where the price is low and the spice is right.

The original Nellie's has long been famous for the heat of its chile-based menu: feverish red salsa with chips starts off the meal, enchiladas topped with a hot red or hotter green elixir of the pods, and burritos smothered with chile sauce. However, the kitchen's secret weapon has no chile in it whatsoever. It is the refried beans that accompany nearly everything: silk-smooth but with just enough bits of unmashed legume to make the texture interesting and the taste irresistible.

Despite its rough-around-the-edges personality, Nellie's serves some specialty dishes with high style. For tacos al pastor, corn tortillas are arrayed with neat little hills of shredded meat festively garnished with chopped tomatoes, slices of radish, wedges of avocado, fresh jalapeños, green onion, and sprigs of cilantro. Even the giant chile cheeseburger is a thing of beauty. Instead of being covered with a mash of chopped peppers as is customary, Little Nellie's Chile CBs come with whole cooked and peeled pods—a rousing complement to meat, cheese, and bun.

Pasqual's

121 Don Gaspar Ave., Santa Fe, NM	$
(505) 983-9340	BL

Pasqual's is a modest corner café with terrific food. At mealtime in this crowded, split-level dining room, you are lucky to find a seat at a small table or at the large shared one where a local yokel or a stranger from just about any part of the world might break bread with you. For breakfast, we love the pancakes, the blue-and-yellow cornmeal mush, big sweet rolls, and giant bowls of five-grain cereal with double-thick cinnamon toast on the side, accompanied by immense bowls—not cups—of latté. And for lunch, we can never resist the expertly made soups. Little things mean so much: good, fresh bread for sandwiches; earthy roasted chiles on quesadillas; even the coffee is a tasty surprise. After a few meals at Pasqual's, it is easy to feel affection for its unpretentious, sometimes clamorous ambiance. This is a restaurant with an adventurous character that perfectly complements the good stuff from the kitchen.

Plaza Café	
54 Lincoln Ave., Santa Fe, NM	$
(505) 982-1664	BLD

The oldest restaurant in Santa Fe (since 1918), the Plaza is a modest luncheonette that caters more to locals than the tourist set. It serves Greek diner standards (souvlaki, Greek salad) as well as New-Mex specialties including chiles rellenos, posole with pork, menudo, and really delicious sopaipillas that are available every day starting at about eleven. Fresh and hot and almost painfully flaky, these little golden pillows are wonderful to eat plain—they are nearly as light as air but with a satisfying bready crust—and are great for dunking, dipping, and mopping in the Plaza's fine red or green chile.

Rancho de Chimayo	
Rte. 520, Chimayo, NM	$$
(505) 351-4444	LD

Up a winding two-lane road into the hills above Santa Fe is the ancient village of Chimayo. The Jaramillo family have lived here for over a century and their home is now a restaurant. Rancho de Chimayo has wide-plank wood floors, hammered tin chandeliers, a capacious fireplace, and a menu of native foods seldom found on ordinary Tex-Mex or southwestern menus. Chile peppers are used in nearly all the good things the Jaramillos serve, from cheese and chile omelets to chile-topped sirloin steak. The best dish is carne adovada (chile-marinated pork), its heat dampened by airweight sopaipillas (pillowy triangles of fried bread) dipped in honey. The place can get overrun by travelers, but there is still something magical about an outdoor table in the high desert air, with candlelight and roving musicians adding to the romance of the Southwest.

Roque's Carnitas

Washington and Palace, Santa Fe, NM	$
(closed in winter)	£

Roque's is a jolly little chuckwagon that serves a great sandwich. Folded inside a sturdy flour tortilla that has been heated on a grate over a charcoal fire is succulent beef, and plenty of it—top round thinly sliced and seasoned, sizzled on a grate along with onions, chiles, and fiery jalapeño salsa. Dining accommodations are park benches in the plaza; your companions are hungry pigeons. Roque, a fifth-generation Santa Fean and a fount of local lore, goes to Mexico each winter, where he runs a pizzeria. To our noses, the smell of his sizzling carnitas on the Santa Fe plaza is as much a sign of spring as singing robins and blooming lilacs.

Santacafe

231 Washington Ave., Santa Fe, NM	$$$
(505) 984-1788	£D

Santacafe is very, very stylish, and the food is very, very delicious, especially the chile-spiked brioche at the beginning of the meal, and the peppery dumplings and smoked pheasant spring rolls with dipping sauces. The kitchen is renowned for combining southwestern flavor with Asian style, but the meal we remember best is one autumn's all-vegetable plate—the very image (and flavor) of a utopian harvest, including all sorts of beans and legumes and the sweetest ear of roasted-in-the-husk corn on the cob.

The old adobe restaurant is a real beauty, and dining here is romantic—indoors is cozy, intimate, elegant; the courtyard is more festive. With a loved one or good friends, a meal at Santacafe is a Santa Fe experience to remember.

Tecolote	
1203 Cerrillos Rd., Santa Fe, NM	**$**
(505) 988-1362 Tues–Sun	**BL**

A casual, family-style café where breakfast is king: atole piñon hot-cakes, made with blue cornmeal and studded with roasted piñon nuts; French toast made from cinnamon-raisin or orange poppy seed bread; corned beef hash atop a hot tortilla, smothered with red or green chile; the "sheepherder's breakfast," which is spuds and jalapeño peppers cooked on a grill until crusty brown, then topped with two kinds of chile and melted cheddar cheese. The only thing wrong with this place is waiting for a table on weekend mornings.

OKLAHOMA

Cattlemen's	
1309 S. Agnew, Oklahoma City, OK	**$$**
(405) 236-0416	**BLD**

In the old (and still thriving) stockyards, Cattlemen's is one of America's best places to eat beef. Its sirloin steak is supremely hedonistic—slow-aged and fast-broiled, with a delirious flavor that flows and flows.

Tex-Mex Lex

A handful of helpful menu terms in Spanish, pigeon-Spanish, Mexican, Cal-Mexican, and Tex-Mexican.

Ajo	Garlic
Carne adovada	Beef or pork marinated in hot chilies
Carne seca	Air-dried beef (a Tucson specialty)
Carne verde	Beef with green chili
Cebolla verde	Green onion, usually grilled in Arizona
Chile con carne	Beef with red chile
Chile colorado	Red chile
Chimichanga	A deep-fried burrito
Chorizo	Spicy pork sausage
Fajitas	Grilled meat served sizzling with vegetables and tortillas
Flauta	"Flute"—a tortilla rolled around beef or chicken
Frijoles refritos	Refried beans
Gordita	Cornmeal pocket filled with meat and/or cheese, grilled

There are plenty of other good cuts of beef on the menu, as well as the Oklahoma favorite, lamb fries—testicles of young lambs that are sliced and deep fried.

Breakfast is a special time here: no tourists, plenty of genuine cowboys and truckers who are their spiritual heirs, and a menu that features crusty breakfast steaks and platters of brains and eggs.

Beyond great chuck, this place has another dazzling attraction: an immense illuminated mural in the front dining room shows cattlemen on horseback many years ago, riding among a vast herd of bovines.

Huevos rancheros	Eggs with salsa, always accompanied by tortilla and fri-joles refritos
Menudo	Tripe soup (a hangover cure)
Molé poblano	A rich sauce of chile, chocolate, and spices (many variations)
Tostada	Crisp-fried corn tortilla, topped with cheese or guacamole
Quesadilla	Tortillas layered with cheese and heated

Some Common Fillings for Tacos

Al carbon	Charcoal-grilled beef or pork
Al pastor	Roast pork
Carne asada	Roasted beef
Carnitas	Small pieces of pork (in California) or beef (farther east)
Frijoles enteros	Whole beans
Hongos	Mushrooms
Lengua	Tongue
Picadillo	Seasoned ground beef
Pollo	Chicken

Classen Grill

| 5124 N. Classen, Oklahoma City, OK | $$ |
| (405) 842-0428 ℬℒ𝒟 Mon–Sat; ℬℒ only Sun | ℬℒ𝒟 |

We like lunch and dinner at Classen Grill—excellent burgers, debonair grilled fish, sophisticated pastas—but breakfast wins our eternal loyalty. Start the day with taquitas (tortilla-wrapped packets of eggs, cheese, and vegetables) or chinook eggs (salmon patties topped with poached eggs) accompanied by a block of lush cheese grits. Insatiable appetites go for "biscuits debris"—two big ones split open and mounded with gravy choc-a-bloc with ham and sausage chunks, cloaked with melted cheddar cheese. On the side you get potatoes, either home fries or Classen potatoes, which are mashed, seasoned with garlic, and rolled into little balls, then deep fried until brittle gold on the outside. The result is a kind of prairie knish.

Del Rancho

301 W. Main St., Moore, OK	$
(405) 794-4131	LD

Del Rancho is a restaurant chain with a handful of branches in central Oklahoma. We're not usually partial to chains, but two things endear this one to us: especially crisp chicken-fried steak (the house specialty), and a weird, old-fangled service system in which each booth telephones its order to the house operator, who then conveys it to the kitchen. A few moments later, it is delivered by a waitress.

Chicken-fried steak connoisseur Karl Rambo of Norman, Oklahoma, originally recommended Del Rancho to us as a convenient stop for interstate travelers. Mr. Rambo advised that in his experience, the Del Rancho in Moore is the one with the best food.

Jake's Rib

100 Ponderosa, Chickasha, OK	$
(405) 222-2825	LD

Jake's serves Paul Bunyan portions of barbecue. It is a polite town café with a television so customers can watch sportscasts as they eat, and a menu that offers mammoth platters of pork ribs, pork chunks, sliced brisket, hot sausage links, and smoke-flavored pink bologna steaks. Side dishes are abundant, too, including curly-Q fries, fried okra, and pinto beans, plus colossal glasses full of iced tea or cold beer.

What Is Chili?

Chili is a fighting word. Devotees to each regional variation swear by their own and damn all others. In the interest of world peace and good eating, here is a rundown of the basic kinds.

Chili Mac: A midwestern urban variant of ground beef in a spicy tomato sauce mixed with spaghetti or elbow macaroni and beans (Bishop's Chili Hut, p. 181)

Cincinnati Chili: Sweet-spiced, finely ground, saucy beef layered onto limp spaghetti noodles, crowned with grated cheese and chopped onion, oyster crackers on the side (Camp Washington Chili, p. 224)

Green Bay (Wisconsin) Chili: Meat and bean chili gilded with a ladle full of hot-spiced oil (Chili John's, p. 232)

New Mexican Chile: Beanless and meatless—a pure puree of pods; always spelled chile and served on the side with other dishes and with soft tortillas for mopping and sopping (Chope's, p. 291)

Texas Chili: Beanless, made with coarse-ground beef or small beef chunks, usually simmered in beer with hot peppers; beans may be served on the side (Pittsburg Hot Link Restaurant, p. 317)

Jigg's Smoke House

Exit 62 off I-40, Clinton, OK	$
(580) 323-5641	£D

This friendly shack by the side of the highway has a single table (made of a construction spool) where customers enjoy excellent barbecue sandwiches of juicy hacked pork in a tangy tomato sauce stuffed inside burger buns. Jiggs's is also an outpost of genuine beef jerky. Using an ultraslow, smoke-drying process, raw beef is reduced to enormous, leather-textured flaps of jerky that smell of smoke and meat for days. It takes two big hands to bend one and a healthy set of teeth to rip off a chaw. Chew, chew, chew—the salty cured flavor inundates the mouth with more intensity than a pinch of Copenhagen Skoal.

Leo's Barbecue

3631 N. Kelley Ave., Oklahoma City, OK	$
(405) 424-5367	LD

Leo's beef is so coarsely hacked that a portion of it, on a platter or in a sandwich, contains some outside chunks with crunchy blackened edges and others that are velvet-soft and dripping natural juice. Sauce is dark and demonically hot with a vinegar punch—good not only on the meat but on the small, buttery baked potato that accompanies all sandwiches and meals. Leo's also offers pork ribs, hot links, and a locally favored treat, bologna. Before you dismiss barbecued bologna as a smoke-house aberration, you need to try it here. This is not bubble-gum-colored supermarket lunch meat; it is a thick-sliced, dark-pink slab with wicked zest, dense and powerfully smoky. We don't like it better than the beef, which is superb, but it is interesting.

The Metro

6418 N. Western, Oklahoma City, OK	$$
(405) 840-9463	LD

A chic bistro where the walls are decorated with posters of French wine labels and the tables are covered with thick napery and clean butcher paper, Metro is an oasis of culinary savoir faire in the meat-and-potatoes belt. Even here, the beef is grand—they make a smoked tenderloin hors d'oeuvre, grilled fillets stuffed with mushrooms and shallots, and a Roquefort burger with pommes frites or lacy fried onions on the side. But the real lure (aside from a list of twenty-five wines by-the-glass and an inventory of essenced vodkas from cilantro/serrano to vanilla bean) is such urbane creations as acorn squash cakes with orange-glazed shrimp and scallops. A menu of seasonal fare is redesigned every two months; last year, it featured roast quail salad, braised tilapia with aromatic herbs, and a dessert feuillete constructed to hold wine-marinated spring berries. Year-round, there is one dessert we can never resist: bread pudding with bourbon sauce. "I don't drink bourbon," revealed the waitress when she brought us a serving of this dark, cinnamon-scented treasure in its liquory pool, "but I sure like to eat it!"

Murphy's Steak House	
1625 W. Frank Phillips Blvd., Bartlesville, OK	$$
(918) 336-4789	£D

Beef is king at Murphy's, a fact made apparent by the giant cow-shaped sign outside; and although we hear the steaks are just dandy, the only thing we've ever eaten here, or ever want to eat is a "hot hamburger." As far as we're concerned, this unique mountain of food is plated perfection: pieces of toasted white bread are topped with French fries, a patty of beef that's been hacked into bite-sized pieces, dark gravy and—if you're smart enough to request them—sautéed onions. It's a magic combination, especially the way the crisp logs of fried potato soften in places where the gravy blankets them, imbibing a rich beefy savor for which the squiggles of onion are an ideal accent. Even folks who come for steak instead of chopped-up hamburger know to order a side dish of fried potatoes with gravy.

Sleepy Hollow	
1101 NE 50th, Oklahoma City, OK	$$$
(405) 424-1614 £D Mon–Fri; D Sat; brunch and D Sun	£D

Food fads come and go, but Sleepy Hollow never changes. Since the 1940s, it has been Oklahoma City's beloved spot for chicken dinner with all the trimmings, meaning a salad, mashed potatoes, gravy, peas, hot biscuits, and pineapple sherbet for dessert. There are a few other items on the menu; the steaks, in fact, are grand. But if you come to Sleepy Hollow only once, make your meal chicken. It is fried in cast-iron skillets until it develops a crisp, golden crust. Sever that crust with a knife and the air all around the table will be perfumed with the nut-sweet aroma of the juicy meat inside. Then put down the knife and

pick up the chicken and eat with your hands. This is food so good you
want to caress it as well as taste it.

The Split-T

57th and N. Western, Oklahoma City, OK	$
(405) 848-2919	LD

The Split-T is a sports bar with a TV in each of the four corners of
each room, just beneath the ceiling. One of a number of joints in
Oklahoma City that serves weird and wonderful hamburgers, it is
known for one called the Caesarburger: a broad patty on a big bun
with a full inch of sopping Caesar-flavored stuff piled inside. We say
"stuff" because the condiment is a sort of cross between salad and
sauce. The combination of this zesty cool garnish and hot beef is inspired. It comes wrapped in paper, but copious spillage is inevitable.

Van's Pig Stand

717 E. Highland, Shawnee, OK	$
(405) 273-8704	LD

Pork shoulder, slow-smoked in the hickory pit, is cut into big, tender chunks and exuberantly sauced, then served with curlique
French fries or a "Vanized" potato (cut open and filled with garlicky
sour cream). It's a superb meal, simple and cheap, and impossible to
duplicate in the northern half of the U.S. Meaty pork ribs and sliced
beef brisket are also available in this pleasant little barbecue, where the
citizens of Shawnee have come to dine for decades.

TEXAS

✩ ✩ ✩

Angelo's	
2533 White Settlement, Fort Worth, TX	$
(817) 332-0357 Mon–Sat	£𝔇

Notwithstanding the sprawl of Angelo's two big rooms and its daunt-ing popularity, and despite the fact that beer flows into frosted gob-lets at an amazing pace, there is something distinctly meditative about this old barbecue parlor. Perhaps its serenity is induced by the haze of hickory-and-brisket vapors that waft from the smoke pit.

"You are in the Land of Brisket," proclaims the counterman when an out-of-towner gets to the head of the line and innocently asks what type of beef is smoke-cooked here. To prove his point, the counterman steps aside, providing a full view of the cutting block behind him, where a kitchen carver plunges his fork into great slab of beef, holds it aloft like a trophy, then plunks it back down on the wood board and begins slicing pieces nearly a half-inch thick. As the knife severs the dark crust and glides into the meat's tender center, each moist slice wants to disintegrate. But miraculously, it holds together enough to make it intact onto a Styrofoam plate, where a row of slices is accom-panied by beans, potato salad, coleslaw, a length of pickle, a thick slice of raw onion, a ramekin of sauce, and two pieces of the freshest, soft-est white bread in America. Tote your own meal to a table, and if you pay an extra twenty-five cents, you can stop at the bar along the way and fill a small cup with scorching hot peppers to garnish the meat.

Bellaire Broiler Burger

5216 Bellaire Blvd., Houston, TX	$
(713) 668–8171 Mon–Sat	£𝔇

The Broiler Burger, a long-respected fast-food joint on Bellaire at Bissonnet, has just what you need if you are a hungry soul in search of a classic 1950s fix. The burgers are thin and cooked through and through, and delicious! The shakes are real, and the French fries are good enough to shame any of us who, at one time or another, have settled for franchised burger-joint spuds.

Bryce's Cafeteria

2021 Mall Dr. (exit 222 off I-30), Texarkana, TX	$
(903) 792-1611	£𝔇

Conversation overheard waiting in line at Bryce's Cafeteria:

"This is the finest food in Texarkana."

"No," a stranger up the line turns to reply. "This is the finest food in Texas."

"I say it's the best in all the South," a third pipes in.

It is hard not to wax rhapsodic waiting at Bryce's Cafeteria, because the waiting line takes you past an array of swoonfully appetizing food, the likes of which has made this place famous since it opened for business some sixty years ago.

There are more vegetables arrayed for the asking than most of us Yankees see in a year. Feast the eyes on purple-hulled peas, fried green tomatoes, red beans, turnip greens cooked with chunks of ham, buttered cauliflower, sauced broccoli, along with a full array of potatoes, cheesy macaroni casseroles, and rice casseroles. Among main courses, fried chicken is stupendously crunchy, and big slabs of sweet ham are sliced to order. For dessert, we like Karo-coconut pie, hot blueberry cobbler, and banana pudding made with meringue and vanilla wafers.

The entire experience is a culinary dream, complete with a smartly uniformed dining room staff (to help old folks and invalids with their trays and to bus tables), and servers who address all men as "sir" and women as "ma'am."

Cattlemen's Steak House

2458 N. Main St., Fort Worth, TX	$$$
(817) 624-3945	£D

Big, beautiful steak is the lure of Cattlemen's, where walls are hung with portraits of prize-winning cattle. Porterhouse, T-bone, sirloin, filet mignon: whatever cut you like, it is broiled hot and fast to pocket all the juices and served with potato and a salad with good blue cheese and sesame dressing. Service can be offhand and fellow diners might be rowdy (in the stockyard since 1947, Cattlemen's draws lots of tourists as well as rodeo folk and ranchers from the outback), but who can worry about such petty concerns when relishing a flavorful forkful of corn-fed, aged beef?

It's nice to walk off a meal with a stroll around the stockyards district, which is populated by a vast number of saddle, boot, and tack shops.

Celebration

4503 W. Lovers Lane, Dallas, TX	$$
(214) 351-5681	£D

Housed in a low-slung stone ranch house in a residential neighborhood, Celebration is a real discovery, for both its ambiance and its good food. The handsome wood-paneled walls are decorated with Indian rugs and evocative black-and-white photographs of contemporary Texas ranch hands, cattle, and life on the range. In the small dining rooms, a meditative calm prevails as gentle western music plays quietly in the background.

In this gracious environment, Celebration serves magnificent home cooking. Pot roast is cooked until ridiculously tender; its profound beefy juices are retrieved and served in a little bowl alongside mashed potatoes that are still a little chunky and freckled with potato skin. Meat loaf is perfumed with spice, lean and beefy. Each piece of fried chicken is massive, nutty-crusted on the outside and dripping moist within. The vegetable selection varies with the season. We have enjoyed an autumn casserole made of sweet, bite-size chunks of squash cooked al dente and veiled in garlic and cheese; and spinach glistening with butter and seasoned just enough to highlight its natural vigor.

Waitress Stephanie offered her advice about dessert. "I'll be honest with you. The coconut cream pie is the best," she said. We wouldn't call her wrong, for this pie is a beauty with a deliriously coconutty filling; but the chocolate cake is equally awe-inspiring. It is a double-layer one, moist and thickly iced, and so tall that it is difficult to cut without carefully positioning the fork on top and gliding it smoothly down through the six inches of devil's food.

Clark's Outpost	
Hwy. 377, Tioga, TX	$
(940) 437-2414	£D

Clark's beef is so delightful to look at with its blackened crust and rosy insides glistening with juice that you want to pick it up in your fingers and fondle it before savoring its incomparable taste. A fine old store with western-theme decor and checked tablecloths, Clark's serves other barbecued things, including pork and pork ribs, and there are some really strange and tasty side dishes—deep-fried corn on the cob and sliced and fried bull's testicles. But it's the beef that is essential.

Del Frisco's Double Eagle Steak House	
5251 Spring Valley Rd., Dallas, TX	$$$
(972) 490-9000 (reservations advised)	D

When a sharp knife penetrates a sirloin's crust at Del Frisco's Double Eagle Steak House and the blade plunges into hot, pink beef, we carnivores are rapt. Juices ooze onto the white china plate and ruddy red-meat perfume fills the air with sure promise of satisfaction.

Del Frisco's is big and expensive, a snapshot of moneyed Texas reminiscent of the TV show "Dallas." Beyond cuts of flawlessly cooked prime beef, which arrive spangled with parsley, the kitchen serves mammoth lobster tails that are amazing to behold, available in two sizes one day last year: twenty-two ounces or two pounds. (The former sold for $77, the latter for $112.) Be sure to start your meal by asking for the off-the-menu platter of three kinds of cool colossal shrimp: with remoulade, a garlicky marinade, and bright red cocktail sauce.

Gennie's Bishop Grill

321 N. Bishop Ave., Dallas, TX	$
(214) 946-1752	£

I F OUR PRICES WERE HIGHER, WE'D BE FAMOUS says the movable-letter menu above the buffet line at Gennie's Bishop Grill. The management is disingenuous. Since it opened in 1970, Gennie's has become quite famous among American café connoisseurs to whom this modest lunchroom is a blue-plate shrine.

Service is cafeteria-style; the line is short and functional. Grab a tray from a pile that includes some plain ones and some with the insignia of an apparently defunct Sirloin Stockade, take a sheaf of silverware wrapped in a paper napkin, then slide toward the food. Tell the server what you want from a selection of that day's three or four entrees. When available, garlic chicken is a must: oozing juice, slipping off its bones as you lift it, fragrant with spice, it is a deeply sensuous eating experience. On the side, you want corn bread stuffing, which is soft and sweet. You also want greens, limp and heavy, sprinkled with peppery vinegar. As for potatoes, Gennie's sweets are brightly flavored, cooked until all tooth resistance is gone; mashed potatoes are glorious—whipped smooth, crowned with a spill of well-peppered cream gravy. Other frequent entrees include spicy beef and macaroni, chicken-fried steak, meat loaf, and liver 'n' onions. All meals are accompanied by your choice of a crisp corn bread muffin or a yeasty round-topped dinner roll that is excellent for mopping up the last streaks of gravy.

Goode Company Barbeque

5109 Kirby, Houston, TX	$
(713) 522-2530 or 523-7154	£ 𝕯

Jim Goode's restaurants have become a small constellation of North Stars in East Texas. Smokehounds from near and far come to the barnlike buildings to pig out on crunch-crusted pork ribs, melt-in-the-mouth brisket, chicken, ham, duck, or turkey with peppery pinto beans and luscious jalapeño cheese bread on the side. The food is sensational, the ambiance is downhome (neon beer signs, stuffed armadillos, cordwood stacked by the outside walls), and the prices are low. Only one problem: the crowds can be daunting, especially on weekend nights.

H & H Coffee Shop

701 E. Yandell, El Paso, TX (915) 533-1144	$
Mon—Sat	𝓑£

H & H Coffee Shop is a hospitable, Mexican-accented cook shop that adjoins the H & H Car Wash, so you can enjoy the sight of vehicles being soaped and toweled while you eat huevos rancheros, burritos, enchiladas, or—Saturday only—menudo, the tripe and hominy stew renowned for its power to cure a hangover. The house salsa, served with nearly everything, is made from finely chopped jalapeño peppers that play reveille on the tongue. H & H is an archetypal hole-in-the-wall, the sort of place you wouldn't likely stop to eat unless you were let in on the secret.

Hammond's Bar-B-Q

U.S. 67, Glen Rose, TX (254) 897-3008	$
£D Thurs–Sat; £ only Sun	£D

In this sawdust-floored country restaurant, you will feast on Texas barbecue—chopped or sliced beef brisket, big hot sausage links, ham, or ribs, accompanied by pinto beans, mustardy potato salad, and Texas toast (thick-sliced white bread cooked in the pit). About that fine beef, A. J. Hammond says he cooks it as slowly as humanly possible, letting it imbibe the flavor of hickory smoke for a full day and a half. The result is meat so tender you literally cannot pick up a piece without it falling into tender shreds, meat so succulent you want to suck on it rather than chew.

Kincaid's

4901 Camp Bowie Blvd., Fort Worth, TX (817) 732-2881	$
Mon–Sat (closes at 6 PM)	£D

Kincaid's added actual tables awhile back, which diminished the thrill of having to dine on your feet, standing wherever you could find a place among the helter-skelter grocery store shelves. Despite the new amenities in this old grocery store, Kincaid's world-renowned half-pound hamburger, dripping juice and stuffed into a warm bun that oozes condiments, remains pure and good and true.

Kreuz Market

208 S. Commerce St., Lockhart, TX (512) 398-2361	$
Mon–Sat	£D

Kreuz (pronounced "Krites") has been smoking meat since the beginning of the century, and they don't even have plates; but they do

Chicken-Fried Steak

To our knowledge, no one has pinpointed the origin of chicken-fried steak, one of the fundamental foodstuffs west of Kansas City. If you are a culinary newbie, you need to know that it isn't chicken, and it isn't steak, and chuckwagon law requires that it be eaten with mashed potatoes and gravy. Technically, it is a cheap piece of beef, breaded and fried like chicken. Culinarily, what it becomes—in the hands of an expert cook—is supreme southwestern comfort food.

We suspect that its origins probably have something to do with the large number of Germans and middle Europeans who settled in the Texas Hill Country, bringing with them a recipe for wiener schnitzel, but finding themselves with tough beef instead of tender veal. Probably some time during the Depression, when times were lean, these ingenious cooks learned to pound the tar out of a cheap cut of beef (classically, using an old-time Coke bottle as a sledgehammer) until it was tender. Then they battered the meat, dredged it in eggs and flour, and skillet-fried it, making gravy from the drippin's.

Make no mistake: chicken-fried steak can be hideous, and we don't recommend ordering one in just any café. But at a restaurant like Threadgill's in Austin (p. 321) or Gennie's in Dallas (p. 309), it is a taste of Texas transcendence with its gnarled tan crust rising in a thousand crisp bubbles melded to the meat so that every mouthful is a perfect mix of crunch and chew. Cut it easily with the edge of a fork, then push the forkful through your gravy. With a heap of black-eyed peas, biscuits, and a tall glass of iced tea (presweetened, natch), this is a four-star Lone Star meal.

twist up the ends of the butcher paper so the meat's juices don't spill when you carry it from the pit to a table. Beef is accompanied by white bread or saltines; and there is a condiment bar with onions, tomatoes, and jalapeño peppers. Kreuz used to be equipped with knives shackled to wood posts; but the sharp knives have been removed and now the management supplies plastic ones. They are not necessary for this meat, which is unspeakably tender, eager to fall apart as soon as you lift it from the paper. Please note: as this book went to print, Kreuz was planning to move to a new location some time in the spring of 1999.

Little Diner

7209 7th, Canutillo, TX	$
(915) 877-2176	£D

This off-the-beaten-path café, which shares a building with a public coin-op Laundromat, serves flautas and gorditas that may be the best in West Texas. Flautas, which means flutes, are tightly rolled, crisp-fried tortillas packed with either seasoned chicken or beef. The chicken is moist and savory; the beef is brisket, cooked until falling-apart tender, then hand-shredded. About the size of a hefty asparagus stalk, this well-nigh perfect piece of food is finger fare: pick it up and crunch away; juices from inside will dribble down your chin. Gorditas are sandwich pockets made of cornmeal, griddle-cooked and stuffed. They have an earthy corn taste and moist insides with just a hint of flaky crispness all around their skin.

Also known as the Canutillo Tortilla Factory, the Little Diner makes flour tortillas every day and corn tortillas (thin and thick) every other day. Both are sold by the dozen across the counter.

Louie Muller's

206 W. Second St., Taylor, TX (512) 352-6206	$
Mon–Sat (until the food runs out, usually mid-afternoon)	£

The walls of this establishment, which was a school gymnasium many decades ago, were once green. But they have been aged in cooking smoke so long that they have developed a resinous patina that looks like tortoiseshell. Louie Muller's dining room—one of the supreme shrines of Texas barbecue—is outfitted with communal wooden tables and is generally as quiet as a cathedral, separated from the kitchen by a counter reminiscent of a chancel rail. Back there is the pit—a long metal box holding a grate where briskets cook slowly over burning

hickory and oak until the meat is so tender it jiggles like Jell-O. There
are no balanced meals, no plats du jour here. Order beef by the pound
or hot sausage links; they are served on butcher paper atop a molded
plastic cafeteria tray. Tote it yourself. Few dining experiences are simpler, or more heavenly.

Mecca	
10422 Harry Hines Blvd., Dallas, TX	**$**
(214) 352-0051	***BLD***

Mecca is a happy-go-lucky roadhouse plastered with Dallas Cowboys
souvenirs, a mounted jackalope, 8 × 10 glossies from celebrity patrons, and wisecracks in the form of bumper stickers (WILL ROGERS
NEVER MET AN AUDITOR) and photocopied manifestos ("I have P.M.S.
and a handgun," says a snarly cartoon character. "Any questions?"). A
squadron of feisty waitresses rules the loose-jointed dining room; and
while these good ol' gals never hesitate to share a piece of their mind,
they also take care of you like mother hens.

"You see that part of your chicken-fry?" says ours, pointing to the
breakfast steak on the plate she carries to our table. It is enveloped in
a golden crust, but one bit along the edge is crustless. "That worried
me," she says, cocking her brow and giving a gimlet eye to the offend-
ing area. "You tell me if it tastes fine. If not, I'll raise hell." It tastes delicious, even the crustless part, a Lone Star delicacy, tender and beefy,
sheathed in breading that cracks into flakes when pressed by fork or
knife. Its natural companion is gravy, which comes in a bowl so you
can spoon it on and use it as a dip for shreds of Mecca's proud, puffy
biscuits.

Cinnamon rolls are a house specialty. Each is a coil of sweet
baked dough veined with cinnamon and frosted, about six inches
across and two inches high, served hot and sopped with melting mar-
garine that forms a golden pool on the plate. Immense and ungainly,
one roll calls for a half dozen cups of coffee to wash it down. No problem: in this joint, waitresses tote coffeepots with the proficiency of a
quick-draw artist twirling a Colt .45.

Norma's Café

3330 Beltline Rd., Farmers Branch (near Dallas), TX	$
(972) 243-8646	BLD

Norma's is a good ol' roadhouse with plenty of personality expressed by signs that hang everywhere:

- LIFE IS LIKE A BLUE PLATE SPECIAL. YOU PICK OUT THE ENTREE AND THE SIDE ORDERS FOLLOW.
- THE DISHWASHER IS THE CREDIT MANAGER. HE IS LOOKING FOR A FEW GOOD MEN.
- YES, WE HAVE GRITS.

The cuisine is haute southwest diner, from giant breakfasts of chicken-fried steak, biscuits, and cream gravy to country catfish or meat loaf with real mashed potatoes at lunch. The long list of burger options is crowned by an "atomic chili cheeseburger" strewn with slices of hot jalapeño pepper. Crinkle-cut French fries are also available in a nuclear configuration, heaped with meaty chili, melted cheese, peppers, and red onions. And of course you can get a hand-dipped milk shake on the side. All this fine food is eaten to the tune of a vintage jukebox featuring the hits of Elvis and Richie Valens. On the way out, the last sign you see says, YOU ARE ABOUT TO RETURN TO THE HARSH REALITY OF THE REAL WORLD.

Otto's

5502 Memorial Dr., Houston, TX	$
(713) 864-8526	LD

Smoked brisket, hot links, and ribs are dished out in a pine-paneled dining room on one side of Otto's; on the other side, hamburgers are served. The burgers are lunch-counter mainstays—thin, cooked-through, and enveloped by soft, spongy buns—and the barbecue is juicy and full-flavored, served with a tangy sauce on the side. Either way, you get a quick, cheap meal that has been satisfying Houstonians for nearly fifty years.

Ouisie's Table

3939 San Felipe Rd., Houston, TX	$$
(713) 528-2264	£ⅅ

Just the right mix of uptown savoir faire and downhome Texas comfort food make Ouisie Cooper's lunchroom a treasured destination in Houston. The hamburger is deluxe; a bowl of simple but elegant black beans, garnished to a fare-thee-well, is a memorable meal; and the BLT sandwich, including a fried egg and jalapeño-spiked mayonnaise, is born again. There is a fresh pasta each day, a glorious grapefruit and avocado salad, and black magic cake to set a sweet tooth spinning. Specials are written on a large blackboard; every local gastronome knows that Tuesday is Ouisie's chicken-fried steak day.

Paris Coffee Shop

704 W. Magnolia, Fort Worth, TX	$
(817) 335-2041 Mon–Sat	ℬ£

Named not for the capital of France, but for the original owners, the Paris Coffee Shop smells delicious in the morning, its air perfumed by sausages, bacon, corned beef hash, as well as tangy biscuits smothered with gravy. Other good breadstuffs include soft, glazed cinnamon rolls and a choice of eight-grain, sourdough, or sun-dried tomato toast. The Paris Coffee Shop is also a legendary lunchroom, known for such stalwart midday meals as roast pork with corn bread dressing and baked short ribs with turnips and their greens, and always an array of oven-fresh pies. When we spotted a piece of pie we wanted behind the counter and ordered it for breakfast, the waitress warned, "It's not today's," but then thought a while and agreed with our choice, declaring, "Hey, yesterday's egg custard pie is better than no pie at all!"

Hamburger Honor Roll

In our book, there is no one platonic hamburger. This honor roll includes dramatically different ones, from Hackney's juicy football-size patty to the flat little sliders of the Cozy Inn. Furthermore, although none of the restaurants are very fancy, some are considerably more déclassé than others (we're thinking of Kewpee Lunch).

- ☛ Cassell's, Los Angeles, CA (p. 334)
- ☛ Conway's Red Top, Colorado Springs, CO (p. 282)
- ☛ Cozy Inn, Salina, KS (p. 285)
- ☛ Feltner's Whatta-Burger, Russellville, AR (p. 129)
- ☛ Goldyburgers, Forest Park, IL (p. 185)
- ☛ Hackney's on Harms, Glenview, IL (p. 185)
- ☛ Kewpee Lunch, Racine, WI (p. 234)
- ☛ Kincaid's, Fort Worth, TX (p. 311)
- ☛ Louis Lunch, New Haven, CT (p. 7)
- ☛ Phillips Grocery, Holly Springs, MS (p. 169)
- ☛ Red Rooster Drive-In, Brewster, NY (p. 71)
- ☛ Solly's Coffee Shop, Milwaukee, WI (p. 239)
- ☛ The Sycamore, Bethel, CT (p. 12)
- ☛ Zaharako's, Columbus, IN (p. 198)

Pittsburg Hot Link Restaurant

136 Marshall St., Pittsburg, TX	$
(903) 856-5765 Mon–Sat (closes at 6 PM)	BLD

Pittsburg is the hot-link capital of the world, where lusciously oily beef sausages are slow-cooked in metal pit and served with stacks of saltines or white bread and accompanied by a beer or sweet soda pop. One of the best places in town to have such a meal is the Pittsburg Hot Link Restaurant, where the never-changing menu is posted on a sign hung on the wall. Also on the menu is genuine all-beef Texas chili (not for the nutritional fussbudget) and that fairly rare Southwestern delicacy, the Fritos pie, which is constructed by topping corn chips with chili, cheese, and diced onion. Such fare won't likely ever get trendy . . . which, of course, is one reason we love it.

Ponder Steak House (Ranchman's Café)	
Ponder, Texas	$$
(940) 479-2221	BLD

Note there is no street address for the Ponder Steakhouse. Find Ponder, about an hour north of the Dallas/Fort Worth Metroplex, and you've found the restaurant. For fifty years, it has been the heart and soul of this sleepy little encampment by the railroad tracks, which beef-eaters from miles around consider nothing short of paradise.

At unclothed tables in a long two-room eatery reminiscent of a wild-west saloon, you'll eat real cowboy-style steaks. Aged and hand cut, then sizzled on a griddle so they develop a wicked crust, they are full-flavored and satisfying in a way that big-city expense-account steaks, at twice the price, cannot touch. Local connoisseurs order quail platters and chicken fried steaks, both of which look delicious; but we've never been able to resist the twenty-four-ounce T-bone. It comes with French fries, but if you call the steakhouse an hour and a half before you want to dine, they'll put a baked potato in the oven and have it ready when you arrive.

Desserts are excellent: homey, homely pies made every day by a pastry chef that everyone knows as Granny. Buttermilk is the flavor we prefer.

Reata	
500 Throckmorton, Fort Worth, TX	$$$
(817) 336-1009	LD

The number-one splurge in Fort Worth, Reata is at the top of a bank building like some colossal ranch dining room with a view for miles through its floor-to-ceiling windows. The menus are leather-framed, the chairs are cowhide-covered, and the walls display leather chaps, burnished six-shooters, and dramatic painted murals of cowboy life. If you watched much television in the 1950s and 1960s, you will likely find yourself humming along with the background music even before you are conscious of hearing it: tasteful interpretations of cowboy-show theme songs.

To call the menu ranch food is a sort of understatement, for traditions here are only the launch pad for inventive Texas meals. Oven-warm sourdough flatbread and fluffy biscuits studded with pecans are presented with a ramekin of garlicky, peppered olive oil for dipping; chicken-stuffed chiles rellenos are served atop corn chowder; beef tamales come with avocado crème fraîche; a tall root beer float is spiked with Kahlúa. No such adornment could improve Reata's exemplary rib eye steak, which the menu warns is well-marbled (praise be!). Cut to whatever size you choose and grilled over mesquite wood, it is tender, full-flavored, and luxuriously juicy. We got a twenty-ounce cut; Reata provided a clever little cardboard saddle bag for leftovers.

Smitty's	
6219 Airport Rd., El Paso, TX (915) 772-5876	$
Mon–Sat	£D

Decor at Smitty's consists of neon beer signs. But if it's beauty you crave, order any dinner platter. Feast your eyes on the smoke-cooked brisket, so tender and moist it seems to melt on the tongue; gaze upon the sweet Texas beans, the slaw, and the magnificent, crusty hunks of German fried potato. Then, after you have feasted your eyes, dig in and really feast. It is superb Texas barbecue, with fiery jalapeño peppers on the side. Located in a strip mall near the airport, Smitty's is our favorite place to while away time waiting for a flight, and the first place we go when we fly into El Paso from any barbecue-deprived part of the country.

Sonny Bryan's

2202 Inwood Rd., Dallas, TX (214) 744-1610;	$
other Dallas locations are 302 N. Market 744-1610,	£Đ
325 N. St. Paul 979–0102, Plaza of the Americas Hotel 871-2097,	
4701 Frankford Rd. 447-0102,	
Macy's Food Court at the Galleria Mall 851-5131	

Wedge yourself into a school desk and experience what cognoscenti consider the best urban barbecue in Texas. Profoundly beefy slices of tender brisket are heaped into gigantic sandwiches, well-sauced and sold with good side dishes such as French fries and pork and beans, as well as tumblers of iced tea.

Only the original Bryan's on Inwood has the school desks and the classic bare-bones atmosphere of an old Texas smokehouse *(and it still tends to close midafternoon),* but all the Johnny-come-lately branches of Bryan's dish out smoky brisket that is as good as it gets. We are especially appreciative of the Frankford Road location, just off the Dallas Parkway. Zooming from the airport toward an appointment in Plano one day awhile back, we had no time for a meal. We hopped off the six-lane, scarfed down a quartet of brisket sandwiches, and headed north again, thanking the good Lord we were chowing down in Texas once again.

Southside Market and B-B-Q, Inc.

| 1212 U.S. 290 W, Elgin, TX | $ |
| (512) 281-4650 | £Đ |

Although the brisket (and even the mutton) is exemplary, the sausages, known hereabouts as Elgin (hard G) hot guts, are what have made the Southside Market a benchmark of smoke-pit quality since 1882. They are all-beef tube-shaped beauties, served with crackers, breathtaking hot sauce made of vinegar and spice, and potato salad and beans. Alas, the colorful old market is shuttered, and Southside now inhabits an airplane hangar–style building on the highway; but despite the lost ambiance, the sausages remain superb.

Threadgill's

6416 N. Lamar, Austin, TX	$
(512) 451-5440	L D

Threadgill's is a hoot. A huge rambling roadhouse loaded with neon beer signs and much Janis Joplin memorabilia (she started her career here on hootenanny night in the 1960s), it is a stronghold of Texas food.

The chicken-fried steak is sublime: a broad slab of beef with a golden crust that's all puckered and puffed, audibly crisp when you crunch down, yet melt-in-the-mouth rich. Push a piece through Threadgill's creamy, pepper-flecked gravy, and fork up some smooth mashed potatoes. Complete this lovely picture with black-eyed peas, a steaming biscuit or square of corn bread, a tumbler of iced tea, and a wedge of cool buttermilk pie for dessert, and you have a quintessential blue-plate feast.

The kitchen's motto is "We don't serve all you can eat. We serve more than you can eat." Meat loaf is massively sliced and smothered with chunky Creole sauce. Sheaves of smoked and glazed ham are piled on a plate under a great spill of Jezebel sauce (named for its sweet and tart blend of horseradish, mustard, and apple jelly). The deep-fried chicken liver platter is one of the most astounding plates of food available anywhere, described on the menu as "more than anyone can eat!"

Despite such excesses, Threadgill's also happens to be a good place to practice nutritional virtue. "Victory with Vegetables" says one side of the menu, where the twenty-three different side dishes Threadgill's offers every day are listed. Many customers come only to eat vegetables: a selection of three, five, or nine, heaped together on a single oval trencher like great colorful globs of paint on an exuberant artist's palette, is called a "vegetable orgy."

Tommy's Bar-B-Que

Rte. 82, Reno, TX (903) 785-2808	$
Tues–Sat closes at 7 PM	£𝒟

East of Paris, Texas, there is a barbecue shack with so much stuff on the walls that it is almost difficult to pay attention to the excellent pit-cooked brisket, hot sausage links, spicy smoked bologna, and tongue-teasing red sauce.

Even before you walk into Tommy's, you know there is someone here with a passion for detail: the small front windows are brimful of taxidermied small game. On the walls inside are rodeo photos, steer horns, horseshoes, collectible cowboy-themed clocks, an autographed picture of Reba McIntyre, a formal portrait of John Wayne, and a funny cartoon that is captioned "Arkansas Motorcycle" and shows a cow wearing socks: Cow-a-socky. What all these items have in common, of course, is that they celebrate cowboy heros, cowboy work, and cowboy humor. The food, including silk-smooth sweet beans and a mighty spicy all-beef chili, is cowboy to the core, too.

UTAH

Arshel's Café

711 North Main St., Beaver, UT	$
(435) 438-2977	ℬ£𝒟

Arshel's Café is a pleasant highway diner with frilly curtains in its window that serves homey hot lunches and hamburgers with fresh-cut French fries. But it's Arshel's pies that snare travelers on their way to or from the parks and canyons of the southland. The lemon meringue is famous, but we were more impressed by crunchy boysenberry with a crumb top, and peanut butter chocolate with a cool, smooth ribbon of fudgy cream mounted atop a pebbly layer of chunky peanut butter.

Capitol Reef Café

360 W. Main St., Torrey, UT	$$
(435) 425-3271	BD

A sophisticated oasis in a spectacular landscape far from everywhere, Southey Swede's dining room (with low-cost lodgings and a nice bookstore attached) is a healthy-eater's destination. It is really quite amazing in a region where meat and potatoes rule to plow into the cornucopic ten-vegetable dinner salad or to find such well-made stir-fries and meatless pastas. Breakfast juices are fresh-squeezed, and espresso is available. At suppertime, beef, chicken, trout, and wonderful shish kebab are also on the menu for vegetable-frowners.

Cowboy's Smokehouse

95 North Main, Panguitch, UT (435) 676-8030	$$
Mon–Sat (closed in winter)	LD

Beef brisket, pork ribs, chicken, and turkey are slow-smoked to succulence in this colorful eatery where the walls are covered with the business cards of friends and fans, and the decor is mounted heads of moose, elk, and deer.

Each table is equipped with a bottle of peppery-sweet, cinnabar-red sauce, but tasty as it is, we recommend savoring the meat pure and unsauced—especially the brisket, which spends a leisurely half-day imbibing warm smoke. Served in slices, each piece has a chewy, blackened rim (delicious to gnaw), and within that crusty exterior is beef that is as soft as brisket can get without disintegrating. Ranch beans are available on the side—simple, peppery, al dente, and there is tasty fruit cobbler for dessert; but it's the barbecued meats and the open-fire-grilled dinner steaks that emblazon the Smokehouse on Utah's good-eats map.

Fat City Smoke House

36 South 100 West, Moab, UT	$
(435) 259-4302	D

Our thanks to Alex Tanford, roving barbecue sleuth, for clueing us in to this fine way station for all sorts of barbecue, but especially sausage. Made on the premises, the sausages are available in two configurations—red hot (but not really incendiary) and garlic (whoo-eey, pass the Breath Assure!). Both are delicious in their own way, served in sandwiches or as part of a plate with potato salad, Texas toast, and a choice of cowboy beans, a sweet potato, a baked potato, or dirty rice. In addition to smoky links, the Fat City pit also yields succulent beef brisket, pork ribs and baby back ribs, slow-cooked chicken, ham, and turkey. Top it all off with a serving of silky sweet potato or buttermilk pie.

For travelers on the go, box lunches are available.

Hires Big H

425 South 700 East, Salt Lake City, UT (801) 364-4582;	$
other locations are at 835 E. Fort Union Blvd., Midvale,	LD
561-2171; and 2900 W. 4700 South, West Valley City, 965-1010	

This bright, cheerful root-beer-and-burger drive-in offers a choice of carhop service or indoor tables. The hamburger, served in a little paper pouch, is a handsome quarter-pound of beef with lettuce, tomato, and special sauce on an extraordinarily fresh floury-topped sourdough bun. There are plain burgers, onion burgers, Roquefort burgers, bacon burgers, and pastrami burgers; and there are excellent French fries or cheese fries or chili cheese fries on the side. Cokes are available with vanilla or cherry syrup added. For what it aims to be, Hires Big H is just about perfect.

Idle Isle Café

24 South Main St., Brigham City, UT	$
(435) 734-2468	LD

Here is the sort of honest town café once found on main streets all across America, but now a rarity treasured by all who yearn for honest food served in a setting of utmost civility. You can have a lovely burger and a malt at the marble and onyx soda fountain; but the choice seats are in the polished wooden booths, each outfitted with a ramekin of Idle Isle apricot marmalade for spooning onto the fleecy, oven-warm rolls that come with dinner. The menu is nothing but expertly prepared blue-plate fundamentals, including divinely tender pot roast with mashed potatoes shaped like a crater to hold gravy as well as such daily specials as Wednesday braised beef joints, Friday trout, and Saturday prime rib.

You must save room for dessert, either Idleberry pie—a resonating dark purple blend of blue-, black-, and boysenberries—or baked custard pudding—which is simply the tenderest comfort food that one can imagine.

Karen's

242 25th St., Ogden, UT	$
(801) 392-0345	BLD

A modest restaurant with cowboy decor (condiments are set on the leatherette tablecloth in a miniature wood corral) and western-landscape paintings signed by Karen herself, this place is a find! When we stopped by one day at noon, the special was pot roast, and it was superb: meltingly tender, dripping juice, heaped on a plate with chunky spuds and carrots. We noticed neighbors' hamburgers served on homemade bulky rolls.

As we left, profusely complimenting Karen, who was busy at her stove behind the counter, she accepted our praise but then said, "Come back tomorrow morning. My breakfast burrito is something else." We had to leave town tht day, but breakfast at Karen's is at the top of our must-eat list in Ogden.

Lamb's

169 South Main St., Salt Lake City, UT	$$
(801) 364-7166 Mon–Sat	BLD

When we tell you that Lamb's is basically a diner, we mean it in the nicest possible way. Open all day every day but Sunday since 1919, it has a long counter up front and a dining room in back, a swift staff of uniformed waitresses, and a menu with something for everyone. You can breakfast on bacon and eggs, milk toast, or grilled mountain trout; eat a lunch of ham on white or liver 'n' onions, and splurge on a deluxe steak dinner (or more of that fine river trout). Accommodations include plush tall-backed booths; and among the civilized amenities is a sound system programmed to soothe and comfort valued customers.

Maddox Ranch House

1900 S. Hwy. 89, Perry, UT	$$
(435) 723-8545	LD

Look for the futuristic spinning sign by the side of the highway and you will find the place north of Salt Lake City for eating immense steaks. OVER 4000 HEAD OF CHOICE BEEF USED ANNUALLY, a sign outside boasts. In business since the 1940s, Maddox is big and popular (you'll likely wait for a table). In the old days, the feed lot was adjacent to the restaurant, allowing customers to look out the window at future steaks on the hoof as they dined. Meals include corn sticks and potatoes, as well as pure drinking water drawn from Maddox's own well.

For those on the go, Maddox has a drive-in adjacent to its restaurant. Here the menu is such classic car-fare as burgers, chicken baskets, long dogs, and cream pies, accompanied by a beverage called "Fresh lime," which is Sprite doctored up with lime squeezin's and sugar.

Mom's

10 E. Main, Salina, UT	$
(435) 529-3921	BLD

Mom's is a vintage crossroads café in an old cow town. Locals as well as travelers congregate in its aqua-upholstered booths for three meals a day, dished out by energetic uniformed waitresses while Mom sits at her desk in the back of the dining room overseeing everything. The menu is basic meat and potatoes. We like the hamburgers and the liver and onions, the latter available, according to the menu, only when the liver is absolutely fresh. For breakfast, there is lush-crusted chicken-fried steak; and there are scones—Utah's own flaky version of the deep-fried dough pastries known in New Mexico as sopaipillas. Mom's scones are accompanied by a squeeze bottle of honey-butter.

Ruth's Diner

2100 Emigration Canyon, Salt Lake City, UT	$
(801) 582-5807	BLD

Ruth's is a diner with a sense of history. Opened in 1930 by Ruth Evans, who developed a reputation as one of the crankiest Pall Mall–puffing hash-slingers in the West, it was bought by a new generation in 1979 and has since become a beacon of sophisticated urban fare. You can still get a hamburger—Ruth's specialty—but burgers at the new Ruth's are available with pasta salad on the side, and topped with Cajun spice and/or blue cheese, fresh guacamole, or melted Swiss. And while Old West biscuits and gravy continue to be a featured attraction of the breakfast menu, you can also eat a luxuriant "Rutherino" omelet with pasta, pesto, cheese, and hollandaise sauce. The dinner menu ranges from liver and onions to Chinese chicken salad and paillard of pork in lemon shallot caper sauce. Recommended: chiles rellenos or roasted garlic chicken.

(Under the same management, the Santa Fe Restaurant adjacent to the diner is a little swanker and features a "private club" where customers can circumvent Utah's strict liquor laws.)

Zoom

660 Main St., Park City, UT	*$$*
(801) 649-9108	*LD*

Zoom is an agreeably casual "roadhouse grill"—come for a sandwich and a beer, sit outside on a heated patio, gab forever over coffee. Yet the setting is western chic (Utahan Robert Redford owns it) and the food smacks of New American creative zeal.

The clever menu is divided into small plates and main plates, so you can have a quick snack of crunchy-topped baked macaroni and cheese or a grand supper of Cuban rubbed pork with papaya relish and black beans. Sandwiches include a thick black Angus burger and a grilled portobello mushroom on focaccia; entrees vary from impeccable leg of lamb served on a bed of minty lentils with yogurt sauce and cheese-dusted pita crisps to ridiculously messy, falling-off-the-bone Detroit-style ribs.

The one dish we cannot resist is grilled tri-tip steak—a cut of beef favored in old vaquero country west of the Rockies. Sided by Zoom's mess o' greens—vivid, tart, incredibly toothsome—this robust platter strikes us as the kind of protein-rich fare that health-food experts used to prescribe for anemic urbanites in need of red meat and fresh air.

Pie Palaces

◀━◆◆◆▶

W hy is pie so especially good when traveling? Even for those of us who don't eat much of it back home (we personally lean more to cake and cookies), pie eating is one of the true pleasures of any road trip. For a lone wedge with a cup of coffee to break up a long stretch of highway, or as the climax of a meal, here is a plethora of pie stops worth inscribing in your little black book.

- ☛ Betty's Pies, Two Harbors, MN (p. 211)
- ☛ Buntyn, Memphis, TN (p. 93)
- ☛ Dodd's Town House, Indianapolis, IN (p. 192)
- ☛ Duarte's, Pescadero, CA (p. 338)
- ☛ Family Pie Shop, De Valls Bluff, AR (p. 129)
- ☛ George's Diner, Meredith, NH (p. 34)
- ☛ Henry's, West Jefferson, OH (p. 227)
- ☛ Jones Café, Pine Bluff, AR (p. 131)
- ☛ Laughner's, Indianapolis, IN (p. 193)
- ☛ Moody's Diner, Waldoboro, ME (p. 23)
- ☛ Norske Nook, Osseo, WI (p. 236)
- ☛ The Owl, Parksley, VA (p. 104)
- ☛ Paris Coffee Shop, Fort Worth, TX (p. 316)
- ☛ Pope's Café, Shelbyville, TN (p. 98)
- ☛ Putney Diner, Putney, VT (p. 46)
- ☛ Stone's, Marshalltown, IA (p. 202)
- ☛ The Village Inn, Middlebury, IN (p. 197)
- ☛ The White Way, Durant, IA (p. 203)

THE DINER
Yountville SACRAMENTO
★ ★ Sutter Creek CHATTER BOX CAFÉ

★ Columbia CITY HOTEL

San Francisco
Pescadero
DUARTE'S

DOIDGE'S
HAYES STREET GRILL
SEARS FINE FOODS
TADICH GRILL

FAR WESTERN TAVERN
Guadalupe
Casmalia
HITCHING POST

DU-PAR'S   DU-PAR'S
Thousand Oaks   Studio City
               Hollywood MUSSO AND FRANK
               ★ Pasadena BEADLE'S CAFETERIA

Los Angeles

CASSELL'S
COLE'S P.E. BUFFET
DU-PAR'S
MAURICE'S SNACK 'N' CHAT
THE ORIGINAL PANTRY
PHILIPPE'S
PINK'S CHILI DOGS

RUBIO'S   THE COTTAGE
BAJA GRILL La Jolla JOHN'S WAFFLE SHOP
Mission Bay
San Diego   Pacific Beach
            ICHIBAN P.B.

EL INDIO
HOB NOB HILL
RAINWATER'S

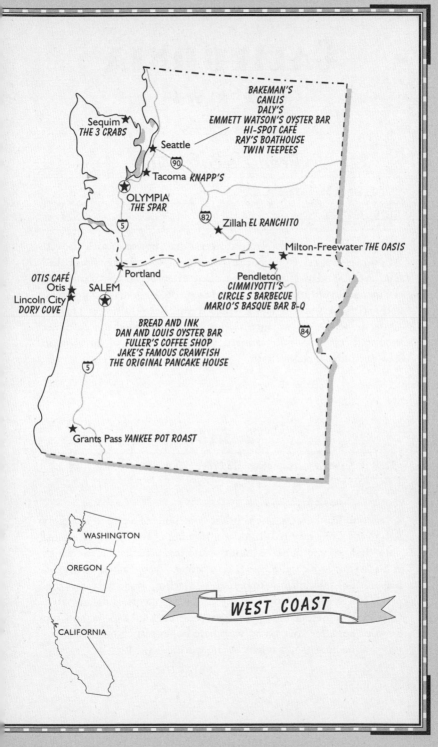

Sequim
THE 3 CRABS

BAKEMAN'S
CANLIS
DALY'S
EMMETT WATSON'S OYSTER BAR
HI-SPOT CAFÉ
RAY'S BOATHOUSE
TWIN TEEPEES

Seattle

[90]

Tacoma *KNAPP'S*

OLYMPIA
THE SPAR

[82]

Zillah *EL RANCHITO*

Milton-Freewater **THE OASIS**

[5]

Portland

Pendleton
CIMMIYOTTI'S
CIRCLE S BARBECUE
MARIO'S BASQUE BAR B-Q

OTIS CAFÉ
Otis
Lincoln City
DORY COVE

SALEM

[84]

BREAD AND INK
DAN AND LOUIS OYSTER BAR
FULLER'S COFFEE SHOP
JAKE'S FAMOUS CRAWFISH
THE ORIGINAL PANCAKE HOUSE

[5]

Grants Pass *YANKEE POT ROAST*

WASHINGTON

OREGON

CALIFORNIA

WEST COAST

CALIFORNIA

⭐ ⭐ ⭐

Beadle's Cafeteria

825 E. Green St., Pasadena, CA	$
(626) 796-3618	LD

Beadle's is a reasonably priced cafeteria that showcases such stalwart dinners as leg o' lamb, pot roast with potato pancakes, and baked ham every Sunday. Hash—beef, turkey, or corned beef—is often on the menu. Roast turkey with aromatic sage dressing, mashed potatoes, and gravy is served five days a week. "People seem to expect Thanksgiving dinner," manager Jane Arvizu told us as she watched a customer vacillate between colorful confetti Jell-O and a dish of carrot-raisin slaw, then finally choose both.

Cassell's

3266 W. Sixth St., Los Angeles, CA (213) 480-8668	$
Mon–Sat	£

Beautiful hamburgers, one-third or two-thirds of a pound of freshly ground beef, rosy red inside a glistening charred crust, are piled onto fresh sesame buns—a mouth-watering presentation, to which you add your own condiments from a buffet. These include *homemade* mayonnaise, high-quality tomatoes, red relish, Roquefort dressing, peach halves and pineapple chunks, and an epicurean potato salad. Cassell's is a rudimentary restaurant—nothing to look at and too crowded any time after noon, with bare-bones seating on a small patio—but its burgers just might be the world's best.

Chatter Box Café

Main St., Sutter Creek, CA	$
(209) 267-5935	BL

This tiny main street café opened for business in 1946, and while the decor is pure nostalgia, the food is a cut above. Enlightened burgers topped with anything from blue cheese or green chilies to sweet Jamaican relish are served on bakery rolls with high-quality condiments and fresh-cut French fries on the side. Breakfast is a bonanza: interesting omelets, delectable corned beef hash, a gold-country version of San Francisco's Joe Special (ground beef, spinach, and onions scrambled with eggs), and a choice of *ten* different kinds of sausage, including spicy andouille, bratwurst, kielbasa, and bangers. Muffins are oven-hot, as are cinnamon rolls . . . but come early, because the good breadstuffs can vanish well before breakfast ends at 11 AM.

City Hotel

Main St., Columbia, CA (209) 532-1479	$$
Sunday brunch	D

This charming little 1856 hotel provides not only the flavor of Gold Rush luxe, but also fine modern food and California wine, all tendered with aplomb by a staff of seasoned professionals as well as students earning their degrees in the Hospitality Management Program of nearby Columbia College. For drinks (vintage or modern), the original What Cheer saloon downstairs is an inviting place to linger; it still has its original cherrywood bar, shipped round the Horn from New England. The second-floor parlor, which serves as a sitting room during the day, doubles as a breakfast room for guests each morning. And the dining room is known throughout the region for its vintner dinners hosted by local wine makers, its "student cookbook" dinners for which Advanced Contemporary Cuisine students prepare four-course meals using recipes from a popular cookbook, and a seasonal menu that reflects enthusiasm for local produce as well as a knowledge of classic cuisine.

Cole's P.E. Buffet

118 E. 6th St., Los Angeles, CA	$
(213) 622-4090　Mon–Sat	LD

The oldest restaurant and saloon in Los Angeles (since 1908), Cole's is a dark and atmospheric hole-in-the-wall cafeteria with sawdust on the floors. Customers pile trays with hot lunches of days gone by: platters of steamed corned beef and cabbage, beef stew, thick-sliced roast beef. The house specialty is the French dip, a West Coast sandwich that might have been invented here. The story is that shortly after Cole's opened for business in the Pacific Electric Railway station, a customer complained that his gums hurt. He wanted a beef sandwich, but feared he couldn't bite through the crusty roll. Chef sliced the roll as usual, but before he loaded it with beef he dipped each half in the pan of natural gravy where the beef sat. The gravy softened the bread . . . and the French dip sandwich was born. It is a splendid concept, particularly well executed by Cole's carvers. When you request a French dip, the man in the toque forks a slab of hot brisket from the steam box and hand-slices a mound of thick, juicy pieces, then spears each half of the sliced roll and holds it in a pan of natural gravy long enough to fully flavor the soft part of the chewy bread but leave the crust crisp. The moistened bread melds with the mellow beef it wraps, and the result is a delicious mess. At the tables, glass jars hold fierce hot mustard—the tender French dip's ideal complement.

The Cottage

7702 Fay Ave., La Jolla, CA	$$
(619) 454-8409　BLD Tues–Sat; BL Sun and Mon	BLD

Only recently did we discover that The Cottage serves lunch and dinner. In our book, it was always a place to go for a breakfast of warm buttermilk coffee cake or brown-sugar-glazed cinnamon rolls or brilliant omelets. But we've come back midday to savor grilled mahimahi tacos served with creamy black beans and papaya salsa and the turkey chili that comes with a sweet, warm corn muffin. At dinner, we have sat down to plates of "Laura's meat loaf" with wild mushroom sauce and creamy mashed potatoes and red curry linguine with grilled tiger shrimp.

A cozy little restaurant with pale yellow walls, low jazz for background music, a sunny patio, and an enchanting staff of waitresses in short-shorts, The Cottage is reason enough to think of La Jolla as paradise on earth.

The Diner	
6476 Washington St., Yountville, CA (707) 944-2626	*$$*
Tues–Sun	*BLD*

The heavenly wine country hash house serves four-star cheeseburgers and shoestring French fries, real cherry Cokes, and fine Mexican dinners. But the stellar meal at this Napa County treasure is breakfast, "served all day." Consider banana-nut pancakes with maple syrup, or buttermilk corn cakes sided by sausage patties seasoned with herbs from The Diner's backyard garden. Eggs and omelets are accompanied by heaps of cheese-draped, onion-laced fried potatoes and toast made from homemade sourdough rye, raisin wheat, or potato bread. The coffee is rich and strong; but if you've got time to linger, you might also favor a mimosa, made with freshly squeezed orange juice and locally bottled champagne.

Doidge's	
2217 Union St., San Francisco, CA (415) 921-2149	*$*
(reservations advised, especially on weekends)	*BL*

Doidge's is a storefront café that is a breakfast boodle. Glorious French toast is made from your choice of bread (raisin-nut, honey-wheat, etc.) and heaped with fresh fruit, nuts, and sour cream. Baked eggs are served in cups made from thick bacon. Corned beef hash comes with crunchy fried potatoes, a garnish of sour cream, and a sourdough roll on the side. Omelets are expertly made with all the usual ingredients and plenty of extraordinary ones. We especially like the peach and walnut chutney omelet, but never can resist that French toast and classic eggs Benedict.

Duarte's	
202 Stage Rd., Pescadero, CA	$
(650) 879-0464	*BLD*

Regular customers often share tables with traveling strangers in this snug 100-year-old tavern, where the specialty of the house is always artichokes (grown in nearby fields). Artichoke omelets are served at breakfast, artichokes are stuffed with fennel sausage later in the day, and every dinner is served with cream of artichoke soup.

Duarte's offers a whole menu of fine square meals, such as pork chops with mashed potatoes and roast turkey with dressing, all served with good, gardeny salads; but beyond the artichokes, the kitchen's main attraction is fresh Pacific seafood. We've eaten impeccable little sand dabs and rex sole in Duarte's pine-paneled dining room; and plump oysters are baked with plenty of garlic in a buttery casserole. Cioppino, made with Dungeness crab, mussels, prawns, and clams, is a weekend specialty.

Pies are hefty and homey, like the best truck stop might serve, made from local berries, rhubarb, apples, and apricots.

Du-par's	
6333 W. Third St. at the Farmer's Market, Los Angeles, CA	$
(213) 933-8446; other locations in	*BLD*
Thousand Oaks and Studio City	

Du-par's is a small chain of old-style coffee shops that specialize in savory pot pies—chicken, steak, or steak and kidney—and a dazzling array of dessert pies including southern pecan, lemon, and coconut custard. It is a three-meals-a-day kind of place: the breakfast pancakes are a Los Angeles legend (you can buy batter ready to take home and pour on the griddle), as is buttered and grilled date-nut bread. Night owls come for fine Welsh rarebit; and there are plenty of regular customers who time their lunch visits according to the immemorial daily specials: Monday fried chicken, Tuesday turkey, Wednesday pot roast, Thursday liver 'n' onions, Friday meat loaf—all accompanied by freshly mashed potatoes.

These hearty foodstuffs are served in spic-and-span surroundings by waitresses who wear tiny yellow hats shaped like cupcakes, white uniforms, and yellow aprons. The West Third Street Du-par's has the added attraction of being at the Farmer's Market, which is a good place to browse among fresh produce and shlock souvenirs and spot the many celebrities who shop here incognito.

El India	
3695 India St., San Diego, CA	$
(619) 299-0333	LD

This breezy taqueria along the Interstate serves fresh Cal-Mex food: carnitas and burritos, guacamole-topped platters of chimichangas, quesadillas, hefty tacos, and diminutive taquitos. Wait in line and tote your own meal to a jammed-together indoor seat or to an open-air patio just across the street. It's cheap, fun, and tasty; and when you're finished, you can heave your disposable plate into the garbage and get back on the highway in a jiffy.

Far Western Tavern	
899 Guadalupe St., Guadalupe, CA	$$
(805) 343-2211	LD

Meals at the Far Western Tavern are served on cowboy-theme dishware emblazoned with little images of brands, spurs, and cows' heads, in a dining room that features a spectacular suite of hairy brown-and-white cowhide curtains. All this could be the decor of a campy new-West restaurant, but here in Guadalupe it is the real Mc-

Coy. This is ranch country, where the vaqueros once rode and where cattle is still big business, so naturally the best thing to order is red meat. In particular, the Far Western features a "bull's-eye" steak cooked on an open grate over flaming live oak logs. It is accompanied by all the companions required at a traditional beef banquet in central California: a tray of relishes to start, zesty little pinquito beans on the side, salsa to heat things up, and crusty bread for mopping juice.

Hayes Street Grill

320 Hayes St., San Francisco, CA	$$$
(415) 863-5545 £ Mon–Fri; 𝕯 daily	£𝕯

Hayes Street Grill has managed to maintain a small-restaurant feeling despite the fact that it is one of the seminal Bay Area kitchens that has defined modern California cuisine. Leave celebrity-chef dining rooms to their gourmet-club clientele. Reserve a table at Hayes Street and start with a marvelous house salad of beets, Stilton, and walnuts, or with simple cracked crab accompanied by red-pepper aioli; then move on to mesquite-grilled halibut, snapper, or scallops with your choice of garnishes that include salsa, lemon-butter, luxurious béarnaise, and peanutty Szechuan. Top it off with crème brûlée, and you will have consumed a sophisticated San Francisco meal to remember.

Hitching Post

3325 Point Sal Rd., Casmalia, CA	$$
(805) 937-6151	𝕯

The Hitching Post's top sirloin is grand—pungent with age, oozing juice, an easy chew—but the filet mignon is even better. Its fibers glow with the flavor of the hard oak wood over which it's cooked, and with the piquant smack of the wine vinegar and oil marinade that is applied as the meat cooks. The beef is served as part of a traditional Santa Maria–style barbecue dinner, which includes relish tray, a cock-

Old California Cuisine

Much as we appreciate the salubrious influence of "New" California cuisine on American menus, we've got a soft spot for Golden State traditions that predate the reign of Alice and Wolfgang, goat cheese, and boutique pizza. An old California meal can be as simple as chicken pot pie at Du-par's or as deluxe as steak and martinis at Musso's. These restaurants are pretty much the same as they were fifty years ago.

- ☞ Cole's P.E. Buffet, Los Angeles, CA (p. 336)
- ☞ Duarte's, Pescadero, CA (p. 338)
- ☞ Du-par's, Los Angeles, CA (p. 338)
- ☞ Far Western Tavern, Guadalupe, CA (p. 339)
- ☞ Musso and Frank, Hollywood, CA (p. 344)
- ☞ The Original Pantry, Los Angeles, CA (p. 344)
- ☞ Philippe's, Los Angeles, CA (p. 345)
- ☞ Tadich Grill, San Francisco, CA (p. 349)

tail of microscopic pink shrimp in red sauce, garlic bread, salsa, and potatoes.

The Hitching Post is one of the few businesses on the main street of Casmalia, a sleepy little town that seems worlds away from modern Los Angeles. Restaurant decor is cow-country casual: linoleum floors and red tablecloths, a TV always on above the bar, a bison head wearing a Buffalo Bills cap, and wall hangings made of cattle hides.

Hob Nob Hill

2271 First Ave., San Diego, CA	$
(619) 239-8176	BLD

Eating in so gentle a coffee shop makes us think of mid-century domestic science brochures that offer advice to the eager new bride who wants to create a happy home: set an attractive table, cook wholesome and well-balanced meals, add a pleasant little garnish to every plate to show you care. So it is at Hob Nob Hill.

There are mouth-watering daily specials (Tuesday short ribs and Sunday sauerbraten are delightful), but the everyday entrees are special, too: chicken croquettes with gravy, mashed potatoes, and tart cranberry relish served in half a hollowed out orange; turkey with sage dressing in the evening; big fruit plates and fiesta salads at noontime.

Hob Nob Hill is a joyous place for breakfast; to start the day with freshly squeezed juice, good coffee, and a wedge of spicy rhubarb sour cream coffee cake or a pumpkin muffin is a taste of California heaven. Amid the rush and crowds, waitresses liven up the room by schmoozing with customers they have served for decades as enthusiastic pastry-hounds rhapsodize out loud over the individual bundt cakes and caramel sticky buns and sweet rolls in the glass case that everyone admires while they wait for a table.

Ichiban P.B.

1441 Garnet Ave., Pacific Beach, CA	$
(619) 270-5755	£D

There are many restaurants around San Diego that serve Japanese fare cheap. Aside from well-made sushi and hot teriyaki at low-low prices, the special charm of Ichiban P.B. is its beachside character. The ocean is blocks away, but Ichiban's counter and booths attract crowds of surfers and a broad assortment of the kind of happy-go-lucky Pacific Beach denizens who give this neighborhood its panache. Japanese though the food may be, the experience of eating a bowl of "stamina noodles" or a platter of California rolls at Ichiban P.B. is way rad—a taste of the sun-drenched essence of surf culture.

John's Waffle Shop

7906 Girard Ave., La Jolla, CA	$
(619) 454-7371	BL

This happy café is reminiscent of the days La Jolla was just a little get-away-from-it-all village by the sea. Nothing fancy about it; you come to John's in the morning for excellent waffles, pancakes, or eggs, or at lunch for such enduring coffee-shop fare as gentle-tempered chili with beans, an avocado-rich Cobb salad, or our personal favorite, the "smart girl sandwich," made with lots of good bacon, grilled onions, tomato, and cheese. On the side, drink a tall chocolate malt or the salubrious West Coast favorite, a smoothie, which is a health shake made with orange juice or strawberries.

Maurice's Snack 'N' Chat

5553 Pico Blvd., Los Angeles, CA (213) 931-3877	$$
(reservations advised)	LD

EAT HERE CHEAPER THAN AT HOME, AND BETTER, TOO says a sign outside. Inside the friendly, unpretentious soul-food landmark, Hollywood celebrities rub elbows with ordinary Angelenos over plates of fried chicken, smothered pork chops, pan-fried fish, short ribs, and meat loaf, all served with heaps of long-cooked, deep-seasoned vegetables. For adventurous eaters looking to get away from fashion-fickle L.A., for homesick southerners in search of comfort food, and for skinny people in search of a serious weight-gain diet, Maurice's is a great place to know about.

Musso and Frank

6667 Hollywood Blvd., Hollywood, CA (213) 467-7788	$$
Tues–Sat (reservations advised)	£D

When Musso and Frank opened for business in 1919, Hollywood was young and fresh and Hollywood Boulevard was a magic address. Hollywood is now an institution and the Boulevard has gone to honky-tonk hell in a handbasket, but step inside Musso's and go back to a wondrous time. Ensconced in a plush leather booth in this wood-paneled institution, you dine on immemorial comfort food that includes svelte lunchtime flannel cakes, sauerbraten with potato pancakes, chicken pot pie every Thursday, and a full menu of broiled steaks and chops with eleven kinds of potatoes available on the side. Old-fashioned cocktails are expertly mixed; and as you sip a martini, manhattan, gibson, or Rob Roy, chances are very good of spotting some of the many show biz celebrities who still come to Musso's. Perhaps they crave the powerful sense of normalcy this old grill radiates.

The Original Pantry

877 S. Figueroa St., Los Angeles, CA	$
(213) 972-9279	BLD

Since 1924, The Original Pantry has been open round the clock, pretty well defining coffee shop cuisine: a cut above café chow (there are no plebeian burgers here), but quick and inexpensive. Full-house egg breakfasts are accompanied by fine sourdough toast, thick slabs of bacon, and piles of good fried potatoes. Such stalwart suppers as roast beef with mashed potatoes or liver 'n' onions are preceded by a delightfully anachronous relish tray; and the dessert of choice is hot apple pie with rum sauce.

Now adjoining The Original Pantry is a more modern dining room called The Bakery, where sandwiches and short-order meals are featured.

Philippe's

1001 N. Alameda St., Los Angeles, CA	$
(213) 628-3781	BLD

Philippe's is a self-service restaurant that is as comfy as an old shoe: sawdust-strewn floors, communal tables, nine-cents-a-cup coffee, and superb French dip sandwiches with roaring-hot mustard on the side. It is as good a people-watching place as Spago, but instead of movie stars, you see the Los Angelenos Raymond Chandler wrote about—downtowners who include municipal employees from the nearby post office and courthouse as well as Santa Anita touts who frequent the bank of old wooden phone booths, racing forms in hand.

Pink's Chili Dogs

709 N. La Brea Ave., Los Angeles, CA	$
(213) 931-4223	BLD

Beautiful, taut-skinned hot dogs are nabbed in spongy buns, then topped with mustard, raw onions, and a spill of Day-Glo orange no-bean chili. Customers eat 'em standing on the sidewalk, sitting in cars parked in the red zone on La Brea, or strolling along Melrose Avenue. These raunchy tube steaks have made Pink's a preferred dive since it opened in 1939, but the menu lists lesser-known breeds of pup worth eating, too: the Guadalajara dog, topped with sour cream; cheese dogs; dogs wrapped in tortillas; chopped dogs in a cup of baked beans. There are even hamburgers and tamales, and a pretty darn good warm potato salad. For dessert, true connoisseurs avail themselves of a Pink's candy machine and top things off with a couple of Atomic Fireballs.

Rainwater's

1202 Ketner, San Diego, CA	$$$
(619) 233-5757	LD
Sat and Sun D only	

Located in a spacious warehouse building outfitted in dark wood and thick white linen, Rainwater's is two restaurants: a downstairs open-kitchen grill with an eclectic menu and an upstairs chop house. At the

Coffee Shop Culture

It is difficult to pinpoint what exactly makes a restaurant a coffee shop (as opposed to a diner, a café, or a lunchroom), but any connoisseur of urban cheap eats knows that a coffee shop is a special kind of place with a soupçon of refinement that always makes for pleasant eating. Some fundamental qualities include three-meals-a-day service, uniformed waitresses wearing name tags, a large and familiar menu (possibly laminated in plastic), a first-come-first-served seating policy, and—of course—hot coffee served before, during, and after any meal.

Nowhere did the coffee shop prosper more than in southern California, particularly in the 1950s and 1960s, when such futuristic Naugahyde-and-Formica shrines as Ship's, Norm's, and Pann's were designed to resemble the offspring of a tail-finned Cadillac mated to a space ship's rec room.

Although no longer the height of culinary modernity, coffee shops still provide a certain basic, casual gratification not available in a diner, a dive, or an ordinary restaurant. Come as you are, eat well and pay little, and walk out with spring in your step.

- ☞ Du-par's, Los Angeles, CA (p. 338)
- ☞ Hob Nob Hill, San Diego, CA (p. 341)
- ☞ John's Waffle Shop, La Jolla, CA (p. 343)
- ☞ Fuller's Coffee Shop, Portland, OR (p. 352)
- ☞ Knapp's Restaurant, Tacoma, WA (p. 359)
- ☞ Sears Fine Foods, San Francisco, CA (p. 348)

latter, customers ensconce themselves in plush leather booths, sip martinis (or one of the 20+ vodkas on ice) and eat posh portions of the best steaks money can buy. "Not for the lean beef eater," the menu warns about the rib eye, which is so nicely accompanied by a crusty cake of rosti potatoes to push through the beefy juices. Huge strips and porterhouses are available for two, and roasted prime rib with horseradish sauce, creamed corn, and mashed potatoes sets the standard. Meals come with sourdough bread and warm corn sticks with creamy insides.

Although the meat menu is universal Americana, there is a curious heartland twist to many of Rainwater's best dishes: "head lettuce" (that's Midwestern for iceberg) is available as a cool, crisp wedge topped with superior Maytag blue cheese from Iowa. The seafood repertoire includes the Great Lakes treat known as a "mess of perch" (crisp-fried filets served with good tartar sauce); and this is the only restaurant outside of Chicago we have ever seen the recherché specialty chicken Vesuvio (white meat chunks sautéed with peas in a garlic wine sauce and served over fettuccini).

Choosing dessert is a dilemma. Rainwater apple pie, served warm, is a classic; so are the pecan pie, the New York cheesecake, and the crème brûlée; but who can resist thin-layered ice cream chocolate lasagna?

Rubio's Baja Grill

4504 E. Mission Bay Dr., Mission Bay (this is the address	$
of the original Rubio's. There are locations throughout	
San Diego and elsewhere) (619) 272-2801	£D

Ralph Rubio didn't invent the fish taco; he brought it back from Baja, where he learned to love it as a vacationing college student. Since he opened his first fish taco stand in San Diego in 1983, San Diegans have come to love fish tacos, too (there are now more than 40 Rubios in Southern California and beyond; and fish tacos are found on menus throughout the city).

The fish taco as served at Rubio's is a thick corn tortilla wrapped around a hunk of fried cod with a tingly mustard-tinged batter that is dressed with creamy white sauce and garnished with rough-cut shreds of cool white cabbage. It is a buck-and-a-half meal that leaves most other fast food in the dust.

Rubio's vacation-themed eat-shops offer many other good meals, including fish burritos (with beans, guacamole, and cheese), shrimp-stuffed quesadillas, "Healthmex" tacos made with char-grilled (not fried) chicken and fish, and even non-fish carne asada (marinated, grilled steak). But if you have time for only one meal at Rubio's, do your tastebuds a favor and choose fish tacos. They're the pride of San Diego.

Sears Fine Foods	
439 Powell St., San Francisco, CA	$
(405) 986-1160	B L

As much a landmark as the cable cars that trundle past its front door, Sears is a modest coffee shop that attracts crowds of tourists as well as non-snob locals for what many consider to be the best breakfast in town: Swedish pancakes. Silver-dollar size, eighteen to an order, and made from a thin batter with a rich dairy savor, they are limp and light and oh-so-easy to eat. Also available for breakfast is excellent sourdough French toast made from thick slabs of bread so deeply soaked before frying that they have a softness reminiscent of custard. Pecan waffles and baked apples are other menu highlights; and side dishes, including smoked ham, fresh fruit cup, and strawberry preserves, are of the highest quality.

Expect to wait for a table most mornings.

Tadich Grill

240 California St., San Francisco, CA	$$$
(415) 391-2373	£D
Mon–Sat	

Formal and first-class, yet democratic (there are no reservations; everybody waits in line), Tadich Grill started as a coffee shop during the Gold Rush. It has grown and moved a few times over the last century and a half, settling in its current clubby location in the Financial District in the 1960s. For perfect Pacific seafood, simply prepared and elegantly presented by white-aproned waiters, it is the best place in town. The cioppino is authoritative, accompanied by good bread; sand dabs, filleted with utmost finesse and presented two at a time on china plates, are exquisite; fried oysters and prawns, accompanied by four-star tartar sauce, are ethereal (and French fried potatoes are huge and tasty); charcoaled swordfish, snapper, and salmon are moist, market fresh, and delicious. A seafood feast in a private booth at Tadich's is a great American meal.

OREGON

Bread and Ink

3610 SE Hawthorne Blvd., Portland, OR	$$
(503) 239-4756	£D

In this civilized storefront café, you can get a deliciously aristocratic hamburger—on a homemade bun, with cheddar or Gruyère cheese or great guacamole on top and served with top-quality condiments, including garlic aioli to die for. Or you can eat food inspired by the cuisines of Vietnam (spring rolls), Italy (anchovy-and-tomato bread), Mexico (chicken enchiladas with tomatillo salsa), or the Pacific Northwest (broiled salmon). Come on Sunday and brunch is traditionally Jewish: cheese blintzes, scrambled eggs with lox and onions, schmaltzy chopped liver.

Bread and Ink is a lovely place to linger over coffee. Magazines and papers are provided and the staff seems to enjoy being part of the nicest restaurant in town.

Cimmiyotti's	
137 South Main St., Pendleton, OR	$$
(541) 276-4314　𝕯 Mon–Sat	𝕯

Eastern Oregon is cattle country, and the beef served in this clubby Main Street steak house—listed on the saddle leather-bound menu under a heading that reads "From the Feed Lot"—is exemplary. There are big New York strips and ladies' tenderloins, filets mignon, chopped steaks and hamburgers, and teriyaki steaks; the specialty of the house is a good-size rib eye that runs with juice when you slice off a hunk.

Cimmiyotti's Italian specialties are guileless Italian-American fare from an age of culinary innocence: soft white spaghetti noodles topped with chunky, oregano-flavored red sauce; lasagna with onions and sausage, made with three stout cheeses; cannelloni; manicotti; ravioli; and fettucine Alfredo. All come with glistening loaves of gentle-flavored garlic bread.

Circle S Barbecue	
210 S.E. 5th, Pendleton, OR	$
(541) 276-9637　𝓑𝓛𝓓 Tues–Sat; 𝓑𝓛 only Sun	𝓑𝓛𝓓

Breakfast is great in this friendly cafe that is loaded to the rafters with western decor, including farriers' tools, vintage saddles, and an inspirational plaque titled CODE OF THE COW COUNTRY ("Always kill a rattlesnake. Never ride a sore-back hoss."). You can eat crunch-crusted chicken-fried steak, a vast platter of pancakes, German sausages, and hash browns, or biscuits and gravy. On the side, many regular customers imbibe a concoction known as red beer, which is a combination of beer and tomato juice.

At lunch and dinner, there is excellent barbecue insinuated with the tang of apple- and cherrywood smoke. We especially like Circle S chicken, which glistens like polished mahogany and is as crisp-skinned as Peking duck, so fragile that you can hear it crackle when you ease a knife down through it and watch the juices flow. Barbecued beef isn't nearly as pretty, but the flat slices have a pleasant smoke flavor nicely complemented by the dark red sauce that comes alongside. You can also get heavily garlicked barbecued German sausage or pork ribs, which are a royal mess to eat and about as porky as a rack can be.

Dan and Louis Oyster Bar

208 SW Ankeny St., Portland, OR	$$
(503) 227-5906	L D

Oyster Stew" are the only words you need to know if you come to Dan and Louis' ancient mariner of an eatery, where the walls are covered, floor to ceiling, with nautical bibelots. The stew is a mild brew of little oysters, warm milk, and melted butter, but can be made brinier by ordering it with a double dose of oysters. Stew has been the specialty here for decades; for a change of pace in winter months, we also like creamed crab—an old-fashioned kind of chafing-dish meal that has virtually ceased to exist as more modern chefs insist on serving seafood that actually looks like fish.

Dory Cove

5819 Logan Rd., Lincoln City, OR	$
(541) 994-5180	L D

Amid marshlands near a clamming beach, this wood-shingled shack is liked by locals for its hefty half-pound hamburgers, available every which way, but especially tasty topped with cheddar cheese and

Canadian bacon on an onion bun. Nor do you want to miss Dory Cove's Oregon-style (ultrathick) clam chowder, and you must save room for dessert. The thing to eat is pie, of which there are nearly a dozen homemade kinds every day, including chiffons, meringues, creams, sour cream raisin, and monumental deep-dish peach or apple, served piping hot.

Fuller's Coffee Shop

136 NW Ninth Ave., Portland, OR	$
(503) 222-5608　　Mon–Sat	B£

When it's time for breakfast in Portland, find this good, old-fashioned luncheonette among the factory buildings and you can't go wrong: freshly made cinnamon rolls, four-star French toast, and omelets accompanied by classic hash browns. At lunch, count on meat loaf with mashed potatoes, corned beef with cabbage, fresh salmon and halibut in season, plus the locally favored treat, fried razor clams. Fuller's is a simple place, easy to love.

Jake's Famous Crawfish

401 SW Twelfth Ave., Portland, OR	$$
(503) 226-1419	£D

Forget the crawfish. Although crawfish pie and étouffée have been on the menu since 1920, they are not what's good about this ever-popular hangout, where many customers come for no reason other than to drink microbrewed beer and eat raw oysters by the dozen and socialize at the back bar. The great things to eat are salmon, Dungeness crab, petrale sole, and a daily blackboard list of a few dozen sea creatures hauled in fresh from the market that day. Jake's also happens to be a fine place to sample the West Coast specialty: hangtown fry, an omelet made with fried oysters.

The setting is Barbary Coast–vintage Pacifica: gold-flocked wallpaper, glittery chandeliers, high-back wooden booths with a patina of decades, and white-jacketed waiters who go about their business with all the efficiency of faro dealers.

Mario's Basque Bar B-Q

3107 Southgate, Pendleton, OR (541) 276-1665	$
open 4 days in September on the Pendleton Round-Up grounds;	
otherwise, call	

Mario Zubiria doesn't currently have a restaurant, but he is well known around Pendleton as a caterer. If you are lucky enough to be in Pendleton during the big rodeo in September, you can sample his robust food; the rest of the year, give him a call and find out where he is cooking, and ask if you can bust in to the event for a taste.

At the rodeo, Mr. Zubiria sets up a big mobile barbecue where he and his men charcoal-grill lamb chunks and chops, beef, and foot-long chorizo sausages, sending mouth-watering smoke signals wafting above the arena. The lamb chunks are chewy and tangy, served in a cardboard boat with charcoal-grilled onions, green peppers, and mushrooms. The hefty chorizo sausage, ground in Boise, Idaho, has an alarming red hue, and is peppery but not very hot. Its crisp skin encloses luscious, coarsely ground and well-garlicked pork, and although it is available on a stick for easy eating, we like it Mario's alternative way: wrapped inside a loaf of French bread and smothered with grilled onions.

The Oasis

State Line Rd., Milton-Freewater, OR	$$
(541) 938-4776 Tues–Sun	£D

The Oasis is like a nice old pickup truck: ramshackle and rugged, but endearingly soulful. Art on the walls includes portraits of John Wayne and Chief Joseph of the Nez Perce; video poker machines in adjacent gaming rooms provide distant boinging background sounds for diners. From our table, we had a good view into the bar. There, perched on stools, were three large X's in a row: suspenders on the broad backs of three gents in cowboy hats having drinks and shooting the breeze. "How-do?" asked one, tipping his hat in our direction.

"Doing fine!" said we as our beef arrived. Beef is king in these parts, and the sirloins, branded with a neat field of crosshatch char marks, were mighty slabs of juicey meat with high flavor and agreeable tooth resistance. Prime rib is opulent; the "ranch cut," in particular, is well over an inch thick, fleshy, and laden with natural gravy.

The Original Pancake House	
8600 Southwest Barbur Boulevard, Portland, OR	**$**
(503) 246-9007	**BLD**

These pancakes are to ordinary restaurant flapjacks what champagne is to grape juice—so good they are almost like another kind of food altogether. Elegant, complex, transcendent . . . and yet utterly satisfying the way only pancakes can be. The secret, other than good recipes for a large variety of 'cakes from simple buttermilk silver dollars to elaborate crepes, is that the kitchen uses the highest quality ingredients. You can taste the freshness of butter and eggs in everything they cook; even cream served with coffee tastes like something from a farm kitchen. The top of the line pancake is baked apple, a vast plateau of deliciousness big enough for two mighty appetites.

A word of warning: the Pancake House gets very crowded on weekends and takes no reservations; come at an off-hour if you can.

Otis Café	
Hwy. 18, Otis, OR	**$**
(541) 994-2813	**BLD**

For big, satisfying food, especially at breakfast time, there isn't a happier place to eat between Coos Bay and Astoria. Lush and crunchy hash browns, topped with melted cheese, are what you want on the side of anything, even sourdough pancakes. There are cinnamon rolls the size of Oregon, excellent whole-wheat black molasses bread, and berry pies to die for. At lunch, to accompany your hot plate or hamburger, have a chocolate malt.

Yankee Pot Roast	
720 N.W. Sixth St., Grants Pass, OR (541) 476-0551	*$$*
Wed–Sun	*LD*

Yankee Pot Roast is a name guaranteed to attract the attention of all meat-and-potatoes fans; and this extremely quaint restaurant in the old brick house on Sixth Street does not disappoint. The atmosphere is Victorian, including period costumes for the staff and the aroma of baking breadstuffs in the vestibule. Pot roast is always on the menu, along with other robust entrees like ham steak with sweet potatoes, meat loaf with mashed potatoes, roast pork, and grilled steak. Good as the meaty meals are, what won our hearts was seafood—lovely plates of fresh halibut and salmon, moist and flavorful, with delicious jumbo biscuits on the side.

WASHINGTON

The 3 Crabs	
101 Three Crabs Rd., Sequim, WA	*$$*
(360) 683-4264	*LD*

There is only one crustacean to focus on when you dine at The 3 Crabs. Dungeness crab, steamed and served "cracked," which means the meat is easily accessible beneath the broken exoskeleton. It is sweet, tender meat, a pure pleasure to savor and a north coast delight all the more enjoyable for the easygoing ways of the pine-paneled dining room of this comfortable old restaurant alongside the Dungeness Spit.

Beyond the crab, The 3 Crabs does offer other tasty shellfish, from raw local oysters and comfortable oyster stew to geoduck chowder. And there are plates of fish, too—salmon, halibut, sole—all simply and expertly prepared, accompanied by creamy coleslaw and followed by high-flavored berry pies.

The restaurant's name, according to a waitress, refers not to denizens of the ocean but to the humans who opened the restaurant decades ago.

Bakeman's

122 Cherry St., Seattle, WA (206) 622-3375	$
Mon—Fri only	£

Listen up: at Bakeman's you want either turkey or meat loaf, on white or wheat, with mayo or mustard; and if you choose turkey, you might want cranberry sauce, too. Make all these decisions before you step down into the subterranean cafeteria known as Bakeman's because the line moves fast and the sandwich makers don't have time to nurse anyone along. The turkey is warm and juicy, sliced fresh; the meat loaf is honest and beefy; the bread is good, too. These simple sandwiches, in this workers' café, are some of Seattle's culinary treasures.

Canlis

2576 Aurora Ave., Seattle, WA (206) 283-3313	$$$
Mon—Sat (reservations recommended, jackets required for men)	D

God bless it, Canlis hasn't changed in the near half-century since it opened. Here is a taste of postwar gourmet living in all its splendor: a debonair dining room with a spectacular view across Lake Union; silk-smooth service by kimono-outfitted waitresses who toss salads tableside with utmost aplomb; and unrepentant steak-and-potatoes (or stellar sautéed prawns and potatoes) meals that conclude with

Grand Marnier soufflés. This classical food is delicious; the setting is romantic; and the whole experience is epicurean Americana at its best.

Daly's	
2713 Eastlake Ave., Seattle, WA	$
(206) 322-1918	LD

Dear to the hearts of grunge-food connoisseurs, Daly's introduced Seattle to the flame-broiled hamburger in 1962. It is nothing but a cheap-eats dive, but the burger it serves is indeed a good one, attended by skinny French fries in a little paper sack, and washed down with a refreshing fruit milk shake.

El Ranchito	
Rte. 12, Zillah, WA	$
(509) 829-5880	BLD

About halfway between Walla Walla and Seattle in the Rattlesnake Hills of Washington, the town of Zillah isn't on most vacationers' itinerary; but if you are a traveler in search of excellent Mexican food, go there and find First Avenue. There is El Ranchito, a restaurant and tortilla factory with a menu of utterly delicious *barbacoa*, tacos, and tamales accompanied by luscious refried beans. Accommodations are casual and prices are low. Your dining companions will be traveling farm workers, local residents, and pilgrims who regularly make the trip from Seattle for the authentic fare.

Emmett Watson's Oyster Bar

Soames-Dunn Bldg., Pike Place Market, Seattle, WA	$
(206) 448-7721	LD

ere are the makings of a carefree Seattle afternoon: a choice from more than three dozen kinds of bottled and draft beer and a half-dozen varieties of oyster on the half shell. That's what's available most days at this pint-size eatery with a scattering of tables in a pleasant off-street courtyard. In addition to impeccably fresh raw oysters, the kitchen makes salmon soup, chowder, and fish and chips.

Hi-Spot Café

1410 34th St., Seattle, WA (206) 325-7905	$
BLD Tues–Sat; Brunch Sun; B and L Mon	BLD

e don't know about lunch or dinner (the menu lists sandwiches, pasta, pizzas), but breakfast at the Hi-Spot is a must-eat Seattle meal. On weekends, you will wait in a line that stretches out the door of the quaint old house in Madrona; once you get a table amid the happy vintage-clutter decor and the fine food starts coming, all minor inconveniences are forgiven. Aromatic cinnamon rolls and fruit-studded scones are the highlights of the baker's yield; off the stovetop come berry pancakes and complex omelets; from the oven emerge swank shirred eggs. Casual but competent service helps make this an easy, fun place to be, whether you are single, on a date, or with the whole family in tow.

Knapp's

2707 N. Proctor St., Tacoma, WA	$
(253) 759-9009	BLD

It is all too easy to take Knapp's for granted: a middle-of-the-road restaurant, neither deluxe and trendy nor colorfully raffish. When you dine in the vintage neighborhood café, you are served by professional uniformed waitresses, at tables clothed with clean white linen. You eat unsurprising meals of roast pork loin (every Wednesday), liver and onions (every day), corned beef and cabbage (the Tuesday special), or turkey with dressing and mashed potatoes. Start with shrimp cocktail or salad, top it off with homemade peach pie and a bottomless cup of coffee. Expertly prepared meals such as these, at honest prices in comfortable surroundings, are not only delicious; they are good for the soul.

Ray's Boathouse

6049 Seaview Ave., NW, Seattle, WA (206) 789-3770	$$
(reservations are essential)	LD

Ray's is the great place to eat seafood in Seattle. Start with oysters galore, steamed clams, or creamy chowder. Exemplary fillets and steaks of all kinds of Pacific salmon are available poached or broiled, plain or fancy; there are tender sautéed scallops, exquisite grilled rockfish strewn with capers and lemon, succulent smoked black cod with wheatberries on the side. The best fish dishes here are the simple ones—neither overdone nor annoyingly undercooked. Meals are deftly served by a helpful staff in the refined downstairs dining room as well as in a more boisterous (and cheaper and easier to get into) upstairs café.

The Spar

114 East Fourth Ave., Olympia, WA	$
(360) 357-6444	BLD

We love this 1930s-vintage lunchroom for its cinnamon rolls, served hot and fresh in the morning, then made into creamy bread pudding for dessert later in the day. We also like the real milk shakes that accompany good hamburgers; and if you are on the lookout for tasty local seafood, you'll get that here, too: pan-fried oysters, crab Louis, or grilled salmon and halibut.

Twin Teepees

7201 Aurora Ave., N., Seattle, WA	$
(206) 783-9740 Tues–Sun	BLD

Ok, so the food won't soon be featured on the cover of *Gourmet*. But it isn't the extraordinary meals that have drawn customers to Twin Teepees since it was built in 1937. The lure is the structure itself—exemplary West Coast roadside kitsch—that suggests you will dine in some sort of Native American mess hall. In fact, once you enter the pointy-topped place, it looks pretty much like any Naugahyde-booth diner, but with an Indian motif; and the cuisine is strictly paleface fare. That includes a large assortment of burgers, from plain and cheese-topped to a Hawaiian burger with a pineapple ring, and a "chicken breast burger," as well as skillets full of hot turkey and roast beef au jus. Although the Teepee Lounge offers highballs and exotic libations, including fuzzy navels and mai tais any time after 11 AM, the meal many devoted customers like best is breakfast, when the place is packed, the coffee flows, and tables are piled high with plates of eggs and potatoes, pancakes and sausage.

Restaurants by Region and State

★ ★ ★

New England

CONNECTICUT

MAINE

MASSACHUSETTS

NEW HAMPSHIRE

Midwest

West Coast